MONUMENTS OF INDUSTRY

an illustrated historical record

CENTRING FOR THE BALLOCHMYLE VIADUCT.

GLASGOW & SOUTH-WESTERN RAILWAY.

Frontispiece: James Newland, *The Carpenter and Joiner's Assistant* (1865)

MONUMENTS OF INDUSTRY

an illustrated historical record

Geoffrey D Hay and Geoffrey P Stell

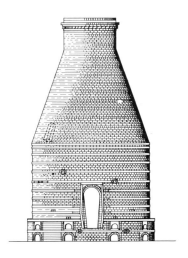

THE ROYAL COMMISSION
ON THE ANCIENT AND HISTORICAL
MONUMENTS OF SCOTLAND
1986

Printed in Scotland for H.M.S.O. by Bell and Bain Ltd., Glasgow.
Dd. 762103/HF 4538 C25 4/86.

CONTENTS

The Royal Commission on the Ancient and Historical Monuments of Scotland

PREFACE

BY THE EARL OF CRAWFORD AND BALCARRES
Chairman of the Commission

The Royal Commission on the Ancient and Historical Monuments of Scotland was established in 1908 to make a record of all the buildings and monuments in the country earlier than 1707, and to specify those most worthy of preservation. In 1948 the limiting date was relaxed to permit inclusion of selected examples of 18th- and 19th-century buildings in the county *Inventories* of monuments. In its survey of Stirlingshire, begun in the early 1950s, the Commission took full advantage of these extended terms of reference by describing a range of monuments which reflected the early industrial development of that county. The results of what might be claimed as pioneering fieldwork in Scottish industrial archaeology were published in 1963,[1] and subsequent topographic surveys in the less heavily industrialised counties of Peeblesshire and Argyll have continued to treat industrial and engineering monuments on a similar basis.[2]

Industrial buildings have also figured prominently in the threatened building surveys carried out by the Commission since 1966, the year when it assumed responsibility for the administration of the former Scottish National Buildings Record, now the National Monuments Record of Scotland. This programme of emergency survey work received statutory recognition in 1969, when a new Planning Act stipulated that no listed building in Scotland should be demolished until the Commission had been given an opportunity to make an appropriate record. Not all industrial monuments fell within the scope of this programme, however, and the heavy and specialised demands of industrial recording led eventually in 1977 to the formation of the Scottish Industrial Archaeology Survey. This unit, originally funded mainly by Scottish Development Department and directed by Mr J R Hume from the Department of Economic History, University of Strathclyde, was transferred to the Commission in April 1985.

Recognising the great importance and interest attached to this subject, the Commissioners have decided to publish a representative selection from the large amount of material relating to industrial monuments amassed during the first thirty years of the Commission's activities in this field. This monograph forms part of a series of occasional publications designed to give fuller treatment to subjects which cannot be embraced within the normal course of the Commission's publication programme.

The monuments described in this volume reflect aspects of the industrial, technological and commercial transformation of Scotland since about the middle of the 18th century. Evidence for earlier remains, other than bridges and a few mills, rests largely upon the techniques of archaeological and historical research. These techniques have been used to assist in the graphic reconstruction of some incomplete or vanished sites of later date, but otherwise the present work is directed principally towards upstanding buildings, machines and processes. These are described and analysed from a structural and technical standpoint, and discussion has occasionally been extended to the wider applications of industrial artefacts.

The collection of case-studies presented here is primarily intended to demonstrate the range of Scottish industrial monuments, the techniques involved in recording them, and the value of the information assembled. It should be stressed, however, that outside the areas covered by the county *Inventories* the material has not accrued as a result of a programme of systematic survey and research. The majority of the subjects in this book were recorded in response to random threats of different kinds; time has been found to make good some deficiencies in the record, but other obvious gaps in the overall coverage of industrial monuments still remain. The variety of circumstances under which these records have been compiled over a thirty-year period also accounts for some inconsistencies in approach and style of presentation. The Commission's aim throughout has been to obtain as full a descriptive record as the subject merited and as time and circumstances permitted; the record of those monuments that were in operation at the dates of survey usually includes an account of the associated industrial processes. For the purposes of this publication an attempt has been made to ascertain what has happened to these buildings and monuments since the surveys were made, and to identify any that are protected by legislation.

For convenience the material has been arranged in seven main sections, each with its own explanatory introduction and summary descriptive accounts of the principal subjects. In almost every case fuller descriptive reports are available for reference in the National Monuments Record of Scotland. This publication differs from previous national industrial surveys, however, in placing considerable emphasis on illustrations, and especially on line-drawings. Most of the drawings have been specially prepared for publication and composed as study-sheets, but several have been deliberately kept in the form of on-site pencil surveys. Photographic coverage includes the results of low-level aerial photography carried out by the Commission's staff, and illustrations of all kinds have been drawn from the archival resources of the National Monuments Record of Scotland. There is a considerable, and growing, literature on Scottish industrial archaeology, but, whilst an immense debt is freely acknowledged to the published works of other scholars,[3] the notes and references cited in support of this text are mainly restricted to the contributions made by the Commission and members of its staff.

Commissioners and staff involved in the preparation of this book would like it to serve as a tribute to the memory of Mr Angus Graham, one-time Secretary of the Commission and a pioneering fieldworker in the archaeology of Scottish transport and industry.

The subject of this monograph serves to illustrate a major aspect of the work carried out since 1954 by one of the Commission's Investigators, Mr Geoffrey D Hay. The compilation of this volume was entrusted to him, and the Commissioners wish to record their deep appreciation of the way in which he has selected the material, especially the illuminating line-drawings which form such a conspicuous feature of this book. Mr Hay has received great support from his co-author, Mr Geoffrey P Stell, who, in addition to writing a substantial portion of the text, has given much help with editorial matters, and from Mr A MacLaren, who has edited the volume. Mention should also be made of the important contributions made by other members of the Commission's staff: by Mr S Scott, Mr D R Boyd, Mr A J Leith, Mr I G Parker and Mr J N Stevenson of the Drawing Office, all under the direction of Mr I G Scott, who was also responsible for the design and layout of the volume; by Mr G B Quick and Mr J D Keggie and their colleagues in the Photographic Department, Mr J M Mackie, Mr S Wallace, Mr A G Lamb, Miss A P Stirling and Mr R M Adam; and by Mrs D D Burton, Miss M Isbister and Miss E J Drysdale, who did the clerical and typing work.

Acknowledgements for assistance or for reproduction of material are also due to the owners and occupiers of all the monuments and buildings recorded in the course of this work, and especially to the managers and staff of those which were in operation at the dates of survey; to members and staff of the Council for British

Archaeology, Industrial Archaeology Research Committee (especially Mr R Wailes and Mr K A Falconer); Her Majesty's Customs and Excise Museum, London (Mr T G Smith); Edinburgh City Libraries; Edinburgh City Museums; Falkirk Museums; Fleet Air Arm Museum, Yeovilton (Commander P J Craig, R N (Retd) and Mr G Mottram); Museum of Flight, East Fortune (Mr D N Brown and Mr A G I Dodds); Mitchell Library, Glasgow; Ironbridge Gorge Museum Trust; Museum of Islay Life; Kirkwall Library, Orkney (Mr R K Leslie); National Library of Scotland; National Maritime Museum; National Museum of Antiquities of Scotland; New Lanark Conservation Trust; North of England Open Air Museum, Beamish (Director, Mr F Atkinson); Prestongrange Colliery Museum of Mining, East Lothian District Council; Public Record Office, London; Royal Scottish Museum (Mr I T Bunyan, Mr J D Storer, Mr J L Wood); Science Museum, London (Mr J B Hill and Dr R F Bud); Scottish Development Department, Historic Buildings and Monuments Directorate; Scottish Industrial Archaeology Survey (Mr J R Hume, Mr G J Douglas and Dr M K Oglethorpe); Scottish Record Office; Her Majesty's Stationery Office; The Fishery Office, Wick; Wick Heritage Museum; Angus District Council; Grampian Regional Council, Roads Department; and to Mr C G Booth, Dr W A Campbell, Lieutenant-Commander D Falkingham, RNR, Mr G R Curtis, Dr J A Iredale, Mr I G McIntosh, Mr E C Ruddock, Mr I Shaw, Mr J C Temple, Professor D G Tucker and Dr D B Walker.

NOTES

n.1 RCAHMS, *Inventory of Stirlingshire* (2 vols, 1963).
n.2 *Inventory of Peeblesshire* (2 vols, 1967); *Inventory of Argyll,* 1 (1971); 2 (1975); 3 (1980); 4 (1982); 5 (1984). For summaries of the Commission's industrial survey work see also Hay, G D, *Transactions of the First International Congress on the Conservation of Industrial Monuments, Ironbridge, 29 May–5 June 1973* (1975), 187–95; Hay, G D, *Scottish Archaeological Forum,* 8 (1977), 1–15; Hay, G D and Falconer, K, *The Recording of Industrial Sites: A Review* (CBA Industrial Archaeology Research Committee, 1981).
n.3 Most notably the gazetteers prepared by Butt, J, *The Industrial Archaeology of Scotland* (1967), and Hume, J R, *The Industrial Archaeology of Scotland* (2 vols, 1976–7).

EDITORIAL NOTES

Presentation

Included in the heading of each of the descriptive articles in the seven main sections will normally be found the National Grid Reference of the monument concerned, the old County, new Region and District in which it is/was situated, and the date(s) on which it was surveyed by the Commission. Information about the condition of the monuments in April 1985 is indicated by the following symbols:

   \#   destroyed
   ●   building listed under the Town and Country Planning (Scotland) Act 1979
   *   monument scheduled under the Ancient Monuments and Archaeological Areas Act 1979
   **   monument in the care of the Secretary of State for Scotland
   ][building or plant partly destroyed or altered

Illustrations and Measurements

All the illustrations are treated as Figures and are integrated with the text. Individual Figures are identified by the number of the page on which they occur, with a distinguishing letter where appropriate, and with the reference usually placed in the nearest margin. Most of the line-drawings are provided with scales in both British and metric units and, in the text, measurements are normally given in British units with the metric equivalent alongside.

Notes and References

These will be found at the end of the section to which they belong. The notes that include additional information are indicated in the text by an asterisk.

Reproductions

Unless specified below, the contents of the volume are Crown Copyright, but copies of the photographs and line-drawings can be obtained from:
   The Secretary
   The Royal Commission on the Ancient and Historical Monuments of Scotland
   54 Melville Street, Edinburgh EH3 7HF.
The records of the Commission, which include a large collection of unpublished illustrations of the monuments described in this volume, may also be consulted in the National Monuments Record of Scotland, 6/7 Coates Place, Edinburgh EH3 7AA.

Acknowledgements for Illustrations

We are indebted to the following individuals and institutions for supplying photographs and for permission to reproduce copyright material:

Bruichladdich Distillery: Fig. 36A.   Viscount Cowdray (Dunecht Estates): Figs. 64A, B.
Mrs P E Durham: Fig. 10A.   Falkirk Museums: Figs. 102A, B.
Mrs R Gibson: Fig. 32D.   Govan Shipbuilders Ltd.: Figs. 126A, B, 128A.
P H T Green Collection: Fig. 236B.   Mr & Mrs T A Jardine: Fig. 97B.
Laphroaig Distillery: Figs. 32B, 34A, 44C, 50A.   Longmorn Distillery: Figs. 50B, 54A, E.
Mansell Collection: Figs. 33A, B.   Mitchell Library, Glasgow: Fig. 154A.
G Mottram Collection: Fig. 233A.   Orkney Library (T Kent Collection): Fig. 235.
Ordnance Survey: Fig. 162 *(with the permission of the Controller of Her Majesty's Stationery Office, Crown Copyright reserved).*
Royal Museum of Scotland (formerly Royal Scottish Museum): Figs. 140A, 201B, 236A.
Scottish Record Office: Figs. 199A, B.   Thomas Tait & Sons: Fig. 181C.
A I Welders Ltd.: Figs. 129A, 130A, B.

A

Grain-mill, East Cluden, New Bridge,
Dumfriesshire
  A.   exterior
  B.   gear cupboard

B

1 FARMING AND FISHING INDUSTRIES

Physical remains of industries, trades and crafts associated with farming and agricultural processing are to be found almost everywhere in the Scottish rural landscape. Such industries were usually, in the initial stages, promoted and organised through the owners of landed estates, but the wider effects came to be felt throughout rural society, from the mains farm down to the humblest smallholding or croft. Market towns absorbed many activities of rural origin, such as tanning and meat-processing, but were themselves supported by the building-trades and specialist crafts within the neighbouring countryside.

Power for the mechanised processes was generally derived from water, wind, oxen or horses and, latterly, steam, petrol or diesel. Since the Middle Ages water-power has probably had the most widespread application, particularly for grain-milling and threshing, although use of wind-power became more common in Scotland during the 18th and 19th centuries.[1] The use of horsepower to drive fixed farm machinery, particularly threshing-mills, has bequeathed a variety of building-forms, ranging from simple open horse-gang platforms of relatively late date to elaborately roofed structures of circular, hexagonal or octagonal plan.[2]

The cultivation of grain in Scotland, as elsewhere, has always been closely associated with the techniques of threshing and milling. The use of the flail and hand-operated quern-stones, just like the earliest use of the plough and the spade, can be traced to the pre-Roman Iron Age in Scotland. Milling lent itself readily to mechan-

isation, and the oldest and simplest mechanised designs are probably those of the water-driven 'Norse', or horizontal mills, with horizontal water-wheels, which now survive mainly in the Northern and Western Isles.[3] A few Scottish mills with vertically set water-wheels incorporate remains dating from the 17th century, sometimes with evidence of detached circular drying-kilns comparable to the small farm kilns of later date.[4]* The vast majority of surviving water-mills, however, belong to the phases of agricultural reorganisation and improvement that took place after 1750; they are usually integrated with stone-built kilns that have their internal drying-apparatus constructed of brick and iron, and are equipped with milling-machinery of varying degrees of complexity and sophistication. The mill at East Cluden, Dumfriesshire (NX 941793), for example, was powered by a wooden upright shaft driving as many as five pairs of stones and ancillary equipment. A few, such as Tangy Mill, Kintyre, Argyll (NR 662277), even had domestic accommodation provided within the same building.

The geographical distribution, size and condition of the mills generally reflect the quality and productive capacity of the surrounding cornlands. In some parts of the country such as the north-east a significant proportion continued in operation until the middle of the 20th century; throughout the country, in fact, a small number of water-powered grain-mills and water- or horse-powered threshing-mills, have survived in working order, their mechanical components generally dating from the last phases of operation

Horse-mill shed, Nether Pirn,
Innerleithen, Peeblesshire

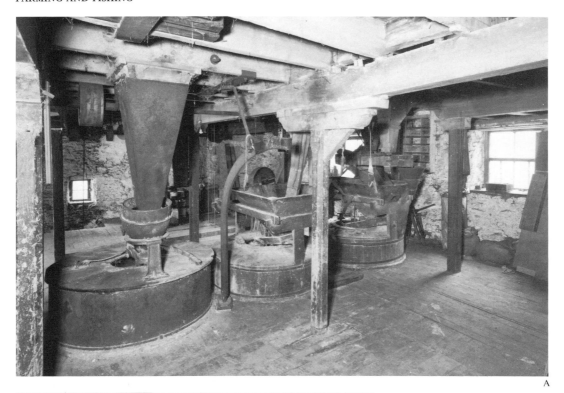

A

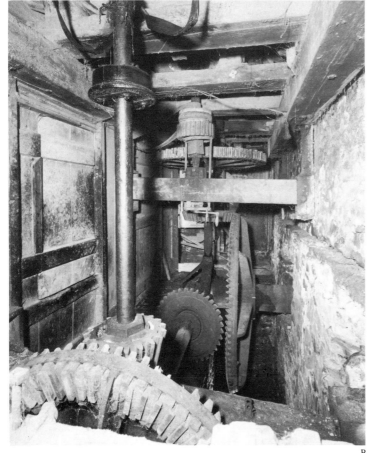

Grain-mill, Craighead, Lesmahagow,
Lanarkshire
    A.   stones floor
    B.   gear cupboard, showing (foreground)
           take-off drive for no. 3 stone

B

A

B

Meat-market, Fountainbridge,
Edinburgh
  A.   external detail
  B.   interior

Tannery, Bonnington, Edinburgh
  C.   tanning-pits

C

in the 19th and 20th centuries. Examples include the water-powered machinery in Craighead Mill, Lesmahagow, Lanarkshire (NS 815407), and the small horse-driven threshing-mill at Conisby, Islay, still in use until the early 1970s and 1980s respectively. Grain-mills became redundant or were converted to other uses as patterns of farming changed; in Galloway, for example, the changeover to dairy farming reduced arable significantly in the latter half of the 19th century.[5]

Livestock husbandry has bequeathed fewer remains that can be classed as industrial, but these make up in variety what they lack in quantity. In some parts of the country, most notably in the north-east, crushed whins formed an important element in winter cattle fodder, and horse-powered whin-mills constitute one of the more unusual relics of pastoral farming in those areas.[6] Cheese-presses,[7*] mechanised butter-churn houses,[8*] elegant model dairies,[9] usually attached to large domestic establishments, and creameries are some of the enduring products of dairy-

farming. Slaughterhouses, meat-markets,[10*] and tanneries which range in size from the diminutive example at Keith, Banffshire, to the large works formerly at Bonnington, Edinburgh (NT 260759), are still to be found in a few provincial centres, reflecting the importance and organisation of the cattle trade within their localities.

Blacksmiths provided essential support for agriculture and transport in rural communities throughout the country, but only a small proportion of smithies still preserve remains of their bellows and other standard features.[11] Nail-making by hand was a specialised metalwork craft centred upon Lennoxtown and Chartershall in Stirlingshire.[12] Sawmills, usually water-powered, were reasonably common on estates that contained significant amounts of timber, but evidence for more specialised rural woodworking crafts is comparatively rare, the bucket mill at Finzean, Aberdeenshire (NO 577912), being a notable exception.[13]

3

Scottish rivers have long been renowned for their seasonal stocks of salmon, while the movement of large herring-shoals around Scotland, especially round the north and east coasts, encouraged much capital investment, large- and small-scale, in the fishing industry in the late 18th and 19th centuries. These abundant resources of fish provided the biggest single impetus to harbour-building, and the *22-30* supporting activities of fish-processing and -curing have bequeathed a whole range of interesting buildings and relics in areas such as eastern Caithness. The physical remains of many such harbours were investigated by Mr Angus Graham during the 1950s and 1960s, and his descriptive and historical accounts[14] provide an excellent basis for the graphic architectural records that the Commission has since *25* undertaken at, for example, Keiss and Wick in Caithness, and Portmahomack (NH 915845) in Easter Ross.

sloping site, with a principal entrance on the E side at mid-floor level. It is constructed of rubble masonry with sandstone dressings and a slated roof, notable features being the characteristic revolving ridge-ventilator above the kiln at the s end, and the windows fitted in the lower part with ventilating shutters.

Water for driving the machinery was drawn from the Corrieglen Water via a lade approaching the mill from the N, and two sluices regulated the water-flow and discharged the excess into the neighbouring burn; at one time the supply was augmented by a large shallow mill-pond long since drained. From the lade the water was carried on to the wheel by a wooden trough, or launder, where it discharged at a point which caused the wheel to turn in a pitch-back action. The water-wheel was equipped with wooden buckets *5(4* but was otherwise of all-iron construction. A waste-water

A

B

Grain-mill, Machrimore, Kintyre, Argyll
  A. exterior, showing pitch-back
       water-wheel and launder
  B. detail of water-wheel

Grain-mill   NR 701092
Machrimore, Kintyre, Argyll
    Strathclyde, Argyll and Bute   ●][1962

Built in 1839,[15] under the terms of a new lease granted by the Duke of Argyll apparently to replace an earlier foundation,[16] this small grain-mill may be regarded as fairly typical of the countless water-powered vertical mills formerly serving country districts during the 19th century. An inscribed stone over the rear ground-floor entrance bears the date 1839 and a mason's mark. In common with the neighbouring mill at Tangy,[17] with which its design had close affinities, it was one of the last two water-mills to remain in operation in Kintyre, finally stopping in the late 1950s; soon afterwards most of its machinery was removed.

Situated in the small township of Machrimore, about 1·2 km NE of Southend, the three-storeyed mill stands on a

trapdoor in the floor of the launder, operated by a system of levers from inside the mill, enabled the flow of water, and *5(2)* hence the speed of the machinery, to be regulated.

The machinery for working the mill and the ancillary processing equipment is detailed in the accompanying drawings,[18*] and is disposed over three storeys known as the *5, 7* bottom, middle and top floors. The transmission on the bottom floor, housed within a stoutly timber-framed gear-cupboard, comprised a bevelled pit-wheel on the *6A* water-wheel axle, meshing with a wallower on the lower end of the upright shaft, the drive to the stones being through the great spur-wheel, cogged to engage with three slotted pinions or stone nuts. All the gearing was of iron construction apart from the spur-wheel, whose mortised iron rim was equipped with replaceable wooden cogs. The stone nuts could be disengaged from the spur-wheel by means of a ring-and-screw lifting-device, and their spindles, carrying the runner stones above, were mounted on timber

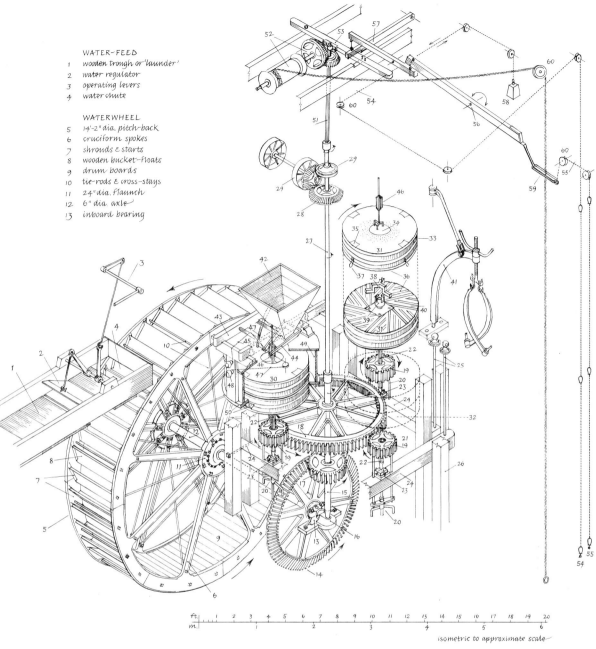

WATER-FEED
1 wooden trough or 'launder'
2 water regulator
3 operating levers
4 water chute

WATERWHEEL
5 14'-2" dia. pitch-back
6 cruciform spokes
7 shrouds & starts
8 wooden bucket-floats
9 drum boards
10 tie-rods & cross-stays
11 24" dia. flaunch
12 6" dia. axle
13 inboard bearing

isometric to approximate scale

TRANSMISSION	GRINDING COMPONENTS	
14 6' dia. bevel pit-wheel	30 animal meal stones	46 revolving cam or 'damsel'
15 4" dia. upright shaft	31 shelling stones	47 wooden spring & tension cord
16 main thrust-bearing	32 finishing stones	48 twist-pegs
17 18" dia. wallower	33 runner stone	49 wooden casing or vat
18 5'-6" dia. great spur wheel	34 'eye' of runner stone	50 skirting & meal outlet chute
19 18" dia. stone nuts	35 balance weights	SACK-HOIST MECHANISM
20 ring & screw engaging gear	*36 furrowed grinding surfaces	51 clutch-shaft & pinion
21 S. stone nut (in gear)	37 grain tags	52 bevel wheel & chain winding drum
22 2" dia. stone spindles	38 three-armed rynd	53 clutch-lever
23 bridging boxes	39 mace-head on spindle	54 engaging cord
24 pivoted bridge-trees	40 bedstone	55 release cord
25 rod tentering screws	41 stones crane	56 balance-beam
26 timber framework	42 wooden hopper	57 gravity locking-bar
27 2½" dia. extension shaft	43 support frame or 'horse'	58 counter-weight cut-out
28 18" dia. crown wheel	44 feed-trough or 'shoe'	59 automatic cut-out point
29 belt & string drives	45 crook-string	60 sheave-blocks
		GDH

* stone dressing conjectural   → direction of rotation

Grain-mill, Machrimore, Kintyre, Argyll

Grain-mill, Machrimore, Kintyre, Argyll
  A. gear cupboard, showing pit-wheel, upright shaft,
       wallower and great spur-wheel
  B. hopper and grain-feed apparatus above shelling-stones

enclosed within a circular wooden casing, or vat, above which was a grain-hopper held within a wooden frame, or horse. From the hopper the grain was shaken into the 6 B centre, or eye, of the stones via a pivoted feed-trough kept in constant motion by means of a cam in the form of a forked iron rod attached to the revolving rynd and spindle turning the runner stone. The trough was held lightly in tension against the cam—known as the damsel—by means of a cord attached to a wooden spring stapled to the side of the horse; a second cord (the crook string) likewise attached to the free end of the trough enabled its angle to be adjusted. The grinding surfaces of the stones were cut with a system of 5(36) lands and furrows to facilitate the grinding action and to cast the meal to the outer edge of the stones; here it was swept along into an outlet chute by a projecting tag affixed to the rim of the runner stone. Also on this floor, situated directly beneath the ceiling and mounted on the head of the upright shaft, was a bevelled crown-wheel which provided 5(28) the main power take-off for driving the auxiliary machinery, namely the bucket elevators, fanners and sieving-apparatus.

On the top floor, mounted high up under the ridge, was the mechanical sack-hoist, driven from a jointed extension 5(51-60) of the main shaft in the form of a clutch-shaft and pinion which by means of a lever was put into gear with a bevel wheel fixed to the winding-drum. Two control cords, running in sheave blocks and accessible to the miller at all levels, enabled him to pull the drive-shaft into gear and to release it by activating a counterweight. The same clutch mechanism could also be worked by an automatic cut-out operated by an ingenious system of levers when struck by the rising sack at its highest point.

The principal stages in the milling process may be enumerated in association with the location points shown on the plans and section. The newly dried grain (A) was 7 raked into the grain-bin (B), where it was bagged (C) and hoisted through double flap hatchdoors to the top floor (D). Here, if the material was intended for animal feed (e.g. pease, beans or grain of inferior quality), it was fed via a hopper (E) into the w pair of stones (F) and, after being ground, passed through the outlet chute into waiting sacks on the ground floor (G on the plan). Alternatively, as the first stage in producing oatmeal, the grain was fed via a similar pair of hoppers and cleaning-sieves into the E pair of stones (H and I), known as shelling- or groating-stones, where the husks were removed from the kernels. The resulting mixture fell through a chute into the fanners or winnowing-machine (J) situated in the ground-floor out-shot, where the chaff was removed and used to supplement the coke as fuel for the kiln. The cleaned grain, then known as groats, was next returned to the loft by the elevator (K) and thence by the hopper (L) into the centre set of finishing-stones (M)—a pair of French block-burrs. The ground meal fell into a sieving-machine (N) on the bottom floor, where it was sorted into different grades and bagged for dispatch. Rejected coarse stuff was passed through a small fanner (O) and then returned to the stones by the elevator (P) for regrinding. For extra refining, the meal could be recycled through the sieving-apparatus by a short elevator at (Q).

The kiln was of the standard pattern, containing at the lower level a central furnace built of stone and lined with

beams or bridge trees, pivoted at one end so that they could also be raised or lowered for adjusting the clearance between the runner and bedstones—a process known as tentering. In addition, the thrust-bearings were housed in bridging-boxes incorporating hackle screws which allowed careful adjustment of the spindle in order to keep the stones rotating in a perfectly horizontal plane.

The middle floor, or stones floor, contained three sets of stones each approximately 3 ft 3 in (0·99 m) in diameter grouped around the upright drive-shaft. Each unit was

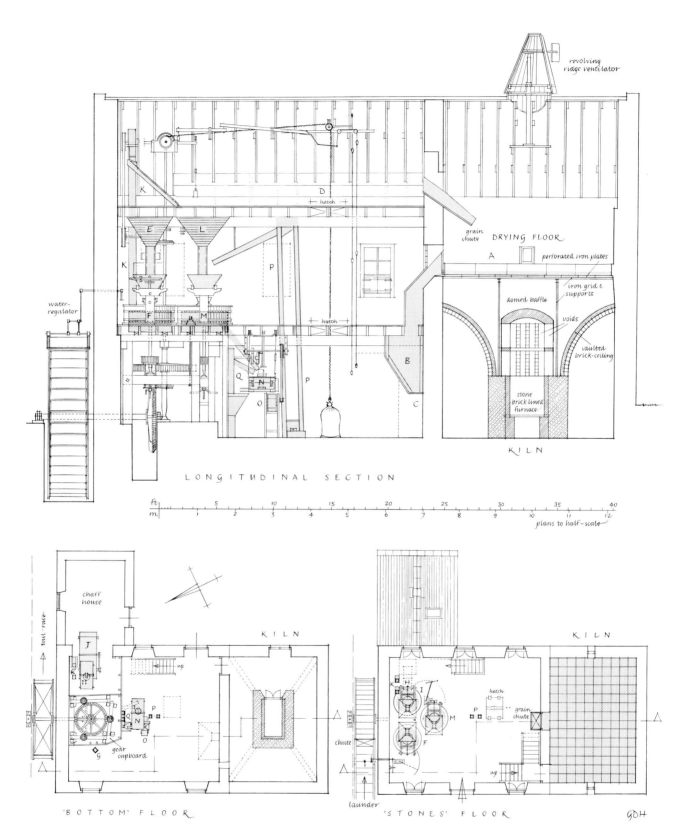

revolving ridge ventilator

DRYING FLOOR

grain chute

A

perforated iron plates

iron grid & supports

domed baffle

voids

vaulted brick-ceiling

stone brick lined furnace

KILN

water-regulator

K

E

L

K

P

F

M

Q

N

O

P

B

C

D

hatch

hatch

LONGITUDINAL SECTION

ft | 5 | 10 | 15 | 20 | 25 | 30 | 35 | 40
m | 1 | 2 | 3 | 4 | 5 | 6 | 7 | 8 | 9 | 10 | 11 | 12

plans to half-scale

chaff house

tail-race

J

K

N

P

O

G

gear cupboard

KILN

np

'BOTTOM' FLOOR

chute

launder

K

I

M

F

P

hatch

grain chute

np

KILN

'STONES' FLOOR

GDH

Grain-mill, Machrimore, Kintyre, Argyll

7

brick. It was surmounted by a flared funnel of brick-vaulted construction, wherein the hot air was allowed to circulate and percolate through the grain spread over the drying-floor, which consisted of perforated cast-iron plates. The revolving ridge ventilator assisted the drying process, which lasted from one to two days depending on the type of grain and the amount of moisture content to be removed.

A

B

Millstones, New Cumnock, Ayrshire
  A. oatmeal runner stone
  B. shelling runner stone

Millstones   NX 617134
New Cumnock, Ayrshire
    Strathclyde, Cumnock and Doon Valley   1970

The two millstones that stand in front of the Crown Hotel, New Cumnock, were taken from New Cumnock Mill (NS 616133), which was gutted in about 1968. They are both runner stones and about 4 ft (1·22 m) in diameter; one is of a pair used for grinding oatmeal, the other for shelling oats. There had been three pairs of stones in the mill, the third having been a general-purpose composition stone faced with emery. The last miller, Mr Robertson, had dressed the stones himself. The working surface of the shelling stone is dressed with lands and furrows arranged in nine sectors ('harps' or 'quadrants'), each comprising a master furrow running tangentially to the eye of the stone, and two secondary or slave furrows aligned parallel. The surface of the oatmeal stone is badly worn, but appears to have been dressed in a similar manner.   8 B

The outer ring of the oatmeal, or finishing stone is 8 A composed of thirteen banded segments of French burr (freshwater quartz from La Ferté-sous-Jouarre). Unlike more conventional French burr-stones studied in other parts of Britain,[19] the inner ring, or hub, is circular, measuring 2 ft (0·61 m) in diameter, and is built up, not of more quartz, but of local sandstone, in this case a pinkish-grey-coloured stone apparently quarried near Largs. The centre of the stone has been mortised to receive a three-arm stiff rynd, and the eye is 1 ft 1 in (0·33 m) in diameter.

The shelling stone also has an outer ring of French burr, 8 B built up with eight less regular segments. It has a four-piece octagonal hub, which varies between 2 ft 4 in (0·71 m) and 2 ft 7 in (0·79 m) in diameter; this is made of burr-stone like the outer ring and is cut to receive a two-arm rynd, extending across an eye 1 ft 1 in (0·33 m) in diameter. Sunk into the top surface of the stone, and spaced equidistantly around the perimeter, are four balance-weights, 8 in (200 mm) by 3 in (80 mm), for keeping the stone in a true horizontal plane.

The use of a sandstone centre or a similar stone of inferior quality in order to economise in the use of the expensive French burr-stone was apparently a distinctive Scottish practice, though isolated examples have been noted south of the Border.

Horizontal Mills   HU 172571
Huxter, Mainland, Shetland   ● 1980

These buildings form a chain of three mills on the burn that empties from the Loch of Huxter into the Sound of Papa. The mills are grouped within a short distance of about 75 m, with the site of a fourth mill, now demolished, a similar distance upstream. They are served by short stone-lined lades, cutting off meanders in the burn, and there is a fall of some 8·2 m between the floor levels of the top and bottom mill. All the buildings are aligned across the lade with the water-courses running transversely beneath the side-walls.

The two upper structures survive as masonry shells, but the lowest building retains its heather- and straw-thatched

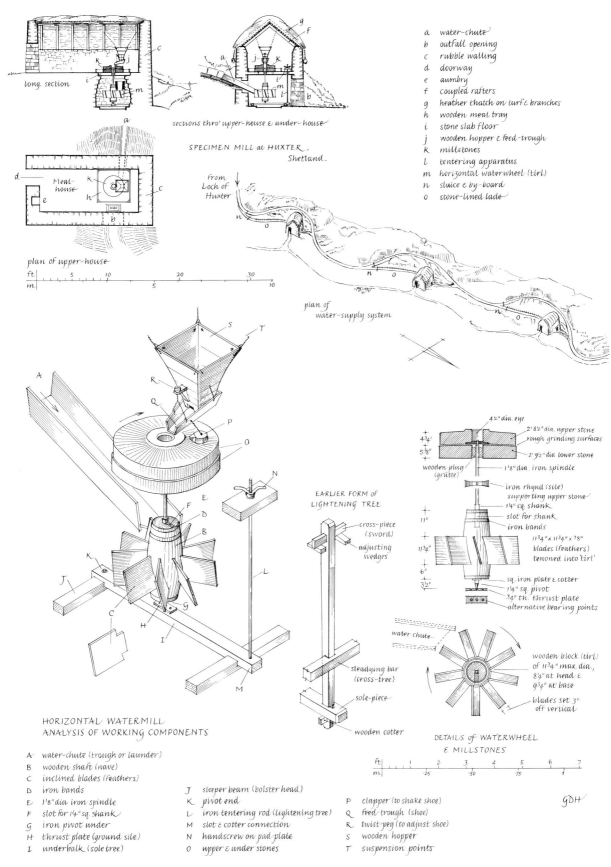

long. section

sections thro' upper-house & under-house

SPECIMEN MILL at HUXTER, Shetland.

d — Meal-house

plan of upper-house

from Loch of Huxter

plan of water-supply system

a   water-chute
b   outfall opening
c   rubble walling
d   doorway
e   aumbry
f   coupled rafters
g   heather thatch on turf & branches
h   wooden meal tray
i   stone slab floor
j   wooden hopper & feed-trough
k   millstones
l   tentering apparatus
m   horizontal waterwheel (tirl)
n   sluice & by-board
o   stone-lined lade

HORIZONTAL WATERMILL
ANALYSIS OF WORKING COMPONENTS

EARLIER FORM OF
LIGHTENING TREE

cross-piece (sword)

adjusting wedges

steadying bar (cross-tree)

sole-piece

wooden cotter

A   water-chute (trough or launder)
B   wooden shaft (nave)
C   inclined blades (feathers)
D   iron bands
E   1'8" dia. iron spindle
F   slot for 1'4" sq. shank
G   iron pivot under
H   thrust plate (ground sile)
I   underbalk (sole tree)

J   sleeper beam (bolster head)
K   pivot end
L   iron tentering rod (lightening tree)
M   slot & cotter connection
N   handscrew on pad-plate
O   upper & under stones

P   clapper (to shake shoe)
Q   feed-trough (shoe)
R   twist-peg (to adjust shoe)
S   wooden hopper
T   suspension points

4½" dia. eye
2'8½" dia. upper stone
rough grinding surfaces
2'9½" dia lower stone
wooden plug (grütte)
1'8" dia. iron spindle
iron rhynd (sile) supporting upper stone
1'4" sq. shank
slot for shank
iron bands
1¾" x 1¾" x ⅞" blades (feathers) tenoned into 'tirl'
sq. iron plate & cotter
1'4" sq. pivot
¾" th. thrust plate
alternative bearing points

water chute

wooden block (tirl) of 11¾" max. dia., 8½" at head & 9¾" at base

blades set 3" off vertical

DETAILS of WATERWHEEL
& MILLSTONES

GDH

Horizontal mills, Huxter, Mainland, Shetland

A

gabled roof. It is oblong on plan, averaging 18 ft (5·49 m) in length by 9 ft 6 in (2·90 m) transversely over walls 2 ft (0·61 m) thick; the entrance is in the E gable-wall. It still has 9 (A) the wooden chute, or pentrough, for directing the water onto the tirl in a clockwise direction. The tirl is of concrete, but an original specimen survives in one of the other mills. 9 (B) This consists of a wooden, elongated barrel-shaped hub (nave) with nine flat paddles. The lower mill also retains a pair of millstones, the bedstone (understone) being 2 ft 9½ in (0·85 m) in diameter and 5⅛ in (130 mm) thick, the runner stone (upperstone) slightly less in each dimension. Until a few years ago it was complete with a square wooden hopper. The drawing is intended to be a general representation of a horizontal mill, based on the Huxter examples and documentary sources.[20]

B

High Mill　　　　　　　　　　　　NS 849507
Carluke, Lanarkshire
　　　　Strathclyde, Clydesdale　　　　● * 1970

Built as a grain mill shortly after 1797, this three-storeyed circular windmill-tower stands complete to the original wall-head some 32 ft 6 in (9·9 m) above ground. The walls have a pronounced external batter, giving the tower an unusually sturdy profile, the overall diameter at the top (14 ft; 4·27 m) being only slightly more than half the basal diameter of 27 ft (8·23 m). At the date of survey, adjacent ranges on the E of the tower contained the remains of a later kiln, threshing-machine and an engine-house, while on the w a two-storeyed dwelling-house and ancillary buildings were grouped around a courtyard.

The interior of the tower retains much machinery and the principal drive-shaft. Previous investigators[21] were misled into believing that some of the mechanism may have been original, but detailed examination showed that the shaft and the stones were driven through gearing from below, not

A. Horizontal mill, Shetland; view by W Collins, c. 1842
B. Windmill tower, High Mill, Carluke, Lanarkshire

A

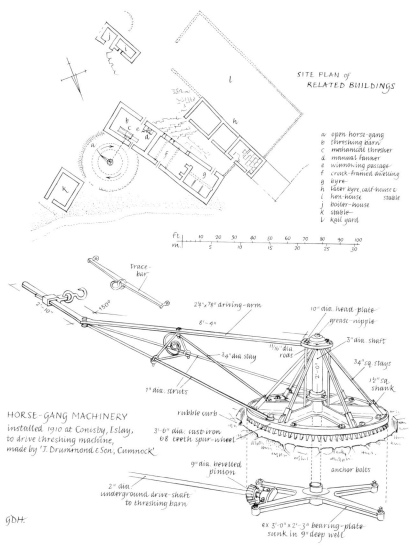

SITE PLAN of
RELATED BUILDINGS

a open horse-gang
b threshing barn
c mechanical thresher
d manual fanner
e winnowing passage
f cruck-framed dwelling
g byre
h later byre, calf-house &
i hen-house   stable
j boiler-house
k stable
l kail yard

ft. 10 20 30 40 50 60 70 80 90 100
m.   5   10   15   20   25   30

trace-bar

2'-10"   150°   2'4"x78" driving-arm   10" dia. head-plate
grease-nipple
8'-4"   3" dia. shaft
11/16" dia. rods
3/4" dia. stay   3/4" sq. stays
1½" sq. shank
1" dia. struts

HORSE-GANG MACHINERY
installed 1910 at Conisby, Islay,
to drive threshing machine,
made by 'J. Drummond & Son, Cumnock'

rubble curb
3'-6" dia. cast-iron
68 teeth spur-wheel

9" dia. bevelled
pinion   anchor bolts

2" dia.
underground drive-shaft
to threshing barn

GDH.

ex 3'-0" x 2'-3" bearing-plate
sunk in 9" deep well

Horse-gang, Conisby, Islay, Argyll
A. drive mechanism and
    open platform
B. site plan and
    working details

B

from above, and none of the components was demonstrably original. Some of the timbers used for framing the machinery may have been in secondary use, but, to judge from the wall-sockets, the original floor-levels appear to have been retained. The mill had been converted to steam-power in about the middle of the 19th century, and subsequently a gas-engine was used. At the wall-head a masonry channel with indented sockets is all that now survives of the kerb of the original rotating cap.

A

Horse-gang   NR 262618
Conisby, Islay, Argyll
    Strathclyde, Argyll and Bute   1980

This open platform, one of two such horse-gangs in
11 Conisby township and characteristic of many small farms
throughout Scotland, was complete with drive mechanism
12 A and threshing-mill in working condition at the date of
survey in 1980.[22] It stands adjacent to a small barn at the
lower (SE) end of a linear range comprising house and
steading. Part of the dwelling is covered with rush thatch
bedded on heather divots, but the barn itself is roofed with
corrugated iron. This horse-powered equipment was introduced in 1910, superseding the traditional practice of
threshing with flails. The platform measures 30 ft (9·14 m) in
diameter overall; the underground drive-shaft, hub, gearing
and harness-bar (swing-tree) are of all-iron construction,
and the spur-wheel measures 3 ft 6 in (1·07 m) in diameter.

Horse-mill   NX 964826
West Gallaberry, Kirkton, Dumfriesshire
    Dumfries and Galloway, Nithsdale   ● 1982

This horse engine-house, situated 1·6 km NW of Kirkton
village and 6·5 km N of Dumfries, is among the last to retain
much of its driving-mechanism, although the threshing-
machine itself no longer survives.[23] Adjoining the outside

B

Horse-gang, Conisby,
Islay, Argyll
  A. threshing-mill in barn

Horse-mill, West Gallaberry,
Kirkton, Dumfriesshire
  B. drive mechanism, showing
      horse-wheel, pinion and
      lay-shaft
  C. exterior of shed

C

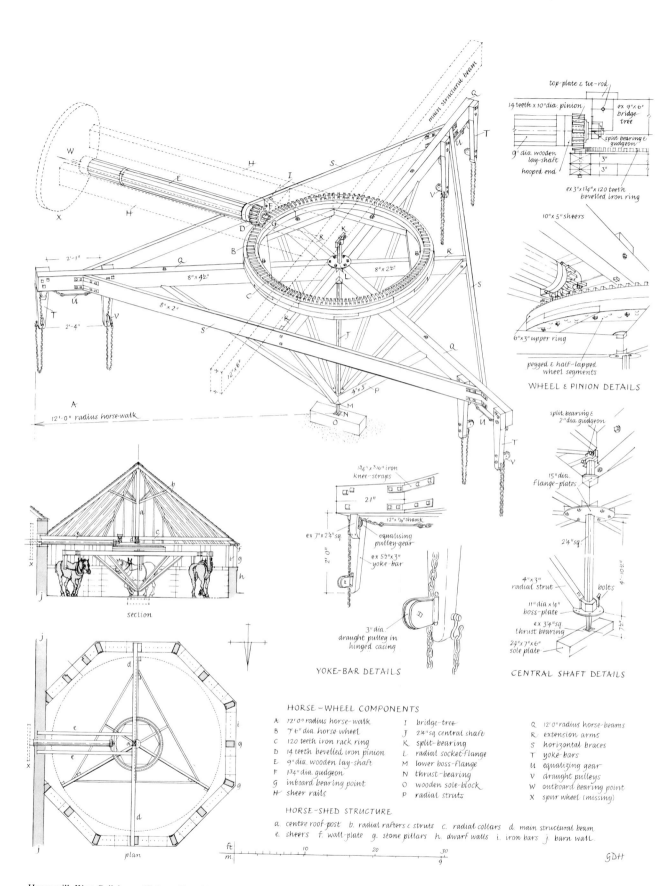

main structural beam

top-plate & tie-rod

14 teeth × 10"dia. pinion

ex 9"×6" bridge-tree

9" dia. wooden lay-shaft

split bearing & gudgeon

hooped end

3"

3"

ex 3"×1¾"×120 teeth bevelled iron ring

10"×5" sheers

6"×3" upper ring

pegged & half-lapped wheel segments

WHEEL & PINION DETAILS

split bearing & 2" dia. gudgeon

15" dia. flange-plates

24" sq.

4"×3" radial strut

bolts

11" dia ×¼" boss-plate

ex 3¼" sq thrust bearing

24"×7"×6" sole plate

CENTRAL SHAFT DETAILS

W

X

H

E

D

G

B

I

H

S

Q

T

V

R

R

L

K

R

S

J

Q

R

S

P

4"×3"

N

O

M

U

T

V

U

T

V

2'-1"

8"×4½"

8"×2"

2'-4"

12'-6"

A

12'-0" radius horse-walk

section

a

b

c

e

d

f

g

h

j

x

1¾"×³⁄₁₆" iron knee-straps

21"

12"×⁷⁄₁₆" shank

equalising pulley-gear

ex 7"×2¼" sq

ex 5½"×3" yoke-bar

2' 0"

3" dia draught pulley in hinged casing

YOKE-BAR DETAILS

plan

j

d

e

e

a

d

i

g

g

x

g

j

HORSE-WHEEL COMPONENTS

A   12'0" radius horse-walk
B   7'6" dia. horse wheel
C   120 teeth iron rack ring
D   14 teeth bevelled iron pinion
E   9" dia. wooden lay-shaft
F   1¾"dia. gudgeon
G   inboard bearing point
H   sheer rails
P   radial struts

I   bridge-tree
J   24" sq central shaft
K   split-bearing
L   radial socket-flange
M   lower boss-flange
N   thrust-bearing
O   wooden sole-block

Q   12'0" radius horse-beams
R   extension arms
S   horizontal braces
T   yoke-bars
U   equalizing gear
V   draught pulleys
W   outboard bearing point
X   spur wheel (missing)

HORSE-SHED STRUCTURE

a. centre roof post   b. radial rafters & struts   c. radial collars   d. main structural beam
e. sheers   f. wall-plate   g. stone pillars   h. dwarf walls   i. iron bars   j. barn wall

ft
m

10
20
30

9

GDH

Horse-mill, West Gallaberry, Kirkton, Dumfriesshire

wall of a barn, which formed one side of an original courtyard layout of farm-buildings, the octagonal shed—rubble-built with sandstone dressings and a handsome slate roof secured by pegs on battens—contains a 12 ft-radius (3·66 m) horse-walk and overhead draught-gear for three horses. Well-executed throughout in dressed pine, the principal mechanical parts consist of a wooden horse-wheel, measuring 7 ft 6 in (2·29 m) in diameter and built up in laminated segments. From this extend three radial arms framed by horizontal braces and supported by radial struts. The square upright iron shaft turns in a thrust-bearing and is secured at the top in a split-bearing fixed to a heavy cross-beam supporting the roof-structure—commonly the only feature of extant horse-mills left *in situ*. The drive transmission from the horse-wheel is by means of a bevelled iron 'rack-ring' and pinion, the latter being attached to a twelve-sided wooden lay-shaft, whose outer end, now sawn off at its bearing-point within the barn wall, would formerly have turned a spur-wheel. The yoke-bars and draught pulleys are about 3 ft 6 in (1·07 m) above the walk and incorporate a system of upper pulleys which allow free running of the draw-chains and thus equalise any uneven strains exerted by the pulling action of the horse.

Kiln-barn HY 266280
Jubidale, Orkney 1968

This is a partly roofless but well-preserved example of a small traditional farm kiln and barn once used for drying oats and bere. It is contiguous with a byre but otherwise stands detached, running parallel with the main farmstead, now ruinous, from which it is divided by a narrow paved close or alley-way. The buildings as a whole are aligned with the gradual fall of the land to the N. Built of random rubble, for the most part composed of slender, knapped stones roughly laid to courses, the barn was evidently roofed with turf thatch laid on a groundwork of thin flagstones supported on timber couples and purlins; a double

oversailing course of flagstones protects the wall-head. Externally, the principal feature is the conical kiln situated at the s end; it tapers upwards to a turf-built chimney, and its lower part merges with the main roof and walls of the barn. The doorway into the barn, in conjunction with an opening, or winnowing-hole, in the opposite side-wall, was used to create a strong draught of air for removing the chaff during the threshing process.[24] A small flagstone (c) in the E wall, known as a gloy-stone or shacking-stone, is evidence of a more specialised method of threshing adopted when the straw was to be kept in unbroken lengths for thatching and other selected work.

Steps and a doorway in the centre of the s gable-wall gave access to the drying-floor of the kiln. The latter was evidently supported on a single beam (kiln-laece), upon which cross-spars were laid and surfaced with a bed of straw for containing the grain. The outer ends of the spars rested on a 4 in-wide (102 mm) ledge or scarcement, situated about 6 in (152 mm) below the door threshold. At this point the kiln-bowl has a maximum internal diameter of 6 ft 6 in (1·98 m) beneath which the sides curve inwards to a basal dimension of about 3 ft (0·91 m), roughly level with the barn floor; above the drying-floor the kiln walls are gathered inwards to join the chimney at the top. A 1 ft-square (0·30 m) opening at the base of the kiln gave access to the horizontal flue, or draught-hole, leading back through the wall-thickness to the ingle fire (g), contained within a square mural recess on the E side at ground level. Directly above is a long, bulbous chamber for storing peat, topped by a smaller recess. These features are partly closed off by an upright partition and a roof of flagstones, which formed a shelter, or neuk, for the fire and also incorporated a stone seat, tucked in the corner for the person watching the fire. On the far side of the kiln, the dried grain could be discharged through a chute, or shoe, for storage in the large mural chamber in the w wall, formed partly as an outshot.

Known examples of a similar regional type have been recorded in Caithness, for instance, at Achalipster (ND 242491) and Bruan (ND 310397).

Kiln-barn, Jubidale,
Mainland, Orkney

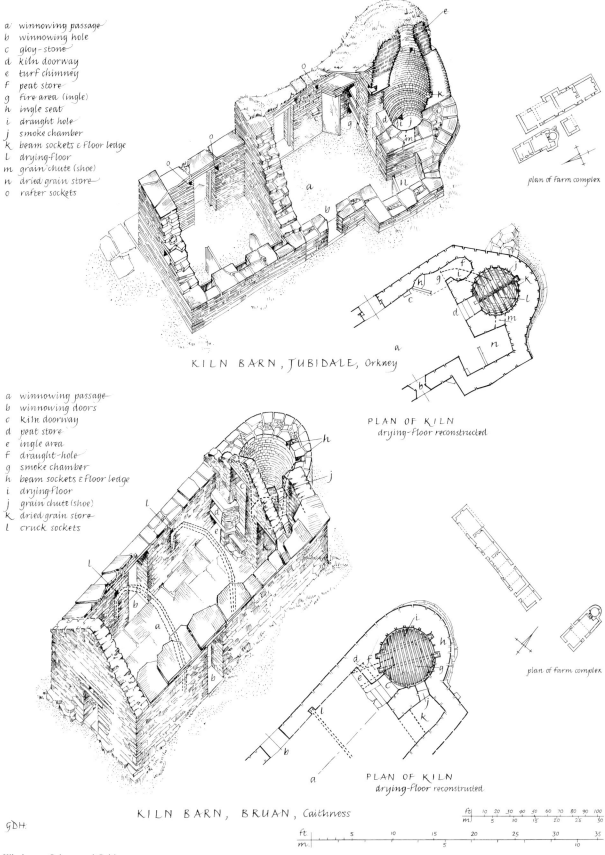

a winnowing passage
b winnowing hole
c gloy-stone
d kiln doorway
e turf chimney
f peat store
g fire area (ingle)
h ingle seat
i draught hole
j smoke chamber
k beam sockets & floor ledge
l drying-floor
m grain chute (shoe)
n dried grain store
o rafter sockets

plan of farm complex

KILN BARN, JUBIDALE, Orkney

PLAN OF KILN
drying-floor reconstructed

a winnowing passage
b winnowing doors
c kiln doorway
d peat store
e ingle area
f draught-hole
g smoke chamber
h beam sockets & floor ledge
i drying-floor
j grain chute (shoe)
k dried grain store
l cruck sockets

plan of farm complex

PLAN OF KILN
drying-floor reconstructed

KILN BARN, BRUAN, Caithness

GDH.

ft 10 20 30 40 50 60 70 80 90 100
m.   5   10   15   20   25   30

ft   5   10   15   20   25   30   35
m.   5   10

Kiln-barns, Orkney and Caithness

15

A

Dairy NH 307270
Guisachan, Tomich, Inverness-shire
Highland, Inverness ●][1972

This small ornamental dairy was erected during the third
quarter of the 19th century, probably in about 1870, when
the Guisachan estate was in the possession of Dudley
Marjoribanks, afterwards Baron Tweedmouth of
Edington. The exterior is of an attractively mannered
Alpine style. Two canopied porticos are supported by rows
of rustic posts, and the main roof, which is slated and of
gambrel type, has a flèche ventilator at the ridge. The
hipped roof of the NW annexe has a chimney-stack with
three twisted 'barley sugar' chimney-stalks.

The interior is divided into a scullery or wash-house at the
NE end, and the milk-room or dairy is at the SW. The

B

Dairy, Guisachan, Tomich, Inverness-shire
  A.   exterior
  B.   milk-room

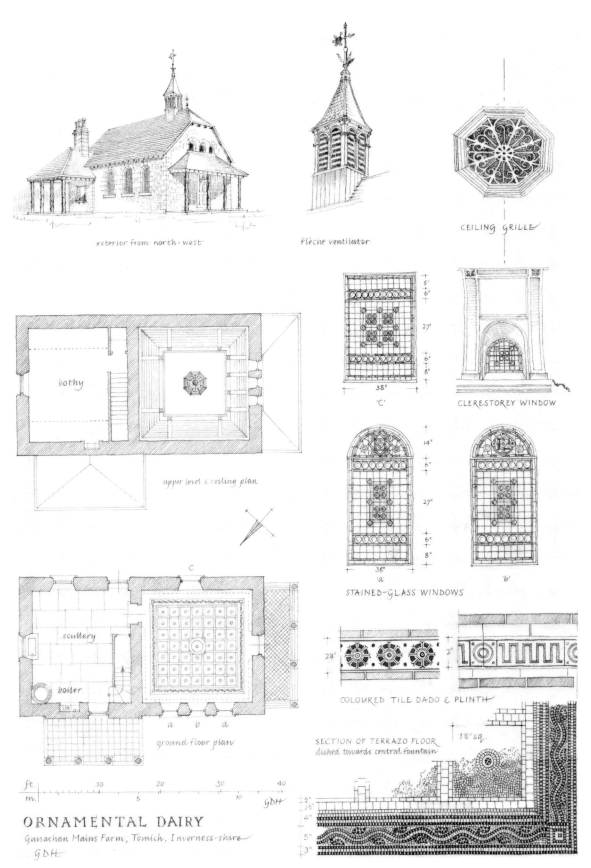

exterior from north-west

flèche ventilator

CEILING GRILLE

bothy

upper level & ceiling plan

'C'

CLERESTOREY WINDOW

8"
6"
27"
6"
8"
38"

14"
6"
27"
6"
8"
38"
'a'
'b'

STAINED-GLASS WINDOWS

scullery

boiler

C

a   b   a

ground floor plan

ft.   10   20   30   40
m.   5   10
GDH

24"
2"

COLOURED TILE DADO & PLINTH

SECTION OF TERRAZO FLOOR
dished towards central fountain

18"sq.

3"
2½"
4"
5"
3"

ORNAMENTAL DAIRY
Guisachan Mains Farm, Tomich, Inverness-shire
GDH

Dairy, Guisachan, Tomich, Inverness-shire (pencil drawing)

17

A. Dairy, Guisachan, Tomich, Inverness-shire; scullery

the inner, and 1 ft 2 in (0·36 m) thick. In the centre of the stone there is a circular hole 8½ in (216 mm) in diameter, through which a wooden shaft was passed in the upright stone and wedged into position. The outer end of the shaft was harnessed to a horse; a swivel-coupling at the inner end was affixed to an iron pin at the hub of the mill. A four-legged iron plate and pivot still survive, set into a sunk granite base some 1 ft 6 in (0·46 m) square.

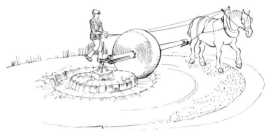

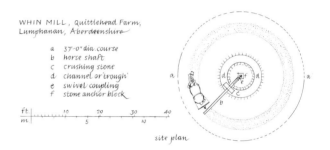

WHIN MILL, Quittlehead Farm, Lumphanan, Aberdeenshire

a 37'-0" dia. course
b horse shaft
c crushing stone
d channel or trough
e swivel coupling
f stone anchor block

site plan

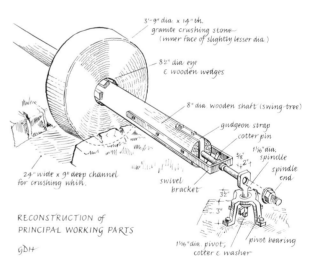

3'-9" dia × 14" th. granite crushing stone (inner face of slightly lesser dia.)

8½" dia eye & wooden wedges

8" dia wooden shaft (swing-tree)

gudgeon strap
cotter pin

1 1/16" dia. spindle

spindle end

24" wide × 9" deep channel for crushing whin.

swivel bracket

pivot bearing

1 1/16" dia. pivot, cotter & washer

RECONSTRUCTION of PRINCIPAL WORKING PARTS

gDH

B. Whin-mill, Quittlehead, Lumphanan, Aberdeenshire

16 B scullery, which has a flagstone floor, contains a small fireplace with a cast-iron hob-grate and range; next to it in the N corner of the NW wall there is an original boiler with a weight-operated lid and a metal pot-lining. A narrow wooden stair leads to a store or bothy on the first floor.

17 The floor of the dairy itself is paved with coloured terrazzo laid in a pattern of squares. It is dished towards the centre of the chamber, where there is a baluster-shafted grey marble fountain which waters the floor and thereby helps to preserve a cool atmosphere. The surrounding walls incorporate two bracketed black marble shelves and above there is a timber shelf, ledged as a plate-rack, with ornamental cast-iron brackets. The walls are lined to the height of the upper shelf with glazed white tiles, which have decorated margins at the brown-glazed plinth and dado. Coloured window-glass set in leaded geometric patterns, including those of the clerestorey windows in the SW wall, helps to reduce the effects of direct sunlight. The plaster ceiling is coved and ribbed, and an octagonal filigree grille in the flat area provides ventilation from the louvred flèche. Wire gauze panels above the external door in the SW wall also admit cooling draughts.

Original utensils still preserved within the dairy and scullery include a range of cooling dishes of white glazed porcelain, various tin containers, two small barrel-churns, a pair of scales and a pine table.

Whin-mill   NJ 567045
Quittlehead, Lumphanan, Aberdeenshire
    Grampian, Kincardine and Deeside   1980

The whin-mill, for crushing whins for cattle fodder, was once a common item of farming equipment, especially in the north-east. In this example, the large granite crushing-stone lies on its side within a kerbed and stone-lined channel.[25] The channel, serving as the crushing area, is surrounded by a circular horse-gang platform some 37 ft (11·28 m) in diameter overall. The stone itself—an edge-stone slightly conical in shape so as to turn in a circle—is 3 ft 9 in (1·14 m) in diameter on its outer face and rather less on

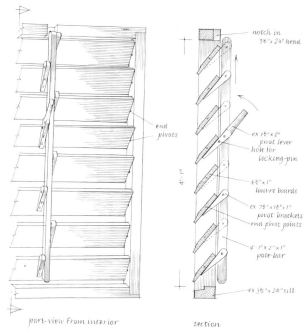

part-view from interior   section

LOUVRE DETAIL, Tannery, Keith, Banffshire   GDH

A

B

Tannery, Keith, Banffshire
  A.   details of adjustable wall-louvre
  B.   exterior from s

Tannery   NJ 428507
Keith, Banffshire
    Grampian, Moray   1980

This is a three-storeyed oblong building, probably of early 19th-century date with some later modifications. It measures 32 ft 9 in (9·98 m) in length by 16 ft 7 in (5·06 m) transversely. The lowest storey and the gables are rubble built; the side-walls of the upper two floors are louvred to provide the necessary ventilation. There are two original adjustable louvres operated by a pole-bar in the westernmost bay of the s wall of the airing loft; the remaining louvres are of the fixed type, and the N elevation is mainly weather boarded. The building has a collar-rafter roof utilising sawn half-log timbers and adzed floor-beams; latterly it appears to have served as a laundry-house with the original airing-loft then being used for drying.

Another provincial tannery, having characteristic louvred frontage and a well-preserved airing-loft with tenter-rails, has been noted at Mill Street, Ayr.[26*]

C

D

E

Tannery, Mill Street, Ayr
  C.   detail of louvred side-walls
  D.   tenter-rails in drying-loft
  E.   street frontage

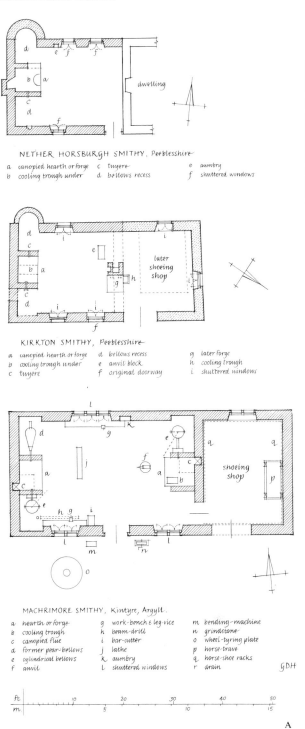

NETHER HORSBURGH SMITHY, Peeblesshire

a canopied hearth or forge   c tuyère   e aumbry
b cooling trough under   d bellows recess   f shuttered windows

KIRKTON SMITHY, Peeblesshire

a canopied hearth or forge   d bellows recess   g later forge
b cooling trough under   e anvil block   h cooling trough
c tuyère   f original doorway   i shuttered windows

MACHRIMORE SMITHY, Kintyre, Argyll.

a hearth or forge   g work-bench & leg-vice   m bending-machine
b cooling trough   h beam-drill   n grindstone
c canopied flue   i bar-cutter   o wheel-tyring plate
d former pear-bellows   j lathe   p horse-trave
e cylindrical bellows   k aumbry   q horse-shoe racks
f anvil   l shuttered windows   r drain

GDH

ft   10   20   30   40   50
m   5   10   15

A

B

A. Smithies; comparative plans
B. Smithy, Nether Horsburgh, Peeblesshire

about 41 m NNE of the neighbouring mill. Adequately lit by a series of mullioned windows fitted with dwarf shutters within, it is planned with two forges, or hearths, backing respectively onto the W gable-wall and an intermediate cross-wall, beyond which is a shoeing-shop. It continued in use until the late 1960s and still preserves the usual original features and its earth floor.

Each forge is equipped with a cylindrical bellows set in a [21 A] side recess; the middle forge incorporates a stone cooling-trough; the gable forge formerly possessed a set of the earlier pear-bellows in the NW corner. Other standard tools [20 C] and equipment include the anvil, mounted on an elm block, a swage block, two work-benches with steel leg-vices, and a roller-type tyre-bending machine. In addition, fixed to the bench beneath the SW window, there is a beam-drill worked [21 C] manually by turning a brace and bit while under pressure from a weighted beam operated by a lever. Outside the smithy, just W of the entrance, is an iron wheel-tyring platform, or plate, and a grindstone.

The shoeing-shop, which is floored with timber planks bedded directly on earth, is also entered externally from a wide segmental-arched doorway in the S wall, and is equipped with high-level wall-racks, once stocked amply with a varied range of ready-made horseshoes; a much rarer feature, set against the E wall, is a well-preserved horse-frame, or trave, for handling difficult horses while they [21 B] were being shod.

C

C. Smithy, Machrimore, Kintyre, Argyll;
    pear-shaped bellows

Smithy
Machrimore, Kintyre, Argyll
Strathclyde, Argyll and Bute

NR 701092

1962, 1983

This estate-built smithy,[27] neatly executed in rubble masonry with dressed offset margins to openings and quoins, and roofed in slate with overhanging eaves, stands

A

B

Smithy, Machrimore, Kintyre, Argyll
   A.   middle forge and bellows
   B.   horse-trave in shoeing-shop
   C.   traditional beam-drill

C

C

A

B

C

D

Ice-house and Salmon-bothy
Dunbeath, Caithness
Highland, Caithness   ● 1970

These two buildings, and a rubble-built warehouse situated a short distance to the N, form part of the herring- and salmon-fishing station which developed in stages around the mouth of the Dunbeath Water from the early 19th century onwards.[28] The large two-chambered ice-house (ND 166294) is built into the side of the headland above the quayside. The W face of the building measures 20 ft 10 in (6·35 m) in width, and the extrados of the semicircular barrel vault is overlaid with turf; the vault incorporates a high-level trapdoor enabling ice to be fed into the inner freezing-chamber. The small outer chamber was evidently used for washing and weighing the fish, and there is a drain-outlet immediately in front of the main doorway. The opening in the cross-wall between the two chambers has an inner and outer stout wooden door, and during the refrigeration process the intervening space was filled with sawdust as an insulator in order to maintain a low temperature within the inner chamber. This chamber measures 18 ft (5·49 m) by 15 ft (4·57 m) internally, and is floored at a slightly lower level to facilitate drainage of the melted ice. The floors throughout are of flagstone.

The bothy (ND 166293) stands on the E side of the mouth of the Dunbeath Water, built partly into the headland with its gable facing seaward. Externally, it is a plain single-storeyed and gabled structure measuring 40 ft 3 in (12·27 m) in length by 19 ft 6 in (5·94 m) transversely. Inside, it has two main compartments divided by a stone cross-wall: an equipment store takes up about two-thirds of the space; the other compartment, which appears to have been re-modelled, includes a foreman's office and bunk-bed in the *22 D* SW quarter, screened by a timber partition, and a range of four wooden bunks lining the E wall. The floors are flagged *22 C* throughout, and there is a fireplace in each gable-wall, that in the store being set across the S angle and having a curved rear wall.

Ice-house and salmon-bothy, Dunbeath, Caithness
   A.   ice-house
   B.   salmon-bothy
   C.   wooden bunks lining E wall of salmon-bothy
   D.   foreman's office and bunk in salmon-bothy

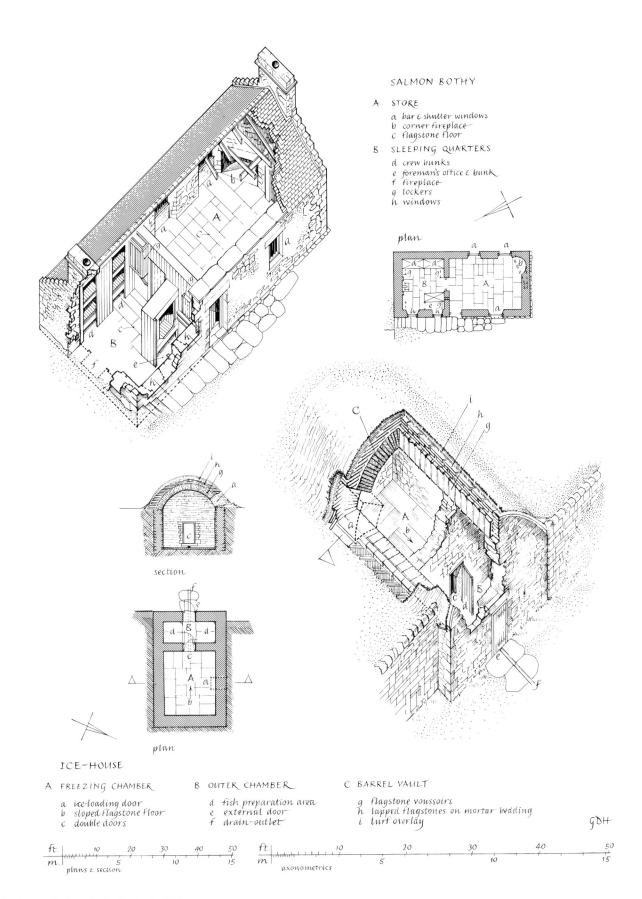

SALMON BOTHY

A STORE
   a bar & shutter windows
   b corner fireplace
   c flagstone floor

B SLEEPING QUARTERS
   d crew bunks
   e foreman's office & bunk
   f fireplace
   g lockers
   h windows

plan

section

plan

ICE-HOUSE

A FREEZING CHAMBER
   a ice-loading door
   b sloped flagstone floor
   c double doors

B OUTER CHAMBER
   d fish preparation area
   e external door
   f drain-outlet

C BARREL VAULT
   g flagstone voussoirs
   h lapped flagstones on mortar bedding
   i turf overlay

GDH

ft | 10 20 30 40 50
m | 5 10 15
plans & section

ft | 10 20 30 40 50
m | 5 10 15
axonometrics

Ice-house and salmon-bothy, Dunbeath, Caithness

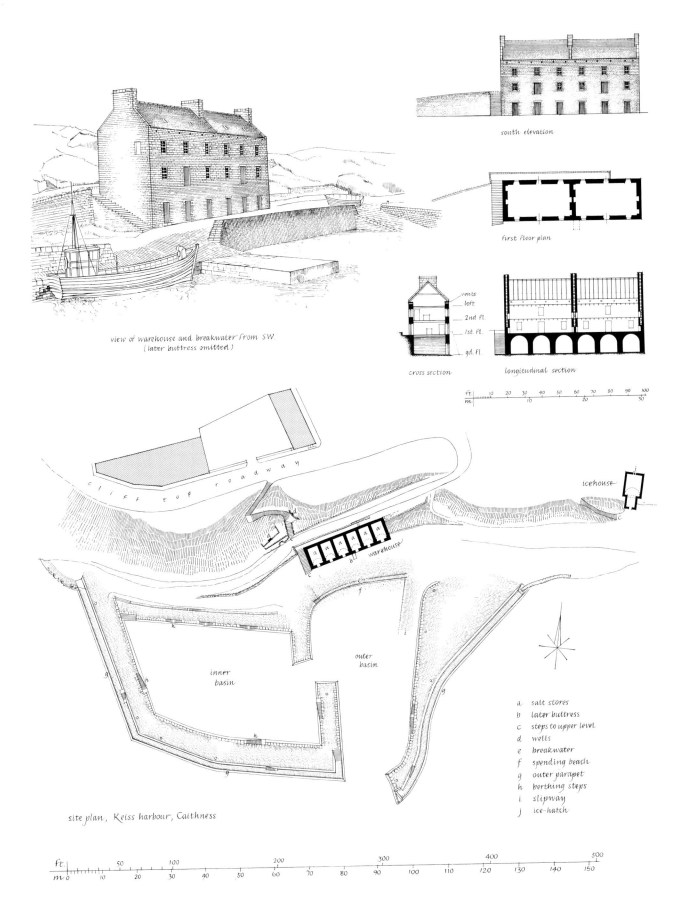

south elevation

first floor plan

cross section

longitudinal section

vents
loft
2nd fl.
1st fl.
gd. fl.

ft.
m

10 20 30 40 50 60 70 80 90 100
10 20 30

view of warehouse and breakwater from SW.
(later buttress omitted)

cliff top roadway

icehouse

warehouse

inner
basin

outer
basin

a   salt stores
b   later buttress
c   steps to upper level
d   wells
e   breakwater
f   spending beach
g   outer parapet
h   berthing steps
i   slipway
j   ice-hatch

site plan, Keiss harbour, Caithness

ft.
m   0

50   100   200   300   400   500
10   20   30   40   50   60   70   80   90   100   110   120   130   140   150

Harbour ND 361609
Keiss, Caithness
Highland, Caithness ●][1968, 1980

Keiss is one of the more picturesque and better-preserved of the small 19th-century herring- and salmon-fishing stations on the eastern coast of Caithness. Keiss Bay was inspected and given qualified approval as a haven by Thomas Telford in 1790, but the small harbour with pier, slipway and stilling-basin was not built until 1820.[29]

The harbour walls and parapets are constructed of coursed rubble masonry, usually comprising large slabs of local flagstone; the walls have battered sides and incorporate recessed stairways. The breakwater at the end of the stilling-basin is built of vertically set masonry. Behind the breakwater there is a three-storeyed six-bay warehouse which measures 80 ft 6 in (24·54 m) by 22 ft 9 in (6·93 m) overall; it occupies a bankside position with the ground-floor and first-floor loading-doors fronting the quayside. The ground floor consists entirely of vaulted cellarage, comprising six transverse barrel-vaulted chambers with independent access designed to serve as salt stores in the herring-curing process. The first floor is flagged and the second floor joisted; the plans at each level are roughly mirrored on either side of a central stone partition, each three-bay unit having a fireplace at opposing ends.

A short distance to the NE of the warehouse and harbour there is an ice-house built into the headland. Behind its gabled outer chamber there is a main vaulted chamber measuring 19 ft (5·79 m) by 14 ft (4·27 m) laterally and served by a high-level hatch beneath the crown of the vault in the landward gable.

Above the harbour, a range of dwellings along the cliff-top terminates at the s end with a yard and an adjoining store and salmon-bothy. The latter is equipped with two pairs of bunk-beds and continued in use until 1940.

A

Fish-curing station, Wick, Caithness
  A. curing-house
  B. plan

Fish-curing Station ND 366510
Wick, Caithness
Highland, Caithness 1983

Situated within the narrow limits of the 'Shore' wharf on the N side of Wick's inner harbour, this former small curing-yard, and its now ruinous three-storeyed building backing on to the cliff face, represents one of the few surviving relics of the port's once flourishing fishing-industry. Close proximity to the wharf and an adequate open area for the storage of barrels and the movement of carts were evidently basic requirements, combined with one or more buildings for preparing the fish, making barrels, and affording temporary lodgings for the large work-force—mainly women—engaged during the brief but hectic herring-fishing season in the summer.[30*]

The majority of indoor activities connected with this particular station appear to have been compactly arranged in one building. It is built of roughly coursed rubble masonry and measures approximately 87 ft (26·52 m) in length by 21 ft (6·40 m) in depth over walls 3 ft (0·91 m) in thickness. Its barrack-like frontage is distinguished by three 10 ft-wide (3·05 m) semicircular-arched openings on the ground floor, and the regulated grouping of windows and doorways on the two upper floors—the latter evidently reached by external stairs and galleries, of which the iron supporting-brackets still remain. Internally, the upper storeys are divided into four main compartments by stout cross-walls, variously splayed and incurved at their inner ends, which, in conjunction with a corresponding but intercommunicating arrangement on the ground floor, act structurally as retaining walls against the cliff outcrop. At a point about midway along its length, the rear wall incorporates a large circular flue partly cut into the rock face. As far as can be deduced, the compartments on the two upper floors, which were equipped with fireplaces in the gable and partition walls, were designed primarily as living quarters, while the ground floor served as a gutting-shed during the season, and as a coopers' shop for the rest of the year. The archways were large enough to admit the end of a cart for unloading the fish into the gutting-trough, or farland, and a planked floor area at the w end may be identified as the salt-store; the circular area beneath the large flue may be identified as the firing-berth in connection with the barrel-making process.[31]

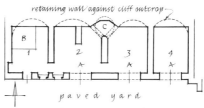

GROUND FLOOR PLAN : gutting-shed & cooperage
A. gutting area B. salt storage C. firing berth
1, 2, 3, 4 : main sub-divisions on upper floors

B

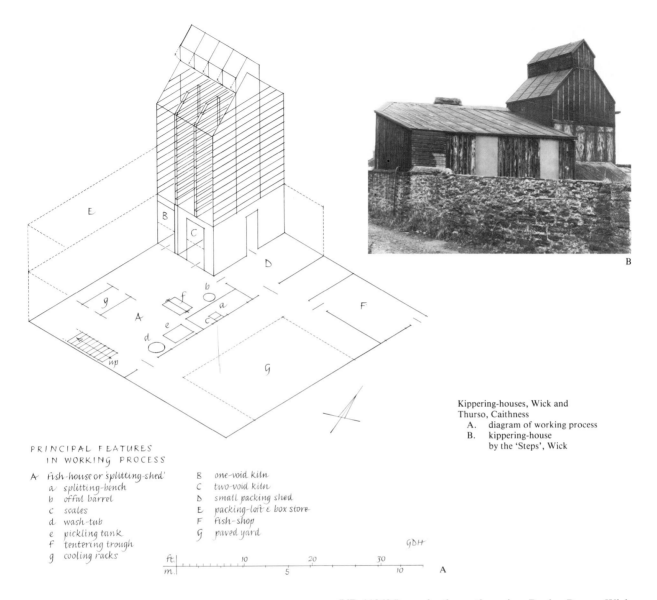

Kippering-houses, Wick and
Thurso, Caithness
  A. diagram of working process
  B. kippering-house
      by the 'Steps', Wick

B

PRINCIPAL FEATURES
IN WORKING PROCESS

A fish-house or 'splitting-shed'
  a splitting-bench
  b offal barrel
  c scales
  d wash-tub
  e pickling tank
  f tentering trough
  g cooling racks

B one-void kiln
C two-void kiln
D small packing shed
E packing-loft & box store
F fish-shop
G paved yard

GDH

A

Kippering-houses
Wick and Thurso, Caithness
    Highland, Caithness   ][1983

The traditional kippered-herring trade, as widely practised
in Wick and the smaller Caithness ports during the 19th
century, has now all but ceased, like the herring-fishing
itself in that region. At its peak, however, during the middle
decades of the century, the tall kipper-kilns of stone or
timber, with their steeply pitched roofs and ridge ventilators, were familiar features, standing either as isolated
units in the smaller harbours, such as Lybster,[32] or clustered
compactly together in Wick and its neighbouring Pulteneytown. Only two working plants now survive in Wick,
namely at the 'Steps' above Harbour Quay (ND 366506)
and in Albert Street, Pulteneytown (ND 366510). Two
earlier specimens, well-preserved but no longer in use, have
also been noted; one is situated in Shore Street, Thurso

(ND 119686) and the other in Bank Row, Wick
(ND 365506), which now forms part of the town's Heritage
Museum.

A detailed examination of the two working units in Wick,
although in their present form dating only from the early
years of this century, reveals all the traditional elements of a
typical kippering-plant.[33] The principal buildings included
facilities for preparing the fish (the fish-house or splitting-
shed), usually with a loft above for packing the kippers and
making up boxes, one or more kilns communicating directly
with the fish-house, and desirably a yard for storage and a
cart.

The 'Steps' example is a small unit with a one- and a
two-void kiln, but in other respects it follows the customary
process, which consisted of splitting the fish, washing and
pickling it, hanging it on tenter-sticks, and then smoking it
in the kiln, after which it was cooled on racks and then
packed. The tenter-sticks for hanging the fish in the kiln
were typically 3 ft 9 in (1·14 m) to 4 ft (1·22 m) long by about

26

A

B

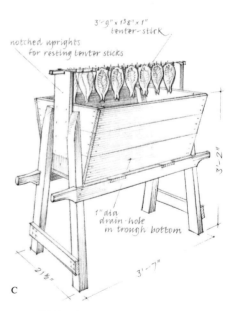

3'-9" x 1⅜" x 1"
tenter-stick

notched uprights
for resting tenter sticks

3'-2"

1" dia
drain-hole
in trough bottom

2'1½"

3'-7"

C

WOODEN TENTERING TROUGH.

Kippering-houses, Wick and Thurso, Caithness
A.   kippering-house, Shore Street, Thurso;
     interior of fish-house
     (entry doors to kiln on rear wall)
B.   rack-frames for holding full tenter-sticks
     before and after smoking
C.   tentering-trough (pencil drawing)

27

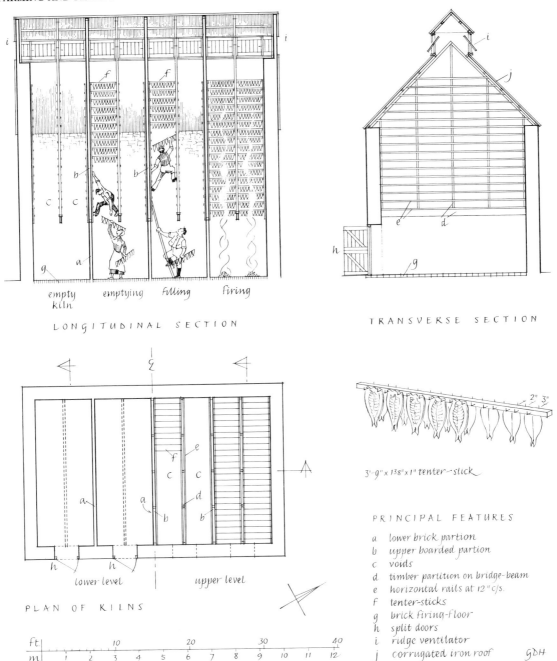

LONGITUDINAL SECTION

TRANSVERSE SECTION

PLAN OF KILNS

3'-9" x 138" x 1" tenter-stick

PRINCIPAL FEATURES

a   lower brick partition
b   upper boarded partition
c   voids
d   timber partition on bridge-beam
e   horizontal rails at 12" c/s.
f   tenter-sticks
g   brick firing-floor
h   split doors
i   ridge ventilator
j   corrugated iron roof   GDH

empty kiln   emptying   filling   firing

lower level   upper level

ft   10   20   30   40
m   1 2 3 4 5 6 7 8 9 10 11 12

2" 3"

Albert Street, Pulteneytown, Wick, Caithness;
reconstruction drawing of kipper-kilns

1½ in (38 mm) by 1 in (25 mm) in section, fitted with sharp angled hooks arranged in eight pairs along each side. The actual tentering operation took place over a trough fitted with a notched upright at each end to hold the tenter-stick.

The Albert Street unit, although far less complete, was originally much larger and housed four two-void kilns. Like the other example cited, they appear to have conformed to a fairly standard pattern and serve to illustrate a typical kiln.

The kiln was approximately 8 ft (2·44 m) in width and up to 18 ft (5·49 m) in length, and about 20 ft (6·10 m) to the wall-head. Its length was subdivided into two voids by a timber-framed partition supported on a beam about 7 ft (2·13 m) above the floor. Solid dividing walls between adjacent kilns, of brick or stone, were built to about the same height and then continued upwards as a close-boarded partition into the roof space. Horizontal rails (stringers)

27 C

28
30

28 (c)
28 (d)

28

A. Domestic fish-smoking kiln,
Lybster, Caithness

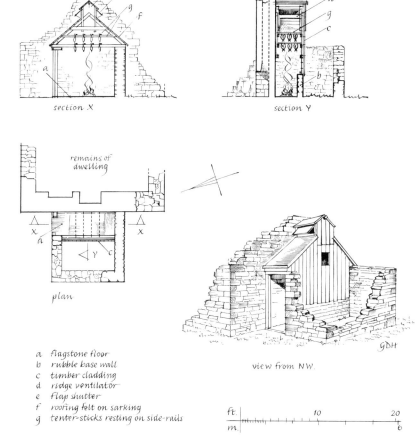

B

Kipper-kilns, Albert Street,
Pulteneytown, Wick, Caithness

B. kiln void, showing side-rails
    for resting tenter-sticks
C. tenter-sticks, wire trays,
    and basket-measures
    for oak-chip fires

a flagstone floor
b rubble base wall
c timber cladding
d ridge ventilator
e flap shutter
f roofing felt on sarking
g tenter-sticks resting on side-rails

section X

section Y

remains of
dwelling

plan

view from N.W.

ft.   10   20
m.   6

A

C

spaced at 1 ft (0·31 m) centres were affixed to the opposing
wall-surfaces for resting the full tenter-sticks. The kiln
floors were of brick, and the door at the end of each kiln
was halved across so that the hinged portions could be
opened independently in order to regulate the draught in
conjunction with the roof ventilator, built along the ridge
and equipped with hinged doors. The outer walls of the
building were usually of stone carried up to the wall-head,
or gave way to timber cladding at about the 7 ft (2·13 m) void
line. In order to fill a kiln with the tentered fish, and likewise
to strip it after smoking, the 'smoker' climbed up and down
the horizontal rails. The smoking process usually took from
six to twelve hours, and consisted of burning successive piles
of oak chips and sawdust, carefully measured in baskets and
disposed in rows of three beneath each void.

A kiln of a domestic scale, situated on the grassy plain at
the head of Lybster harbour has also been noted
(ND 245348). Probably used for smoking finnan haddock
and herring, it is built against the gable of a former dwelling
within the walls of a roofless outhouse. It measures 7 ft
(2·13 m) by 3 ft (0·91 m) internally, and although of
rudimentary construction it incorporates all the features of
the commercial kiln: a solid floor (of flagstones) and a
dwarf wall with timber-clad frame above, fitted with a
number of rails for tenter-sticks, and a ridge ventilator on
the pitched roof.

29 B,C

29 A

Kippering-house, Albert Street,
Pulteneytown, Wick, Caithness

NOTES

n.1 Shaw, J P, *Water-power in Scotland 1550-1870* (1984);
Donnachie, I L and Stewart, N K, *PSAS,* **98** (1965-6), 276-99;
Douglas, G J, Oglethorpe, M K and Hume, J R, *Scottish Windmills* (SIAS, University of Strathclyde, 1984).

n.2 Walker, D B, *SAF,* **8** (1977), 52-74.

n.3 See Cruden, S H, *PSAS,* **81,** (1946-7), 43-7; Curwen, E C, *Antiquity,* **18** (1944), 130-46; Dickinson, H W and Straker, E, *Transactions of the Newcomen Society,* **13,** (1932-3), 89-94; Goudie, G, *PSAS,* **20** (1885-6), 257-97; Maxwell, S, *TDGAS,* 3rd series, **33** (1954-5), 185-96; Cheape, H, *Kirtomy Mill and Kiln* (Scottish Vernacular Buildings Working Group, 1984).

n.4 E.g. Preston Mill, East Lothian (NT 594778), kiln refloored; Benholm Mill, Kincardineshire (NO 806690); and other examples noted by SIAS.

n.5 Donnachie, I L, *The Industrial Archaeology of Galloway* (1971), 39-40.

n.6 Ritchie, J, *PSAS,* **59** (1924-5), 128-42; and see Fenton, A and Walker, D B, *The Rural Architecture of Scotland* (1981), figs. 147-9.

n.7 For a regional survey, see Michie, G and Fenton, A, *Scottish Studies,* **7** (1963), 47-56. Specimens recorded by RCAMS include that built into a wall at Brackside, Reay, Caithness (NC 956646) and a free-standing press at Rothes Glen Hotel, Moray (NJ 254525).

n.8 E.g. Livingston Mill, West Lothian (NT 033668).

n.9 For a general account, see Robinson, J M, *Georgian Model Farms* (1983), 92-100.

n.10 E.g. behind 16 High Street, Peebles (NT 252404); meat-market, formerly at corner of Dundee Street and Fountainbridge, Edinburgh (NT 247729).

n.11 See also, e.g., *Inventory of Peeblesshire,* **2,** No. 591.

n.12 *Inventory of Stirlingshire,* **2,** Nos. 263, 267, 276; see also Graham, A, *Scottish Studies,* **5,** (1961), 117-19.

n.13 Walker, D B, *Folk Life,* **21** (1982-3), 71-82.

n.14 Graham, A, *PSAS,* **95** (1961-2), 300-3; **97** (1963-4), 212-25; **99** (1966-7), 173-90; **101** (1968-9), 200-85; **108** (1976-7), 332-65; *TDGAS,* 3rd series, **52** (1976-7), 109-42; **54** (1979), 39-74; and *Old Ayrshire Harbours (Ayrshire Collections,* **14,** No. 3, 1984).

n.15 This account and the drawings have been prepared in consultation with Mr R Taylor and Mr D Martin, the former miller, and with Mr A C S Dixon, who conducted the Commission's original field survey in 1962.

n.16 Reference dated 1836, formerly in the possession of the late Mr Duncan Colville, Machrihanish, relating to negotiations made by his family for a new lease of the mill.

n.17 *Inventory of Argyll,* **1,** No. 352.

n.18 In the isometric drawing, certain distance points (e.g. that between the wallower and great spur-wheel) have been adjusted for clarity.

n.19 Cf. Russell, J, *Transactions of the Newcomen Society,* **24** (1943-5), 55-64; Tucker, D G, *Post-Medieval Archaeology,* **11** (1977), 1-21; idem, *Industrial Archaeology Review,* **6** (1982), 186-93; and see idem, *PSAS,* **114** (1984), 539-56.

n.20 Based on SIAS survey of 1981, and Goudie, G, *PSAS,* **20** (1885-6), 257-97.

n.21 Donnachie, I L and Stewart, N K, *PSAS,* **98** (1965-6), 276-99 at 288, No. 10.

n.22 Cf. *Inventory of Argyll,* **1,** No. 351.

n.23 Stephen, H, *The Book of the Farm* (1844), 318-22. See also Fenton, A, *Scottish Country Life* (1976), 83-8, and Fenton, A and Walker, D B, *The Rural Architecture of Scotland* (1981), 167-81.

n.24 A detailed account of threshing and drying grain is given by Firth, J, *Reminiscences of an Orkney Parish* (1922), 17-19. See also Fenton, A, *Scottish Country Life* (1976), 80-3, 95-7. For grain-drying in Caithness, see Henderson, J, *General View of the Agriculture of the County of Caithness* (1812), 106-7, cited in Baldwin, J R (ed.), *Caithness, A Cultural Crossroads* (1982), 102. For the Hebridean type of kiln see, e.g., *Inventory of Argyll,* **3,** No. 371, and discussion in *Gwerin,* **1** (1956-7), 161-70.

n.25 For the different methods of crushing whins or gorse into cattle food, see Ritchie, J, *PSAS,* **59** (1924-5), 128-42.

n.26 In the airing loft of the former tannery at Mill Street, Ayr (NS 340216), wooden rails furnished with closely spaced tenter-hooks are secured to the roof tie-beams and aligned parallel to the long axis of the building.

n.27 This account has been prepared in consultation with Mr R Taylor senior (1984).

n.28 *NSA,* **15** (Caithness), 104; Dunlop, J, 'Pulteneytown and the planned villages of Caithness', in Baldwin, J R (ed.), *Caithness, A Cultural Crossroads* (1982), 130-59 at 147.

n.29 Dunlop, op. cit., 136-7.

n.30 A photograph in the Alex Johnston Collection, Wick Heritage Museum, shows this building in a ruinous condition as early as 1900.

n.31 Duthie, R J, *The Art of Fishcuring* (1911), 5-11.

n.32 Anson, P F, *Fishing Boats and Fisher Folk on the East Coast of Scotland* (1930), illustration on p. 252.

n.33 Duthie, op. cit., 33-44.

2 MALT WHISKY DISTILLING

Although growing out of the farming economy described in the previous section, the practice of making pot-still malt whisky has become a sufficiently renowned and distinctive feature of Scottish industry and commerce to merit detailed treatment in its own section.

Until the end of the 18th century, especially in the Highlands, private distillation for home consumption was common, and as whisky, traditionally known as aqua vitae (Gaelic *uisge beatha*), became increasingly recognised as a marketable commodity, even more was made illicitly in 61 contravention of the stricter Excise controls imposed during the latter half of the century. Against this background the legalised industry developed only slowly and did not really 52 gain a foothold until new legislation was enacted between 1816 and 1823. Thereafter the erection of licensed distilleries for commercial production was rapid, and by the later 1880s the style and pattern of the typical Victorian malt-whisky distillery had become fully established. In general, their character remained largely unchanged until well into the 20th century, but since the 1960s they have been extensively modernised, particularly with regard to plant and internal equipment. Although the basic techniques of the whisky-making process have been carefully preserved, few, if any, distilleries now retain their full range of older working-methods. Initially, this survey was confined to the distilleries in Islay,[1] but it soon became apparent that in order to obtain a comprehensive picture of the traditional malt pot-still distillery it was necessary to select the evidence from a wider field, where specific features and parts of the older plant are still in use or survive.[2]

Barley, peat and a suitable water-supply are the essential ingredients for making pure malt-whisky, and in the past their local availability was largely responsible for the main geographical areas of the industry being established in the w and NE Highlands and selected parts of the Lowlands. By far the most important single factor influencing their location was the water-supply, which was drawn from the neighbouring uphill lochs, burns and springs. Water of superior quality was reserved exclusively for making the whisky, whose character was demonstrably affected by it, but water was also required in large quantities for general purposes such as cooling, washing and originally for supplying the motive power for the premises. Several distilleries were obliged to guard against drought by conserving the water-supply in nearby dams, and at others, when there was no direct water-link the nearest source was tapped by man-made lades or culverts. Thus, at the small distillery of Edradour, near Pitlochry, Perthshire, the dam 56 continues to be used, as also at Balvenie, Dufftown,

A. Edradour, Pitlochry, Perthshire; dam and malt-barn

B. Balvenie, Dufftown, Banffshire; general view of dam and distillery

31

Banffshire (NJ 324414); and in earlier times artificial lades were cut at both Ardbeg (NR 415462) and Bowmore (NR 309598), both on Islay, while at Royal Lochnagar, Deeside, Aberdeenshire (NO 266938), an underground culvert was made of hollowed-out tree sections tapered with spigot ends.

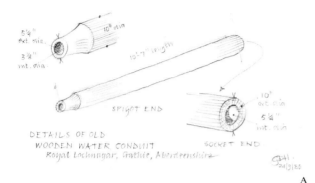

A

Proximity to a good transport system also became an increasingly important factor as the industry expanded and looked to wider marketing areas. On Islay and in Campbeltown, Kintyre, Argyll (NR 7120)[3]—regions once renowned for smuggling—it is significant that the surviving distilleries are situated on the coastline, all but one being equipped with nearby piers or jetties for direct access to shipping-services. The exception was the long-established business of Laphroaig, Islay (NR 387451), where coal and other supplies were delivered by Clyde 'puffers' and then

transhipped into small boats, or landed in carts at low tide; the whisky was floated out to the ships in casks lashed together. In the Lowlands and NE Highlands the landward distilleries came to rely increasingly on an efficient rail or road system. Mortlach, Dufftown, Banffshire (NJ 326396), for example, had its own railway sidings linked to the main line, and the juxtaposed distilleries of Tamdhu (NJ 189418) and Knockando (NJ 195414), Moray, were built adjacent to the main railway. For the more isolated distillery of Glenlivet, Banffshire (NJ 195290), the only means of transport was by road, the vehicles graduating from the horse-drawn cart to the steam-tractor and steam-lorry.

33 A

D. Bowmore, Islay, Argyll, c. 1890

B. Laphroaig, Islay, Argyll;
coaling, 1937

C. Bunnahabhainn,
Islay, Argyll;
general view
from seaward

A

B

Glenlivet, Minmore, Banffshire
- A. general view, 1890
- B. worm-tubs, 1890

A. Laphroaig, Islay,
Argyll, *c.* 1900

The form and layout of distilleries were largely determined by the main stages in the whisky-making process,
which may be summarised as germination, extraction,
fermentation, distillation, and maturation. The principal
38,39 buildings are the multi-storeyed malt-barns, the extensive
53 A,B warehouses and the distillation block itself. In general, they
present attractive groupings with neat regular fenestrations
to the barns and the warehouses, characterised usually by
34,36 the tapered roof of the kilns and by the tall chimney-stacks.

In historical and physical development they tend to fall into
two main categories, one comprising the earlier distilleries,
which evolved piecemeal over a long period and often from
primitive beginnings, and the other being the later distilleries built from the outset as rationally planned units, often
with their own self-contained communities. On Islay, the
former is best represented in detail by Laphroaig, whose *34* A
development from a modest farm-unit is well documented *35*
from 1840 onwards through a sequence of building-phases

B. Lagavulin, Islay, Argyll;
view from across the bay

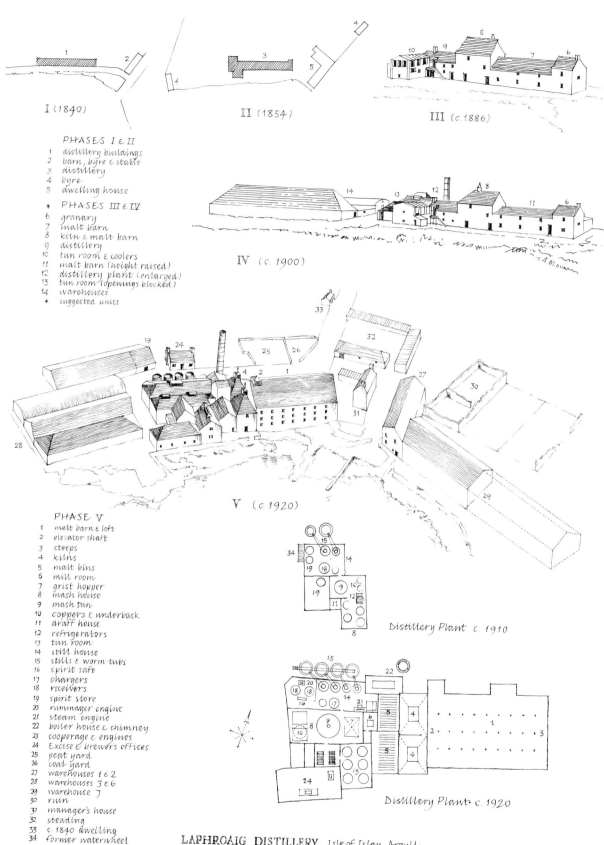

I (1840) II (1854) III (c.1886)

IV (c.1900)

V (c.1920)

PHASES I & II
1 distillery buildings
2 barn, byre & stable
3 distillery
4 byre
5 dwelling house

* PHASES III & IV
6 granary
7 malt barn
8 kiln & malt barn
9 distillery
10 tun room & coolers
11 malt barn (height raised)
12 distillery plant (enlarged)
13 tun room (openings blocked)
14 warehouses
* suggested units

PHASE V
1 malt barn & loft
2 elevator shaft
3 steeps
4 kilns
5 malt bins
6 mill room
7 grist hopper
8 mash house
9 mash tun
10 coppers & underback
11 draff house
12 refrigerators
13 tun room
14 still house
15 stills & worm tubs
16 spirit safe
17 chargers
18 receivers
19 spirit store
20 rummager engine
21 steam engine
22 boiler house & chimney
23 cooperage & engines
24 Excise & brewers offices
25 peat yard
26 coal yard
27 warehouses 1 & 2
28 warehouses 3 & 6
29 warehouse 7
30 ruin
31 manager's house
32 steading
33 c.1840 dwelling
34 former waterwheel

Distillery Plant c. 1910

Distillery Plant c. 1920

LAPHROAIG DISTILLERY, Isle of Islay, Argyll.
known phases of development and suggested plant layout

GDH

A. Bruichladdich, Islay, Argyll, before alterations, c. 1960

to a complex nucleated layout by about 1900.[4] Bruichlad-
36 A   dich, Islay (NR 264611), on the other hand, is a distillery of
37   comparable size built in the 1880s to a preconceived plan,
with the main processing-units disposed in a regular
courtyard layout, in common with many others of the later
32 C   period. Bunnahabhainn (NR 420732), also on Islay, built in
1881 may be cited as a grander example of this category,
verging on the institutional in character, while on the
36 B   mainland the smaller distillery of Speyburn, Moray
(NJ 272503), designed by C C Doig and opened in 1897, is
celebrated for its classic functional profile.

In general, the building-materials are composed of local
rubble masonry and slate, and for the newer establishments
exposed masonry of snecked rubble and ashlar became the
rule. Latterly, brickwork was also used, notably for
alterations and extensions, and at both Caol Ila, Islay
(NR 428700) and Bruichladdich the main buildings erected
in the 1880s were designed in concrete, then a relatively new

material, the walling at Bruichladdich being constructed of
two-leaf precast blocks. Invariably the rougher walling and
any admixture of building-materials are rendered uniform
by applications of whitewash, several distilleries, such as
Lagavulin, Islay (NR 404457), and Caol Ila, using the plain   34 B
wall-surfaces to advertise the name of the distillery.   53 B
Internally the floors and roofs are framed in timber,
supported on rows of cast-iron columns over the wider floor
areas of the maltings and warehouses, while in the more   40 B
confined space of the tun-room and still-house an open   53 D
king-post roof truss was once a common feature. Good
roofs of the king-post type exist at Longmorn, Moray
(NJ 234583), Dallas Dhu, Moray (NJ 035566) and   46 A
Tamdhu, and the Lagavulin malt-barn preserves a very fine   47
range of queen-post trusses.

The economic advantages of centralised mechanical
maltings of the pneumatic and 'Saladin' type have caused a
steady reduction in the number of maltings located at

B. Speyburn, Rothes, Moray; general view

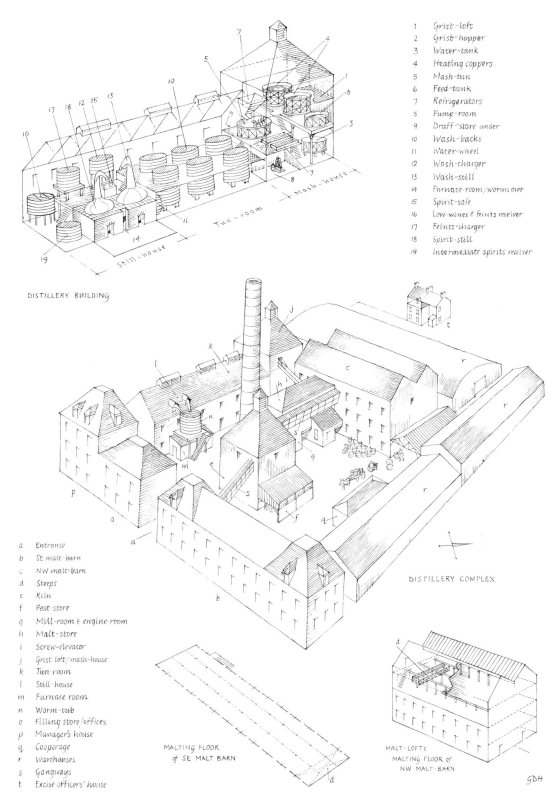

1 Grist-loft
2 Grist-hopper
3 Water-tank
4 Heating coppers
5 Mash-tun
6 Feed-tank
7 Refrigerators
8 Pump-room
9 Draff-store under
10 Wash-backs
11 Water-wheel
12 Wash-charger
13 Wash-still
14 Furnace-room/worms over
15 Spirit-safe
16 Low-wines & feints receiver
17 Feints-charger
18 Spirit-still
19 Intermediate spirits receiver

DISTILLERY BUILDING

DISTILLERY COMPLEX

a Entrance
b SE malt-barn
c NW malt-barn
d Steeps
e Kiln
f Peat-store
g Mill-room & engine-room
h Malt-store
i Screw-elevator
j Grist loft/mash-house
k Tun-room
l Still-house
m Furnace room
n Worm-tub
o Filling store/offices
p Manager's house
q Cooperage
r Warehouses
s Gangways
t Excise officers' house

MALTING FLOOR
of SE MALT BARN

MALT-LOFTE
MALTING FLOOR of
NW MALT-BARN

GDH

Bruichladdich, Islay, Argyll; reconstruction drawing of original layout

A. Port Ellen, Islay, Argyll; malt-barn and kiln

B. Ardbeg, Islay, Argyll; malt-barn and kilns

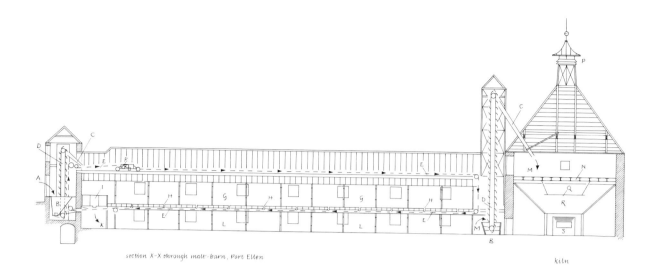

section X-X through malt-barn, Port Ellen

kiln

A   barley intake
B   hopper
C   chute
D   elevator
E   barley band
F   barley bogie
G   barley loft
H   floor chutes
I   cast-iron steeps
J   modern steeps
K   steeped grain
L   malting floor
M   green malt

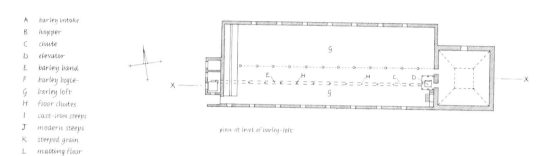

plan at level of barley-loft

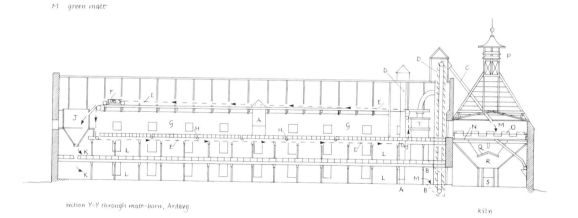

section Y-Y through malt-barn, Ardbeg.

kiln

N   drying floor
O   mechanical plough
P   roof vent
Q   baffle plate
R   smoke-chamber
S   furnace
T   dressing machine

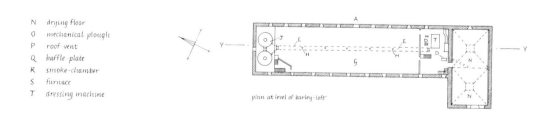

plan at level of barley-loft

scale for sections — plans to half-scale

Port Ellen and Ardbeg, Islay, Argyll; malt-barns and kilns

A

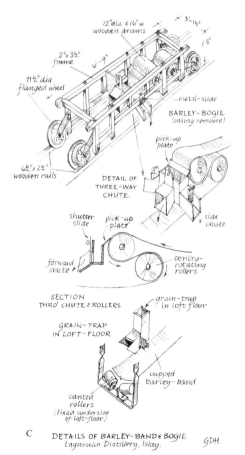

Ardbeg, Islay, Argyll
  A.   malt-loft interior
  B.   malting-floor

B

C   DETAILS OF BARLEY-BAND & BOGIE.
      Lagavulin Distillery, Islay.   GDH.

individual distilleries in recent years, but until the 1950s the malt-barn and associated kiln and malt deposit store were almost indispensable preliminaries in the working process.

38

39

40 A
The typical malt-barn is of two or three storeys, including a barley-loft for initial storage of the grain, originally delivered in sacks and transferred to the loft through the loading-door with block and tackle. The lower or malting-floors, surfaced with quarry tiles or slate slabs bedded in sand, usually have restricted head-room and are subdivided into long working-aisles by regular rows of columns. The floors are sparingly lit from the side-walls by small regularly spaced windows fitted with internal wooden shutters for controlling the temperature conditions within. Additional working-space in the two-storey arrangement, for example at Port Ellen, Islay (NR 359457), and Benriach, near Elgin, Moray (NJ 230585), is achieved by having one or more parallel ranges, each capable of functioning separately.

40 B

39

It is important to keep the grain well aerated and fresh before the germinating process, and for this purpose the barley-loft was equipped with a continuous conveyor belt, or barley-band, running centrally over its length within the roof-space and directly beneath the loft floor. It worked in conjunction with bucket elevators and small outlet-chutes spaced at intervals in the loft floor, and at the upper level was trained through contra-rotating drums set in a railed bogie. Incorporated in the bogie was a device for directing the grain into chutes which by a system of adjustable slides could discharge it to either side or forward. In effect, the bogie and barley-band acted as a pick-up and spreader, initially to spread the newly delivered grain on the loft floor, then to recycle it through the floor chutes, and ultimately to transfer it to the steeps.

39 (E)

40 C

41 B

The steeps, used for soaking the barley to promote germination, are situated at one end of the loft floor and consist of long rectangular tanks about 3 ft (0·9 m) deep, traditionally constructed of cast-iron flanged panels or slate slabs. They are equipped at the base with a central channel for drawing off the water, and traps or sluice-valves for

41 C

41 A

A. Bruichladdich, Islay, Argyll; cast-iron steeps

A

Benriach, Elgin, Moray
  B. barley-bogie
  C. concrete steeps

B

C

B

releasing the steeped barley into wheeled hoppers below for spreading it over the malting-floors. A more novel arrangement for spreading the malt and conveying it to the kilns is to be found at Lagavulin, where an overhead monorail system was used for carrying the grain in wicker baskets with a tip-up action, named elsewhere by Alfred Barnard as 'travellers'.[5]

The barley is left on the malting-floor for between seven and fourteen days, during which time it is regularly turned traditionally by hand, using wooden shovels, or shiels, in order to maintain an even germination and temperature. Normally contiguous with the malt-barn, and at the opposite end to the steeps, is the kiln for drying the green malt, which is collected in two-man hand-barrows, or malt-boxes, and then transferred to the kiln by elevator and overhead chute.

Kilns may range from 25 ft (7·6 m) to about 40 ft (12·2 m) square and are frequently arranged in pairs, sometimes with a common drying-floor. At ground level the kiln contains a central brick-furnace surmounted by a hopper-shaped smoke-chamber whose sheet-metal sides spread outward to encompass the drying-floor, usually no less than 14 ft (4·3 m) above in order to prevent the malt from being scorched; as a further safeguard a square horizontal baffle-plate may be suspended about 10 ft (3 m) above the furnace in order to deflect the heat and smoke to the outer limits of the chamber. Extant drying-floors are constructed of perforated wire, referred to as 'patent German wire tiles' when introduced in the 1880s; but earlier materials evidently included perforated clay-tiles, slates or iron plates, overlaid with loosely woven horsehair matting to retain the finer particles of grain.[6] The tall tapering roof of the kiln, elaborately framed in timber and latterly distinguished by a pagoda-style ventilator, is designed to draw the hot air upwards, while at the same time causing it to linger long enough for the peat smoke to flavour the drying malt.

In earlier times peat was the sole fuel used, burnt in open braziers or chauffeurs,[7] and although vast stocks are still required it is now reserved for the initial flavouring effect, the main source of heat being provided by other fuels such as coke and anthracite. Originally the malt was turned periodically by using hand-rakes, and after the drying stage it was shovelled out of the kiln through a wall-hatch. At the time of survey, home-maltings using the methods and features just described were seen working at Ardbeg, Bowmore and Laphroaig on Islay, and at Benriach.

C

Bowmore, Islay, Argyll
  A. malting-floor; wheeled hoppers and shiels in use
  B. kiln-furnace
Lagavulin, Islay, Argyll
  C. basket traveller

A. Port Ellen, Islay, Argyll;
   interior of kiln, showing
   drying-floor, open timber roof
   and grain-chute

B. Dallas Dhu, Forres, Moray;
   kiln

Usually adjacent to the kiln are the malt deposit store and
35 mill-room, where the dried malt is left for a period of about
   six weeks, after which it is passed through a dressing-
44 B machine to clean it of impurities and then it is ground to a
   coarse flour or grist in a roller-mill. Originally this was done
   between common millstones, but the operation has long
   since been performed by pairs of steel friction-rollers in a
   compact mechanical unit, of which early examples exist at
44 A Royal Lochnagar, and Edradour, Perthshire, the former
   dating from 1919 and made by R Boby, Ltd., of Bury St
   Edmunds. The traditional method for controlling the grain
   consistency, which becomes a critical factor at the mashing
   stage, was to use a small device known as a separator or
45 A sampling box, and these continue to be used at many
   distilleries, including Royal Lochnagar and
   Bunnahabhainn. After being ground, the malt is transferred to the grist bins, or hoppers, ready for the distillation
   process.

   The mash-house, tun-room, and still-house are invariably
35 grouped together under one or more roofs, to form the
37 distillation block. Ideally the various units and processing
57 vessels are linked to a gravity-flow system, as for example at
   Oban, Argyll (NM 859301), but where the site and gradient
59 do not allow, one or more reciprocating pumps have to be
   used for moving the grain or liquid to the different levels.

Most of the plant has to be renewed periodically, and hence
the few early features that survive are no older than the
1880s; in general, however, the major components preserve
much of their traditional style and character.

   The mash-house contains the vessels necessary for the
extraction process, which include one or more hot-water
tanks, or coppers, for initially heating the water, and the   37(4)
mash-tun, a larger circular vessel of cast iron, equipped with 37(5)
a revolving rake or stirrer for mixing successive batches of   45 C,D
malt with hot water; the resulting liquid extraction, or wort,
is run off into an adjacent tank, or underback, and the spent 57(14)
grain or draff disposed of for cattle-food. Old-style coppers 45 B
are still in use at Bowmore and Bruichladdich, and many
distilleries retain traditional mash-tuns. The early method
of cooling the wort—an essential preliminary to fermentation—was by running it into extensive shallow tanks,
exposed to the fresh air, sometimes equipped with revolving
fans, and usually situated above the mash-house or the   35
tun-room.[8] During the 1880s they were progressively
replaced by a much more compact device termed a   37(7)
refrigerator,[9] consisting of an intricate arrangement of   57(17)
copper pipes through which the wort passed while cold   44 C
water flowed over them. These in their turn have been   56 A
superseded by modern equipment.

B. Bruichladdich, Islay, Argyll;
   grain-dressing machine
C. Laphroaig, Islay, Argyll;
   'refrigerators', c. 1920

A. Royal Lochnagar, Deeside, Aberdeenshire;
   roller malt-mill

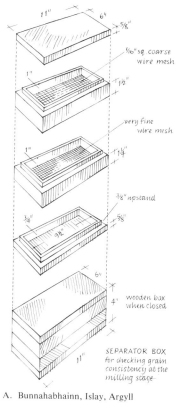

A. Bunnahabhainn, Islay, Argyll

Bowmore, Islay, Argyll
  B.   hot-water tanks
Edradour, Pitlochry,
Perthshire
  C.   mash-tun
  D.   mash-tun, stirring-
      mechanism

B

C

D

The tun-room, divided into two levels by iron gratings, normally adjoins the mash-house, and contains the large circular vessels, or washbacks, used in the fermenting *37(10)* process, which may range in number from two to as many as *56 A* fourteen or more. Made of wooden staves, of oak, pine or *57* larch, bound together with iron hoops and covered with *46 A,B* heavy sectional lids, the traditional washback is still favoured in many distilleries because of its good insulating properties. The mixture of wort and yeast pumped into each vessel is never higher than 3 ft (0·9 m) from the top so that no spillage occurs from the froth and turbulence caused during the fermentation process, a behaviour further kept under control by revolving arms, or switchers, fitted to each *57(22)* vessel.

The older still-house is usually a complex array of vessels *47* and apparatus linked at different levels by ladder-stairs and *48* gangways, often with much doubling back and crossing of *50* pipe-runs to accommodate everything in a limited space.

A. Dallas Dhu, Forres, Moray;
   tun-room at upper level
B. Bruichladdich, Islay, Argyll;
   tun-room at lower level

A

B

Tamdhu, Knockando, Moray; still-house (early riveted still in foreground)

Balvenie, Dufftown, Banffshire; still-house

Wood, copper and iron as the principal hardware largely shape its internal character in conjunction with the distinguishing labels and colours applied to the different vessels and circuits—an Excise requirement. The most prominent objects are the copper pot-stills, which until well into the 20th century were coal fired, and in the smaller *37* distilleries normally confined to a single wash-still and spirit-still—the minimum required for distillation. The *57* traditional still has changed little in general design since it was first evolved for the purpose of intensive distillation at the turn of the 18th century, when duty was charged according to the still capacity as opposed to the quantity of spirit that could be produced. In essence it has a broad, *49 A* shallow body with a domed bottom to afford the maximum *59* firing surface, and an elongated neck terminating in a bent pipe, or lyne-arm. But in its finer detail, notably the angle of the lyne-arm, it varies considerably from one distillery to another, a fact which accounts appreciably for the individual characteristics of malt whiskies, and hence the inveterate practice of renewing a still with one of matching design. Stills are exclusively made of copper, shaped and *47* built up in a number of sections riveted or welded together, and ranging in thickness from ⅝ in (16 mm) at the base to ³⁄₁₆ in (5 mm) at the neck. The wash-still initially separates the crude alcohol from the water and solid matter, and *49 C* when coal fired has to be equipped with a rummager, which is a device composed of three or four rotating arms fixed within the body of the still, to which chain mesh or sheeting is attached for scouring the bottom to prevent any sediment

B. Balvenie, Dufftown, Banffshire:
   still; man-door dated 1884

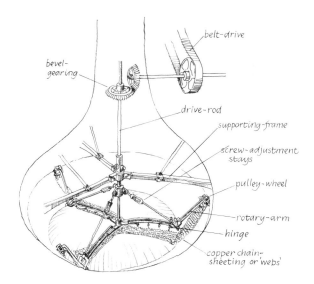

DETAIL OF 'RUMMAGER' IN WASH-STILL

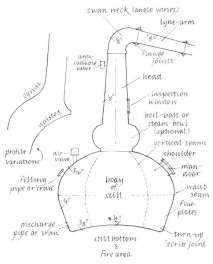

* sheet copper thicknesses graded as specified

A. Principal features of traditional
   pot-still

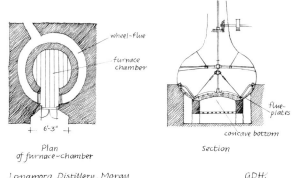

Plan
of furnace-chamber

Section

C   Longmorn Distillery, Moray   GDH.

A

from caking on the surface. The spirit-still receives the product from the wash-still, known as low-wines, and is usually of a smaller capacity owing to the absence of solid impurities in the liquid. Old coal-fired stills, formerly at Laphroaig and Glenlivet, are recorded in photographs taken about 1920, and working examples exist at Glen Grant, Moray (NJ 275495), and Longmorn; Bruichladdich and Ardbeg both retain specimens of the earlier type of riveted still, which are probably the last ones in service.

37

57

50 A,B

B

A. Laphroaig, Islay, Argyll;
   still-house, *c.* 1920
B. Glenlivet, Minmore, Banffshire;
   stills, *c.* 1920

A. Dallas Dhu, Forres, Moray;
   interior of worm-tub
B. Speyburn, Rothes, Moray;
   worm-tubs for wash-stills
   and spirit-stills

A

As part of the distillation process, each still is attached to a condensation unit for converting the vapour into liquid again after passing over the lyne-arm. Several distilleries *33 B* continue to use the old method, which consists of directing *37 (n)* the distillate through a coil of copper pipes, tapered in diameter from about 12 in (305 mm) to 5 in (127 mm) at the outlet, and immersed in a stave-built vessel, or worm-tub, of cold running water standing against the outside wall of *51 A* the still-house. Good specimens of the traditional worm-tub *51 B* continue to be used at Dallas Dhu, Speyburn and Mortlach.

Apart from the spirit-receiver—a stave-built vessel of *35,37* oak, secured with Excise padlocks—the other main feature *57* in the still-house is the spirit-safe, a locked brass box with *60 B* glass sides through which the successive distillates from the *55 C* stills are passed for sampling and directing to the appro- *60 B* priate receiver.

Water-power was commonplace for driving the plant and pumping-machinery until well into the 1870s, when it was increasingly replaced by the steam engine. The latter in turn has now been ousted by electricity, but Laphroaig and Bruichladdich, among others, were powered by steam within living memory, and Longmorn is one of the four to retain its engine in working order, together with an earlier water-wheel. Moreover, until quite recently the once standard practice of driving the rummager apparatus from a small auxiliary water-wheel powered from the overflow of the worm-tubs, was employed in several distilleries, for example Glen Grant and Longmorn.

B

A

A. Knockdhu, Knock,
Banffshire;
filling-store

B. Port Charlotte, Islay, Argyll:
bonded warehouse; locking-bar and padlock

Adjoining the still-house, or situated nearby, is the
37 filling-store, where the newly made spirit is put into casks.
57 Good traditional examples are to be seen at Dallas Dhu, and
52 A at Knockdhu, Banffshire (NJ 547528). Its main feature is
the spirit-receiver, a large wooden staved vat elevated on
piers and partially encircled by a wooden gallery; the other
standard features are the weighing-scales, the stock-cask
store, and a booth for the Excise Officer and his
measuring-instruments. The cask-filling operation remains
under manual control in many smaller distilleries, as also is
the traditional method of weighing the cask empty and full
to determine the spirit content.

The 1823 legislation included provision for the storage of
31 whisky in bond without payment of duty, and warehouses
progressively became more numerous and space-
consuming. Many were of the single-storeyed type, disposed in long, contiguous ranges, having earth floors to
preserve a moist atmosphere; but after the 1850s, with the
growing demand for malts in the blending industry, larger
warehouses of two or more storeys became more common,
notably in the Lowlands. All are characterised by their
barred and louvred windows; they also have stout wooden
doors, secured with heavy locking-bars and double
52 B shrouded padlocks. Attractive examples of single-storeyed
type, dating between 1846 and 1907, are to be seen at Port

Ellen, all immaculately whitewashed, and also on Islay 53 A
there is a superior example of the multi-storeyed type at
Caol Ila. Dating from about 1900, the latter is a three- 53 B
storeyed building of brick, designed with timber-slatted
floors at the upper levels for promoting good air circu-
lation. The traditional method for stowing the casks, called
dunnage warehousing, is by stacking them in tiers of four or 53 D
five with timber rails in between. They are graded in a
variety of sizes which include: butts (exceeding 110 gal./500
litres); puncheons (90–120 gal./410–545 litres); hogshead
(55 gal./250 litres); American barrels (40 gal./182 litres);
and the smaller quarter casks (28 gal./127 litres) and octaves
(14 gal./64 litres), now rarely used.

A

B

C

D

A. Port Ellen, Islay, Argyll;
    bonded warehouses
B. Caol Ila, Islay, Argyll;
    multi-storeyed warehouses, *c.* 1900
C. Bruichladdich, Islay, Argyll; cask stencils
D. Ardbeg, Islay, Argyll;
    dunnage warehousing

E

A. Glenlivet, Minmore, Banffshire;
   cooperage repair-shop, c. 1920
B. Port Ellen, Islay, Argyll; peat-store
C. Bunnahabhainn, Islay, Argyll;
   front of manager's office and flat
D. Caol Ila, Islay, Argyll;
   Excise Officer's house
E. Glenlivet, Minmore, Banffshire;
   Excise office, c. 1920

Of the various ancillary buildings, every distillery at one
54 B time possessed a peat-shed, with open or ventilated sides to
allow the huge stocks of peat to dry out and mature.
Another essential unit is the cooperage repair-shop, whose
54 A earlier character and functions may be judged from the one
formerly at Glenlivet. Suitable offices and living-
54 C accommodation for the resident manager and Excise
62 A Officer also formed part of the complex, and living-quar-
54 E ters for the Excise Officer were a statutory requirement.
After 1893 a standard design was specified for this
purpose,[10] normally a substantial house of four bedrooms,
54 D of which examples are to be found at Caol Ila and
Laphroaig, dating from about 1896 and 1905.

A B

A. Royal Lochnagar, Deeside,
   Aberdeenshire;
   glass whisky dispenser
B. Lagavulin, Islay, Argyll;
   malting-implements

C

Most of the older distilleries retain a variety of traditional malting-implements, which include malt ploughs, wooden *55 B* hand-shovels, or shiels, wooden-wheeled hoppers, two-man box-barrows, bushel measures and peat barrows. In addition, several specific features, now preserved as relics, are worthy of mention. Perhaps the earliest spirit-safe to *55 C* survive is now preserved in HM Customs and Excise Museum, London, and formerly belonged to Port Ellen Distillery; it is uniquely small in capacity, measuring 14½ in by 7 in by 13 in high (369 mm by 178 mm by 330 mm), with holders for three hydrometers. An old wooden staved vat at Laphroaig was used in 1928 for making the first blend of 'Islay Mist' whisky, and good specimens of copper cask-pumps were noted at Caol Ila and Speyburn. Royal *62 B* Lochnagar preserves a very fine urn-shaped glass whisky dispenser, engraved with the Royal coat of arms—a relic of *55 A* the pre-1914 era, when it was customary to supply whisky to inns and public houses in barrels, often of glass or china. Both Caol Ila and Glenlivet have old-style beam-scales *55 D* formerly used for the cask-weighing procedure in the filling-store.

Among the interesting relics in the museum at the Glenkinchie distillery, East Lothian, (NT 443668), is the string-and-ball apparatus one used by the stillman for sounding the neck of the wash-still to test the level of the boiling liquid, prior to the introduction of inspection windows.

C. Port Ellen, Islay, Argyll;
   early spirit-safe, *c.* 1824
D. Glenlivet, Minmore, Banffshire;
   beam-scales

D

Edradour, Pitlochry
Perthshire
A. tun-room;
    'refrigerator' on left
B. general view from w

B

Edradour Distillery   NM 959579
Pitlochry, Perthshire
        Tayside, Perth and Kinross   ][1980

Alfred Barnard had little to say about this distillery during
his celebrated tour of the Scottish whisky distilleries in 1887,
possibly because it was then operating on a modest scale
which would fail to impress him.[11] Founded in 1837, it is
now acknowledged to be the last of the small farm
distilleries, and until the 1960s continued to employ all the
traditional methods and equipment for distilling malt

whisky. Although no longer relying upon water-powered
machinery or home malting, virtually all the plant and
buildings remain intact. The latter are recorded in the
drawing and the photographs, as are the more complex 57
elements of the distillation plant, and collectively they serve 59
to delineate the full range of stages in the whisky-making
process.

The distillery preserves several early features of special
interest. The two-roller malt-mill, or bruiser, is now
perhaps the smallest and earliest of its type. For cooling the
wort prior to fermentation, an old-style refrigerator is used, 56 A
patented by Robert Morton and Co., which is the last of its
kind in the industry. The two washbacks, each of a modest 57(19,20)

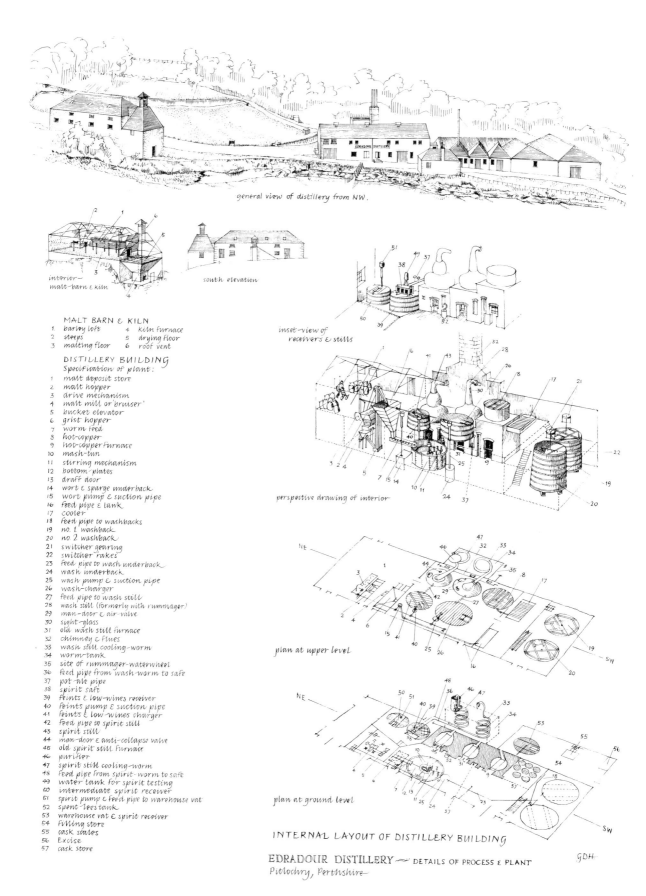

general view of distillery from N.W.

interior—
malt barn & kiln

south elevation

inset view of
receivers & stills

perspective drawing of interior

plan at upper level

plan at ground level

MALT BARN & KILN

1.	barley loft	4	kiln furnace
2.	steeps	5	drying floor
3.	malting floor	6	roof vent

DISTILLERY BUILDING
Specification of plant:

1. malt deposit store
2. malt hopper
3. drive mechanism
4. malt mill or 'bruiser'
5. bucket elevator
6. grist hopper
7. worm feed
8. hot-copper
9. hot-copper furnace
10. mash-tun
11. stirring mechanism
12. bottom plates
13. draff door
14. wort & sparge underback
15. wort pump & suction pipe
16. feed pipe & tank
17. cooler
18. feed pipe to washbacks
19. no. 1 washback
20. no. 2 washback
21. switcher gearing
22. switcher rakes
23. feed pipe to wash underback
24. wash underback
25. wash pump & suction pipe
26. wash-charger
27. feed pipe to wash still
28. wash still (formerly with rummager)
29. man-door & air-valve
30. sight-glass
31. old wash still furnace
32. chimney & flues
33. wash still cooling-worm
34. worm-tank
35. site of rummager-waterwheel
36. feed pipe from wash-worm to safe
37. pot ale pipe
38. spirit safe
39. feints & low-wines receiver
40. feints pump & suction pipe
41. feints & low-wines charger
42. feed pipe to spirit still
43. spirit still
44. man-door & anti-collapse valve
45. old spirit still furnace
46. purifier
47. spirit still cooling-worm
48. feed pipe from spirit-worm to safe
49. water tank for spirit testing
50. intermediate spirit receiver
51. spirit pump & feed pipe to warehouse vat
52. spent-lees tank
53. warehouse vat & spirit receiver
54. filling store
55. cask scales
56. Excise
57. cask store

INTERNAL LAYOUT OF DISTILLERY BUILDING

EDRADOUR DISTILLERY — DETAILS OF PROCESS & PLANT
Pitlochry, Perthshire

GDH

A

C

B

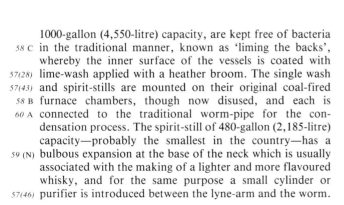

D

1000-gallon (4,550-litre) capacity, are kept free of bacteria
58 C in the traditional manner, known as 'liming the backs',
whereby the inner surface of the vessels is coated with
57(28) lime-wash applied with a heather broom. The single wash
57(43) and spirit-stills are mounted on their original coal-fired
58 B furnace chambers, though now disused, and each is
60 A connected to the traditional worm-pipe for the condensation process. The spirit-still of 480-gallon (2,185-litre)
capacity—probably the smallest in the country—has a
59 (N) bulbous expansion at the base of the neck which is usually
associated with the making of a lighter and more flavoured
whisky, and for the same purpose a small cylinder or
57(46) purifier is introduced between the lyne-arm and the worm.

Edradour, Pitlochry, Perthshire
  A. still-house; neck and lyne-arm of stills
  B. still-house; coal-fired furnaces
  C. tun-room; 'liming the backs'
  D. measures and cooperage equipment

Another once important feature, situated between the
filling-store and the warehouse range, was a small contiguous building which originally served as the whisky store
or shop, where, prior to the Maturation Act of 1915, whisky
was sold direct from the cask.

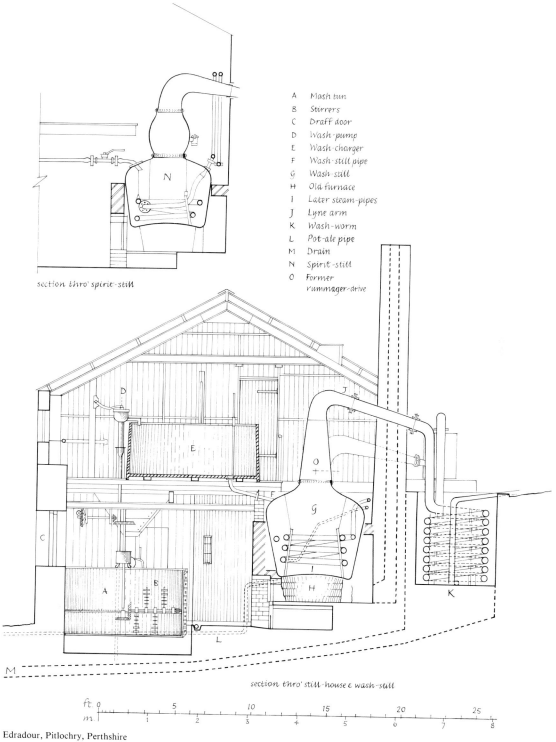

section thro' spirit-still

A   Mash tun
B   Stirrers
C   Draff door
D   Wash-pump
E   Wash-charger
F   Wash-still pipe
G   Wash-still
H   Old furnace
I   Later steam-pipes
J   Lyne arm
K   Wash-worm
L   Pot-ale pipe
M   Drain
N   Spirit-still
O   Former
     rummager-drive

section thro' still-house & wash-still

ft 0   5   10   15   20   25
m 1   2   3   4   5   6   7   8

Edradour, Pitlochry, Perthshire

A

B

C

Edradour, Pitlochry, Perthshire
A. worm-pipes against external wall of
    still-house
B. still-house; spirit-safe and receivers
C. filling-store

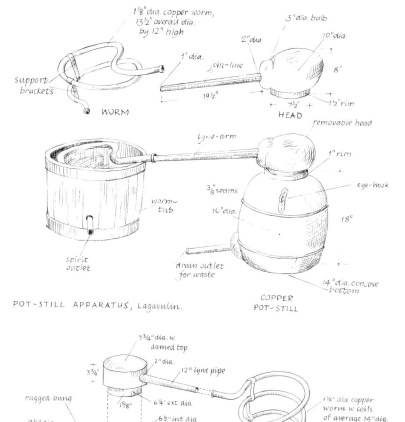

WORM

1⅛" dia. copper worm, 13½" overall dia. by 12" high

support brackets

HEAD

3" dia. bulb

2" dia.

10" dia.

1" dia.

join-line

19½"

8"

7½"

½" rim

removable head

POT-STILL APPARATUS, Lagavulin.

lyne-arm

worm-tub

spirit outlet

1" rim

eye-hook

3⅜" seams

10" dia.

18"

drain outlet for waste

14" dia. concave bottom

COPPER POT-STILL

7¾" dia. w. domed top

2" dia.

12" lyne pipe

3¾"

15⅝"

6¼" ext. dia.

ragged bung

2½" dia. vent pipe

3"

6½" int. dia.

1¾" h. neck w. bead rim

8½"

eye-hook

7" waste-outlet

1¾" dia.

stopper

1¼" dia.

22½" dia. flat bottom

1⅛" dia. copper worm w. coils of average 14" dia. by 15" overall height

WORM

'TIN' POT-STILL

POT-STILL APPARATUS, Ballygrant.

GDH

Illicit Still Apparatus

Islay, Argyll

Strathclyde, Argyll and Bute   1979

Of the two examples illustrated—now preserved respectively at Lagavulin distillery (NR 404457) and the Museum of Islay Life, Port Charlotte (NR 252585)—the former is believed to have been used in the Lagavulin region and the other near Ballygrant. Their precise dates are unknown but in basic design both examples are doubtless modelled on the small pot-still apparatus of earlier times used originally by the private distiller and increasingly by his illegal counterpart, whose trade went largely unchecked until the effective legislative measures of 1823. Apart from a need for seclusion, the location of an illicit still was dependent on a suitable water-supply, desirably with provision for a small dam and a working-area for handling the whisky-making process through its various stages from initial steeping of the barley to the final product. Two sites answering to these requirements have been recorded in Argyll, one situated in a narrow gorge near Skipness (NR 921599), and another occupying the ruins of a former click-mill on the Druim a' Mhuilinn Burn, Isle of Jura (NR 564735).[12]

The majority of bothies were equipped with a single still and cooling worm, so that actual distilling had to be conducted in two separate operations, the still having to be thoroughly cleansed between the alternate charges of wash and low-wines. The principal components of the distilling apparatus, traditionally made of copper, were the pot-still, the combined head and lyne-arm, and the coiled pipe or worm, the three separate units being easily joined together or dismantled at short notice. The Lagavulin apparatus is the more complete and has a deep pot-still of conventional pattern, while the other is of the later, crudely made 'tin' variety and has a modern head. A pair of eye-hooks on both stills were probably an aid to carrying the vessels by attaching them to a loop of rope or an iron handle.

A. Edradour, Pitlochry, Perthshire;
Excise and distillery manager's offices
B. Caol Ila, Islay, Argyll;
cask-pump

NOTES

n.1   *Inventory of Argyll,* **5,** No. 437 and p. 45. The Commissioners
       wish to record their special gratitude to the directors, managers
       and staff of all the whisky distilleries visited in the course of this
       survey during the period 1979–81.
n.2   For earlier comprehensive accounts of Scottish distilleries, see
       Barnard, A, *The Whisky Distilleries of the United Kingdom* (1887,
       reprinted 1969). Moss, M S and Hume, J R, *The Making of
       Scotch Whisky* (1981), provide the most recent account, embracing
       all aspects of the process and business history of the industry.
n.3   *Inventory of Argyll,* **1,** No. 348.
n.4   Plans at Laphroaig Distillery: estate plans by William Gemmil,
       surveyor, 1840, and by ?J Young, surveyor, 1854; distillery plans
       dated 1910, 1924 and 1928. Information from the late Mrs
       Wishart-Campbell, managing director of Laphroaig Distillery
       1954-72.
n.5   Barnard, op. cit., 302, 340.
n.6   Ibid., 69.
n.7   Ibid., 89, 99.
n.8   Barnard mentions several mainland distilleries, op. cit., 50, 121,
       235, 250; Bremner, D, *The Industries of Scotland* (1869), 452.
n.9   Barnard, op. cit., 90, 94, 96, 101, 105, 110, 113; Bremner, op.
       cit., 452.
n.10   Smith, T G, *Something to Declare* (1980), 126.
n.11   Barnard, op. cit.
n.12   *Inventory of Argyll,* **1,** No. 350; 5, No. 431.

3 TEXTILES

Prior to the emergence of a fully mechanised factory system, the making of textiles was fundamentally a cottage-based industry, widely dispersed throughout the country, with the spinning and weaving done entirely by hand. In the case of flax and wool, this practice persisted well into the 19th century, and cotton, too, evidently remained part of the home-weavers' craft for a limited period. Late 18th- and early 19th-century cottages associated with the woollen trade were recorded in the small villages of Torbrex (NS 788919) and Cambusbarron (NS 7792), both in Stirlingshire;[1] and attractive examples of cotton-weavers' cottages are to be found in Carlops village, Peeblesshire.[2] In the tartan-making village of Cambusbarron, a two-storeyed structure, well supplied with windows and a hoisting-door, was identified as a former weaving-

70

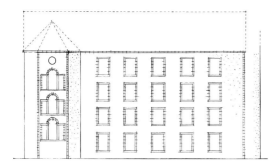

East Elevation – partly re-constructed

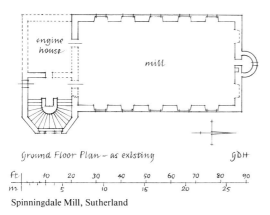

engine house

mill

Ground Floor Plan – as existing   JDH

| ft | 10 | 20 | 30 | 40 | 50 | 60 | 70 | 80 | 90 |
| m | | 5 | | 10 | | 15 | | 20 | | 25 |

Spinningdale Mill, Sutherland

shed, and may perhaps represent one instance of the industry's gradual mutation to factory-style premises.[3]

Cotton, as the cheaper, more tractable textile, lent itself readily to the new improved machine processes, and cotton-spinning, from its extensive introduction in Scotland during the latter half of the 18th century, operated on a full-time factory basis. Initially, water-power and reasonable access to the raw material were the major factors governing the location of the large purpose-built mills, which caused a profound change in the landscape over an area stretching from the Glasgow hinterland eastwards to Perthshire and north to Aberdeen. Model factories of the water-powered phase, built during the 1780s by such entrepreneurs as David Dale, George Dempster and Claude Alexander to house Arkwright's water-frame and Crompton's spinning mule, included New Lanark, Lanarkshire; *76-83* Catrine, Ayrshire (NS 526258) and Deanston (NN 715015) *65* and Stanley (NO 114328), both in Perthshire. A smaller *84* isolated venture, aimed at promoting employment in the Highlands, was the spinning-jenny factory erected at Spinningdale, Sutherland, on the shore of the Dornoch *63* Firth (NH 675894). Designed with considerable architectural character, this is a multi-storeyed structure incorporating a circular latrine-tower at one end, but it has lain ruinous since 1808 following an accidental fire.[4*]

With the introduction of the rotative steam-engine, early 19th-century mills began to be built specifically for the new motive power and, as a consequence, location of the cotton industry gradually became more concentrated in the vicinity of Glasgow and the neighbouring coal measures. Water-power, none the less, remained a major resource until well after the 1850s, particularly in the woollen industry, and many factories, such as the now vanished Garlogie Mills, *131-5* Aberdeenshire, used steam-power simply as a stand-by *64* before moving directly from water-wheel to turbine. The outstanding feature of the water-power era was the pair of high-breast wheels, 50 ft (15·24 m) in diameter and 10 ft 6 in *65 A* (3·20 m) wide, capable of developing 240 horsepower, which *66 A* was installed at Claude Alexander's Catrine Works between 1825 and 1827. Acknowledged in 1861 by their designers Fairbairn and Lillie as 'even at the present day among the best and most effective structures of the kind in existence',[5] these wheels were demolished in 1945, and the heart of Claude Alexander's immaculately planned industrial village—the elegant five-storeyed mill itself—suffered a *65 B* similar fate some twenty years later.

Although technological change began later in the traditional textiles than in cotton, the woollen and linen industries became no less mechanised and sophisticated by

63

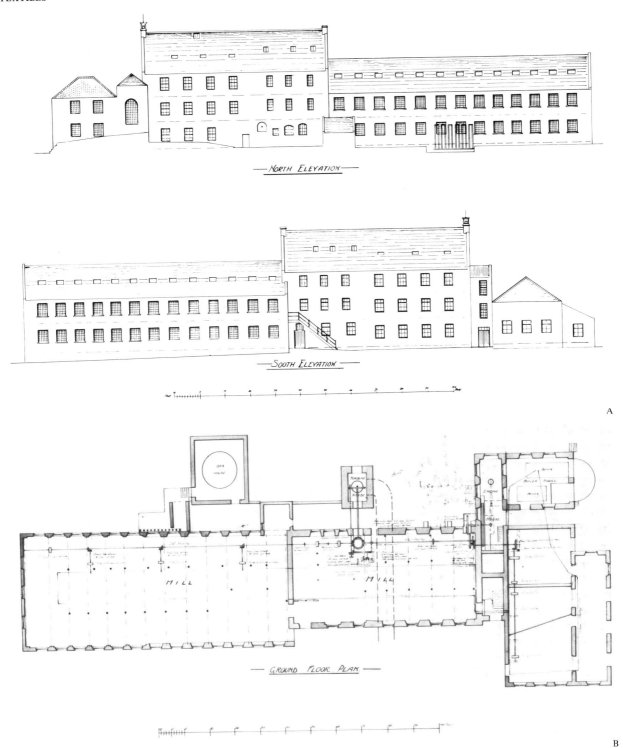

NORTH ELEVATION

SOUTH ELEVATION

A

GROUND FLOOR PLAN

B

Woollen mills, Garlogie, Aberdeenshire
A, B. survey drawings, c. 1910, Dunecht Estates

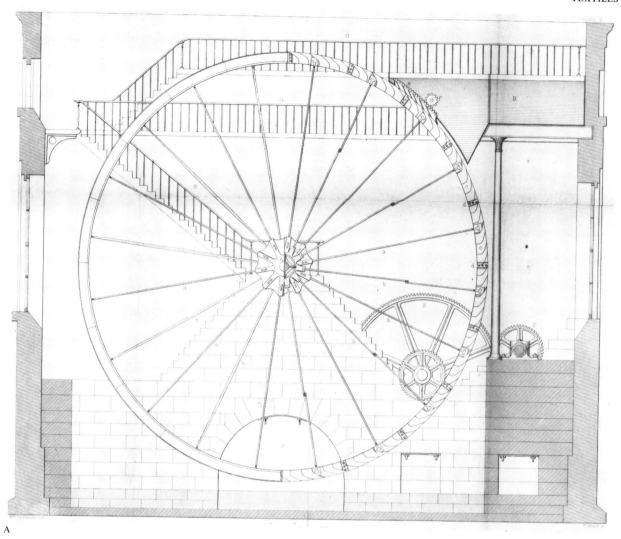

A

B

Catrine Mills, Ayrshire
  A. design drawing of water-wheel
      (Fairbairn and Lillie, 1827)
  B. view from NE

A. Catrine Mills, Ayrshire; view of the two wheels

Skeoch Mill, Bannockburn, Stirlingshire
B.   general view from s
C.   design drawing of workers' dwellings,
        c. 1780 (redrawn)

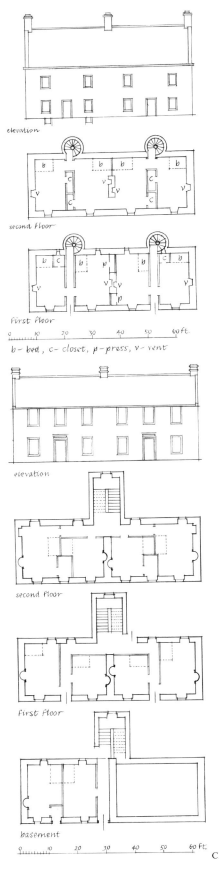

elevation

second Floor

First Floor

b – bed, c – closet, p – press, v – vent

elevation

second floor

First floor

basement

B

C

66

Mills, Blairgowrie, Perthshire; aerial view from N

the middle of the 19th century, by which time they were consolidated respectively in the Border towns and the Fife–Angus area. Previously, the works tended to be on a modest scale and more widespread. Skeoch Mill, Bannockburn, Stirlingshire (NS 809904), recorded in 1960,[6] may be cited as a medium-sized family business, established by William Wilson about 1770 and developed by the turn of the century into a compact industrial complex comprising a spinning-mill, weaving-sheds, and dye-houses, together with an associated range of workers' dwellings—another essential element of most factory enterprises. On the other hand, the somewhat later group of flax and jute mills dispersed on each side of the River Ericht, just above Blairgowrie, Perthshire, originally all driven by waterwheels, is a classic instance of a large colony of mills sited expressly for the purpose of exploiting a good water-supply.

Whatever the raw material, the various stages in its conversion to the finished product, particularly with regard to the central processes of spinning and weaving, were basically the same for all textiles. Consequently, both the machinery and power-plant used, together with the buildings containing them, conformed to a fairly universal pattern. Spinning, as the first process to be mechanised, required a linear layout for accommodating the rows of machines and working-aisles for the operatives; thus from the outset the standard spinning-factory tended to be a long multi-storeyed structure, built with external load-bearing walls of brick or stone and provided with regular and ample fenestration to admit good natural lighting. Iron tie-plates

B

A. Cast-iron wall-tie, New Lanark, Lanarkshire
B. Royal George Mill, Bannockburn, Stirlingshire

A

or discs for stabilising the broad wall-surfaces at upper floor levels were often a feature of the exterior. A particularly interesting example was the now vanished Garnock Mill, Kilbirnie, Ayrshire (NS 316544), built in 1834,[7] whose walls were braced internally across the corners by tie-rods secured with massive 2 ft 3 in (0·69 m) by 1 ft 4 in (0·41 m) elliptical cruciform wall-plates and bosses fixed on adjacent wall-surfaces. The earlier mills contained wooden beam-and-joist floors spanning from wall to wall, but in the course of evolution the overall width was extended by the insertion of one or more rows of intermediate columns of cast iron. Presaged by the erection of Houldsworth's Cotton Mill, Glasgow, by the 1820s these internal frames were often rendered fireproof by the use of a cast-iron framework and jack-arch floor construction, though timber floors remained a common alternative; the refinements achieved in the development of the fireproof iron frame by the end of the 19th century may be deduced from that employed in the engine-house of the Atlantic and Pacific Mills, Paisley. For a time the spinning-mill also made provision for hand-

looms, usually on the lower floors, but once the power-loom became widely adopted in the 1850s, rows of single-storeyed weaving-sheds, with roofs of saw-tooth profile incorporating north lighting, became a standard feature of the larger factory complexes, particularly the Border woollen mills. In contrast, the earlier Royal George Mill, Bannockburn (NS 808904),[8] built c.1822, is a tall, narrow four-storeyed structure with clear-span timber floors and a wheel-house at one end, typical of the more elementary style of factory used for both spinning and hand-loom weaving.

With the advent of steam-power, the engine-house and the tall factory chimney eventually became familiar features. In common with the water-wheel, the rotative beam-engine and the later horizontal compound engine were sited at the centre or at the end of the building, and the engine-house tended to be singled out for special architectural emphasis, either as an integral part of the building, as at the now demolished Ferguslie Mills, Paisley (1826–1858), or simply as a detached structure. Transmission from the power source to the horizontal line-shafting and machinery on each floor was by means of a vertical shaft and bevel-gearing until about the 1860s, when the larger mills adopted the more efficient rope-drive—a series of ropes running to each floor and driven from the flywheel of the steam-engine (e.g. Atlantic and Pacific Mills, Paisley).

An important branch of the coarse-textile industry to emerge during the middle decades of the 19th century was the hemp and jute trade for the manufacture of canvas, bagging and ropes, which became centred on Dundee and its environs. This in turn led to further offshoots, such as the linoleum trade in Kirkcaldy, where, from its erection in 1900, the towering mass of Walton's factory—a stone multi-storeyed building with well-proportioned fenestra-

A

B

A. Walton Linoleum Factory, Kirkcaldy, Fife;
   view from NE
B. Ferguslie Mills, Paisley, Renfrewshire;
   mills 1 and 3 from SW
C. Templeton Carpet Factory, Glasgow, c. 1898

tion and internal fireproof floor construction—proclaimed
one of the town's major industries. The factory was
designed and erected specially to house the inlay linoleum
machinery, invented and patented by Frederick Walton,
who first established the process under the name of the
Greenwich Inlaid Linoleum Company. The commercial
show-piece of the late textile era, however, is James
69 C Templeton's carpet factory overlooking Glasgow Green—a
bizarre rendering of Venetian Gothic in polychrome brick
and stone designed by William Leiper in 1889.

C

69

F

A

street frontage

box bed

box bed

work area

parlour

kitchen

specimen plan of dwelling in terraced row

Ft. 10 20 30 40 50
m. 5 10 15

Details of kitchen fireplace

corbelled lintel

4'-4"

12"

elevation

section

GDH
ft 1 2 3 4 5 6 7 8 9 10
m. 1 2 3

20"

7½"

plan of jamb

4"

B

Weavers' cottages, Carlops, Peeblesshire
  A.   E side of main street
  B.   survey drawings

Weavers' Cottages   NT 161560
Carlops, Peeblesshire
     Borders, Tweeddale   ● 1963

Founded in 1784 as a cotton-weaving community by the local laird, Robert Brown of Newhall, the village of Carlops retains three terraced rows of weavers' cottages of that date on each side of the main street.[9] Built in 2 ft-thick (0·61 m) lime-mortared rubble, with sandstone dressings, they are single storeyed and may originally have been covered with pantiles, though they all are now slated. The frontages are whitewashed and their neat, regular fenestration reflects the main subdivisions of the rooms within. The original layout of a typical cottage appears to have comprised a kitchen and a combined workshop and parlour separated by a through passage and adjacent box-beds or bed-closets. A central feature of the kitchen was the wide lintelled fireplace projected on rounded corbels, all executed in dressed sandstone, though not a single example now survives.

C. Woollen mill, Bridgend, Islay, Argyll;
    water-wheel; chain-drive mechanism

A

B

Woollen Mill　　　　　　　　　　　　　NR 352632
Bridgend, Islay
　　Strathclyde, Argyll and Bute　　　　　　1979

This mill, built 1883 on the E bank of the River Sorn, is typical of the smaller country business and primarily of interest for the machinery it contains and the traditional methods employed for processing the wool from its raw state, through the various stages, to the finished product.[10] Plainly constructed of local rubble masonry, it comprises a gable-ended main block of three storeys, and a single-storeyed s wing, all originally slated. The upper floors are of wooden beam-and-joist construction carried on two intermediate rows of posts, and the E gable incorporated a loading-door at each level designed initially for admitting machinery.

　The layout of the machinery and equipment, some of *72* which are among the last specimens of their kind to survive in Britain, is noted on the plans in their sequence of use. All the powered machinery was driven by a low breast-shot iron *70 C* water-wheel with an unusual chain-drive mechanism, situated against the wall inside the s wing. Briefly, the process involved preparing the raw wool by breaking it down into smaller pieces in a teasing-machine, carding it in *71 A* a scribbler to remove its initial coarseness, then in a similar *72(2)* two-cylinder carder to form it into more uniform strips, *71 C* which were cast automatically on to a piecing-machine *74 A* designed to join them into continuous strands. The bulky nature of the strands, or rovings, required them to be

Woollen mill, Bridgend,
Islay, Argyll
　A.　teasing-machine *(1)*
　B.　sprinkler-box for
　　　oiling wool before
　　　teasing
　C.　wooden-framed
　　　carder *(3)*

C

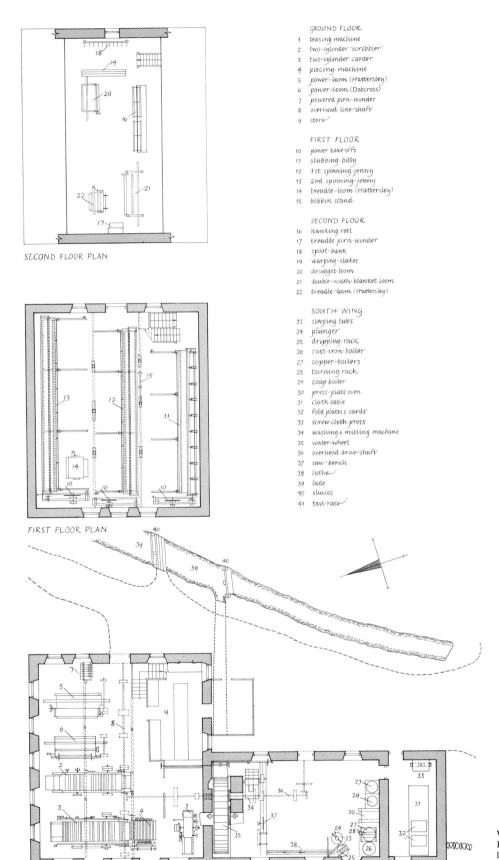

SECOND FLOOR PLAN

FIRST FLOOR PLAN

GROUND FLOOR PLAN   SOUTH WING

GROUND FLOOR
1   teasing machine
2   two-cylinder 'scribbler'
3   two-cylinder carder
4   piecing-machine
5   power-loom (Hattersley)
6   power-loom (Dobcross)
7   powered pirn-winder
8   overhead line-shaft
9   store

FIRST FLOOR
10 power take-offs
11 slubbing-billy
12 1st spinning-jenny
13 2nd. spinning-jenny
14 treadle-loom (Hattersley)
15 bobbin stand

SECOND FLOOR
16 hanking reel
17 treadle pirn-winder
18 spool-bank
19 warping-stakes
20 drugget loom
21 double-width blanket loom
22 treadle-loom (Hattersley)

SOUTH WING
23 steeping tubs
24 plunger
25 dripping-rack
26 cast-iron boiler
27 copper-boilers
28 turning rack
29 soap boiler
30 press-plate oven
31 cloth table
32 fold plates & cards
33 screw cloth press
34 washing & milling machine
35 water-wheel
36 overhead drive-shaft
37 saw-bench
38 lathe
39 lade
40 sluices
41 tail-race

Woollen mill, Bridgend
Islay, Argyll;
layout of machinery

A

B

processed into a leaner yarn in a slubbing-billy on the first
floor, before the yarn was suitable for spinning in the jenny; *73 A*
it could be further refined in a second jenny. The spun yarn *72(13)*
was next formed into hanks on the second floor and then *75 A*
washed and dyed in the dye-house. Having been woven in *75 B*
one or other of the power- or hand-looms, the finished
cloth, whether of tweeds, rugs or blankets, went through a
final process of washing and shrinking in the milling- *72(34)*
machine, following which it was dried on tenter frames, *73 C*
situated on high ground behind the weaver's cottage.
Suiting material went through a further stage of being
folded and pressed in a cloth-press worked by means of a *73 B*
turn-screw which compressed a series of heated metal plates
inserted between the folds of cloth. The piecing-machine,
slubbing-billy and jenny have been selected for more *144-50*
detailed study in Section 5.

Woollen mill, Bridgend, Islay, Argyll
    A.   first floor from NE, showing no. 1 spinning-jenny *(12)*,
           slubbing-billy *(11)* and power-drives *(10)*
    B.   cloth-press *(33)*
    C.   tenter-frames

C

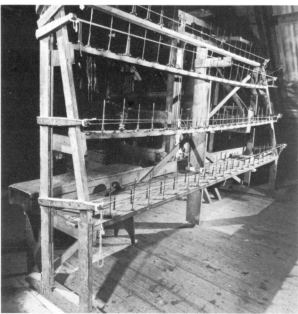

C

A

D

E

B

Woollen mill, Bridgend, Islay, Argyll
A.   piecing-machine *(4)*, two-cylinder carder *(3)*,
      and scribbler *(2)* in background
B.   warping-stakes *(19)*
C.   custom card
D.   unwinding-machine
E.   treadle pirn-winder *(17)*

A

B

Woollen mill, Bridgend, Islay, Argyll
    A.   second floor from NW, showing treadle-loom *(22)* and blanket-loom *(21)* to right
    B.   dye-house *(23–30)*

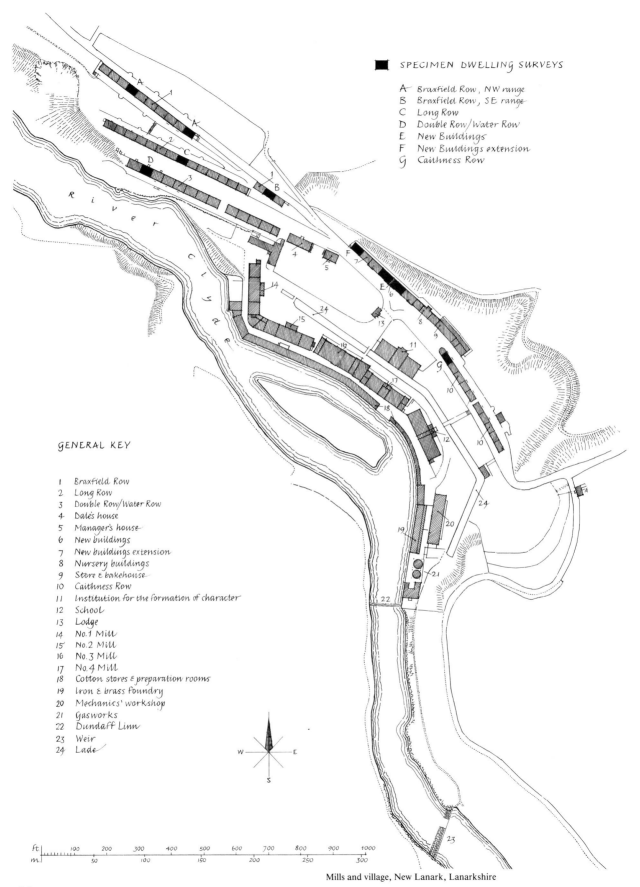

A Braxfield Row, NW range
B Braxfield Row, SE range
C Long Row
D Double Row/Water Row
E New Buildings
F New Buildings extension
G Caithness Row

GENERAL KEY

1   Braxfield Row
2   Long Row
3   Double Row/Water Row
4   Dale's house
5   Manager's house
6   New buildings
7   New buildings extension
8   Nursery buildings
9   Store & bakehouse
10 Caithness Row
11 Institution for the formation of character
12 School
13 Lodge
14 No.1 Mill
15 No.2 Mill
16 No.3 Mill
17 No.4 Mill
18 Cotton stores & preparation rooms
19 Iron & brass foundry
20 Mechanics' workshop
21 Gasworks
22 Dundaff Linn
23 Weir
24 Lade

ft 100 200 300 400 500 600 700 800 900 1000
m   50   100   150   200   250   300

Mills and village, New Lanark, Lanarkshire

A

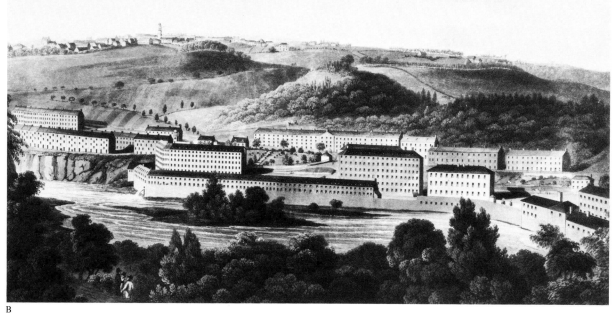

B

Mills and village, New Lanark, Lanarkshire
  A.   aerial view from sw
  B.   view from s by J Clark, *c.* 1825

Mills and village,
New Lanark, Lanarkshire
A. view from NE by J Winning, c. 1818
B. store, c. 1895

Mills and Village   NS 880425
New Lanark, Lanarkshire
    Strathclyde, Clydesdale   ●][1967–79

The importance of New Lanark as a pioneering enterprise of industrial and social organisation is well known.[11] Founded in 1785 by David Dale in association with Richard Arkwright, and profoundly influenced by the social and educational ideals of Dale's son-in-law Robert Owen, by 1825 it had become a model industrial village complete with mills, church, school, community buildings, including shop and bake-house and workers' dwellings. The site occupies a narrow stretch of ground beside the River Clyde, just below *76-83* B Corra Linn Falls, and the close inter-relationship between the mills, community buildings and lade system is best appreciated from the illustrations and site plans. Although the mills themselves have been subjected to alteration and reconstruction, the whole complex apart from No. 4 mill, which was burnt down in 1883, remains much as Dale and Owen planned it. A current programme of restoration by the New Lanark Conservation Trust in association with the Scottish Development Department, has been accompanied by a series of measured surveys undertaken by the Commission, which have included Owen's New Institution, *79* erected between 1813 and 1816, and his School *c.*1819. The *80*

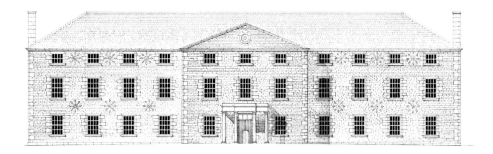

north-east elevation

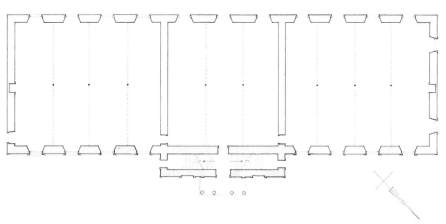

first-floor plan

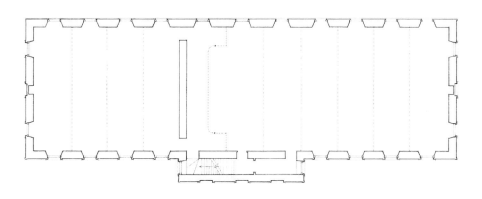

ground-floor plan

The New Institution for the Formation of Character, New Lanark, Lanarkshire–
drawing partly reconstructed

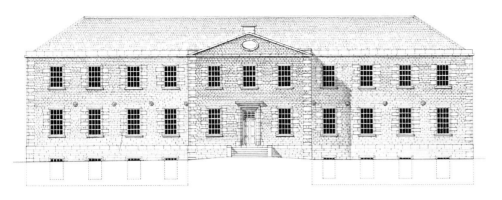

east elevation

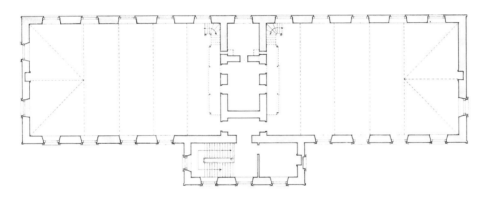

first-floor plan

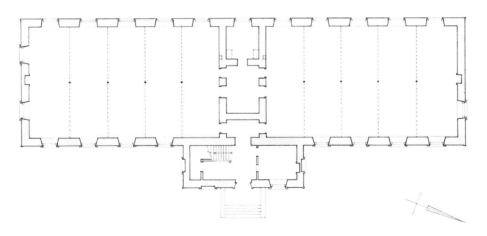

principal floor plan

The School, New Lanark, Lanarkshire — *drawing partly reconstructed.*

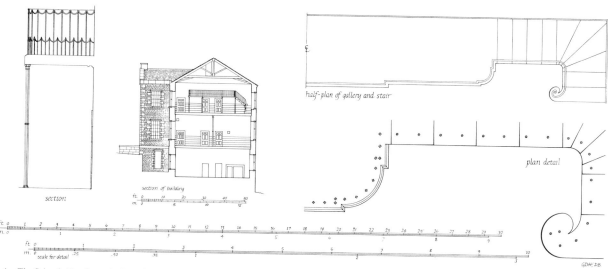

half-plan of gallery and stair

plan detail

section of building

ft. 0   10   20   30   40   50
m. 0   5   10   15

section

ft. 0 1 2 3 4 5 6 7 8 9 10 11 12 13 14 15 16 17 18 19 20 21 22 23 24 25 26 27 28 29 30
m. 0   1   2   3   4   5   6   7   8   9

ft. 0   1   2   3   4   5   6   7   8   9   10
m. 0 scale for detail .25   .50   .75   1   2   3

GDH/DB

A. The School, New Lanark, Lanarkshire;
details of musicians' gallery

81 A

82 (A)

81 B
82 (D-F)

83 B

81 C

83 A,B

two principal floors of the institute, each 140 ft (42·67 m) long by 19 ft (5·79 m) wide, were designed for educational and recreational purposes, the 21 ft-high (6·40 m) upper floor being formerly divided into two apartments with side-galleries; the 150 ft by 42 ft (45·72 m by 12·80 m) first and second floors of the school were each divided into two large rooms and furnished at their inner ends with a musicians' gallery enclosed by delicate iron balustrades.

The terraced rows of workers' tenements provide a remarkable insight into the living standards of the times. Apart from Braxfield Row, which is stepped along the descent of the approach road, the remainder of those here illustrated are built into the sloping hillside, and consequently the rear of the terraces usually incorporate one or more floors below street level with independent access. Flatted throughout and approached by communal stairs, the buildings fall into two main categories, the central blocks of New Buildings and Double Row/Water Row being of double-room depth, often allowing a four-square arrangement on each floor, and the remainder of single-room depth. Each dwelling incorporated from one to four rooms, the principal elements being the fireplace, scullery and box-beds, the last especially affording a flexible unit for several permutations of house-layout. Flagged floors and a more limited window area made the basements less suited for habitation, and they appear to have been soon relegated to the function of wash-houses and possibly latrines, although the existence of no fewer than eight box-beds in two rooms in the basement of Water Row point to their possible use as pauper dormitories. The original domestic fittings were of a fairly standard character: the fireplaces had plain stone surrounds and latterly an iron range equipped with swey and smoke-board; another universal feature was the hurley-bed (Scots), or truckle-bed—a wooden drawer or box mounted on wheels capable of accommodating two persons, and low enough to be slipped under the fixed bed when not in use.

B

Mills and village,
New Lanark,
Lanarkshire
B.   New Buildings from s
C.   specimen fireplace

C

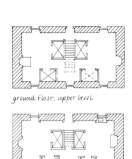

ground floor, upper level

ground floor, lower level

A BRAXFIELD ROW, NW RANGE

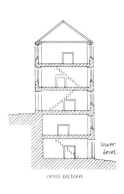

cross section

lower level

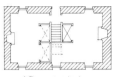

ground floor, upper level

ground floor, lower level

B. BRAXFIELD ROW, SE. RANGE

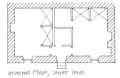

First Floor, upper level

ground floor, upper level

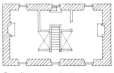

ground floor, lower level

C. LONG ROW

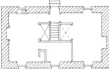

cross section

lower level

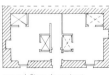

G CAITHNESS ROW, second Floor

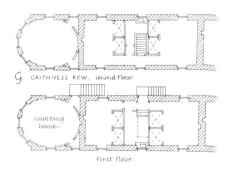

counting house

first Floor

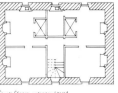

First Floor, upper level

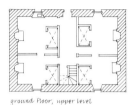

ground Floor, upper level

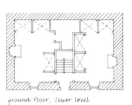

First Floor, lower level

ground Floor, lower level

D. DOUBLE ROW / WATER ROW

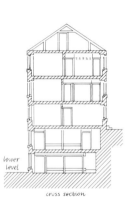

cross section

lower level

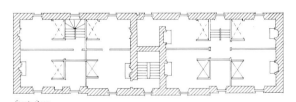

First Floor

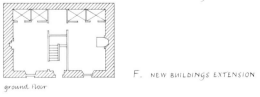

ground floor

E. NEW BUILDINGS

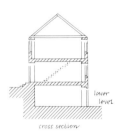

ground floor

F. NEW BUILDINGS EXTENSION

⊠ box-bed units   ⊡ former box-beds or closets

SPECIMEN DWELLING-UNITS, New Lanark

ft | 10 20 30 40 50 60 70 80 90 100
m | 5   10   15   20   25   30

Mills and village, New Lanark, Lanarkshire;
comparative plans

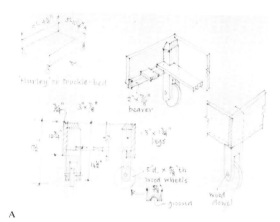

A

Mills and village, New Lanark, Lanarkshire
A.   sketch details of hurley-bed
B.   box-beds and hurley-bed

B

C. Mills and village, Stanley, Perthshire;
aerial view of mills from NE

Mills and village, Stanley, Perthshire;
Bell Mill from NE

Mills and Village
Stanley, Perthshire
    Tayside, Perth and Kinross

NO 114328

● 1981

Founded in the same year as New Lanark by George Dempster, in association with Arkwright and a group of Perth merchants, upon land feued from the Duke of Atholl, the cotton mills and factory village of Stanley constitute another early industrial enterprise developed on model lines.[12] The existing mill complex, which is situated in a steep wooded valley on the N bank of the River Tay consists principally of Bell Mill, or West Mill, completed by 1790, East Mill (c.1840), and Mid Mill (c.1850), the buildings being ranged round three sides of an irregular courtyard with a tall free-standing chimney in the centre. The mills were originally powered by seven giant water-wheels generating a total of 400 horsepower, and linked to an underground conduit system some 800 ft (244 m) in length, which drew the waters from the River Tay on the N side of Sheil Hill. The village occupies a level site on higher ground to the w and comprises neat rows of two-storeyed terraced houses laid out on a regular plan, some of stone and others of brick; evidently by 1828 it also included a church, school and shops, and a tenement block.

The most noteworthy building is Bell Mill, which is perhaps the best surviving example in Scotland of the earlier narrow mill with wooden floors and limited headroom. Originally of six storeys and measuring 90 ft by 28 ft (27·43 m by 8·53 m) internally, the building has a modest width relative to the substantial cross-beams (14 in by 10¼ in; 356 mm by 260 mm) which were probably designed to span from wall to wall; in the existing arrangement, however, the basement and ground storey are combined into one, and the floors supported on a central row of cast-iron columns.

The external walls are built in masonry to first-floor level and in brick above—the latter being made on site from local

ENTRANCE LODGE CIRCA 1876 & WEST ELEVATION OF
part of the Stanley Mills complex, Stanley, Perthshire

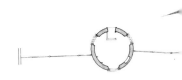

clays and laid in Flemish bond. Other salient characteristics are the slated and gabled roof capped by a handsome belfry and weather-vane at the s end; and an ample regular fenestration composed of segmentally arched sash-windows. The w elevation, with its slightly advanced central portion, and the small circular, ogival-roofed lodge-house (c.1876), standing a short distance to the s, makes a fitting architectural frontispiece to the mill complex.

MILL CIRCA 1790

ground floor plan

transverse section & north elevation

Mills and village, Stanley, Perthshire; Bell Mill

A

B

C

Houldsworth's Cotton Mill, Glasgow
A. E façade
B. pilaster capital
C. pilaster base

Houldsworth's Cotton Mill   NS 578651
Glasgow
    Strathclyde, City of Glasgow   # 1967

Henry Houldsworth's cotton spinning mill, formerly situated in Cheapside, Anderston, was one of the small but important group of buildings whose evolution over little more than a decade produced an effective form of fireproof construction for the multi-storeyed factory.[13] It was built in 1804–5, its nearest contemporaries being the Salford Twist Mill, Manchester (1799–1804), the flax mill at Meadow Lane, Leeds (1802–3) designed by Charles Bage, and the North Mill at Belper (1803–4) by William Strutt. Measuring 232 ft by 43 ft (70·71 m by 13·11 m) on plan, and rising to seven storeys above a sub-basement, it has a brick façade,

86 A-C treated uniformly with a giant order of pilasters and entablature, but concealing a two-period structure. Had it

87 been completed as originally planned, it would have comprised a central two-bay engine-house and a twelve-bay fireproof range on each side, but in the event only the northern half was built in that manner, and a s range with conventional timber floors and iron columns was subsequently added in the mid-19th century.

As in the forementioned English examples, the floors of

88 the northern section of the building were of brick jack-arch construction supported on an internal cast-iron frame composed of cross-beams and two rows of columns set on *89* stone pad foundations. Successive column lengths were shouldered at the head and rendered continuous from floor to floor by spigot joints; the beams were of inverted T-section and each row was cast in three lengths with half-round sockets at the end to clasp the column head. The resultant flexible joints and the simple bending moment thus imposed were factors that determined the shaped longitudinal profile of the beam, which increased to a depth of 15½ in (394 mm) at the centre. Another technical refinement was the longitudinal tie-rods restraining any unresolved thrusts from the jack-arches, which in this case were completely embedded in the arch core in order to protect them from fire.

The roof was supported on a series of cast-iron trusses, *90 A,B* each made up of four prefabricated sections strapped and bolted together and stilted above the wall-head on open web-pieces. Initially, the trusses had two intermediate supports provided by extensions of the main columns, but they were subsequently modified and mounted at a slightly higher level.

The motive power for the mill was a Boulton & Watt engine, which also exhausted steam through the hollow structural columns to provide a novel central-heating system; the firm's draughtsman, William Creighton, supervised the erection of the engine on site but it is not known who was wholly responsible for designing the building.

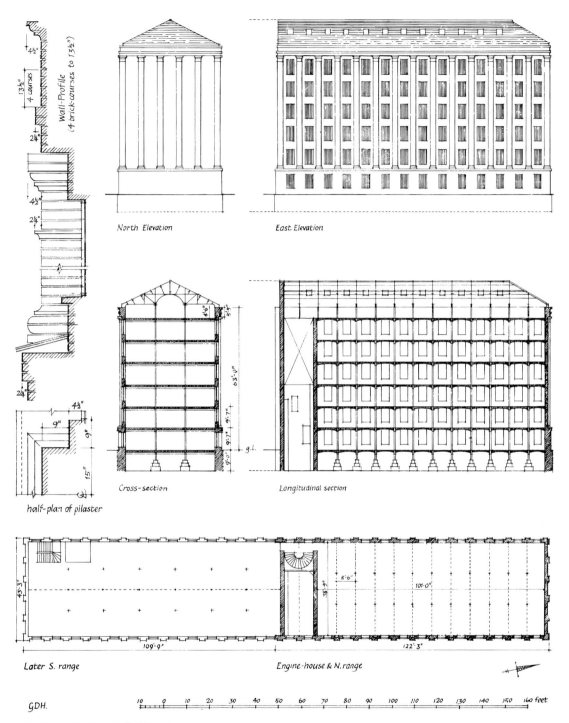

Wall-Profile
(4 brick-courses to 13½")

13½"
4 courses
4½"
2⅛"
4½"
2⅛"
4½"
2⅛"

North Elevation

East Elevation

Cross-section

Longitudinal section

half-plan of pilaster

4½"
9"
9"
15"

4'6"
5'5"
63'-0"
9'-7"
9'-7"
9'-0"
g.l.

Later S. range

Engine-house & N. range

43'-3"
38'-9"
8'6"
101'-0"
109'-9"
122'-3"

GDH.

10 0 10 20 30 40 50 60 70 80 90 100 110 120 130 140 150 160 feet

Houldsworth's Cotton Mill, Glasgow

87

Houldsworth's Cotton Mill, Glasgow; exposed floor-sections

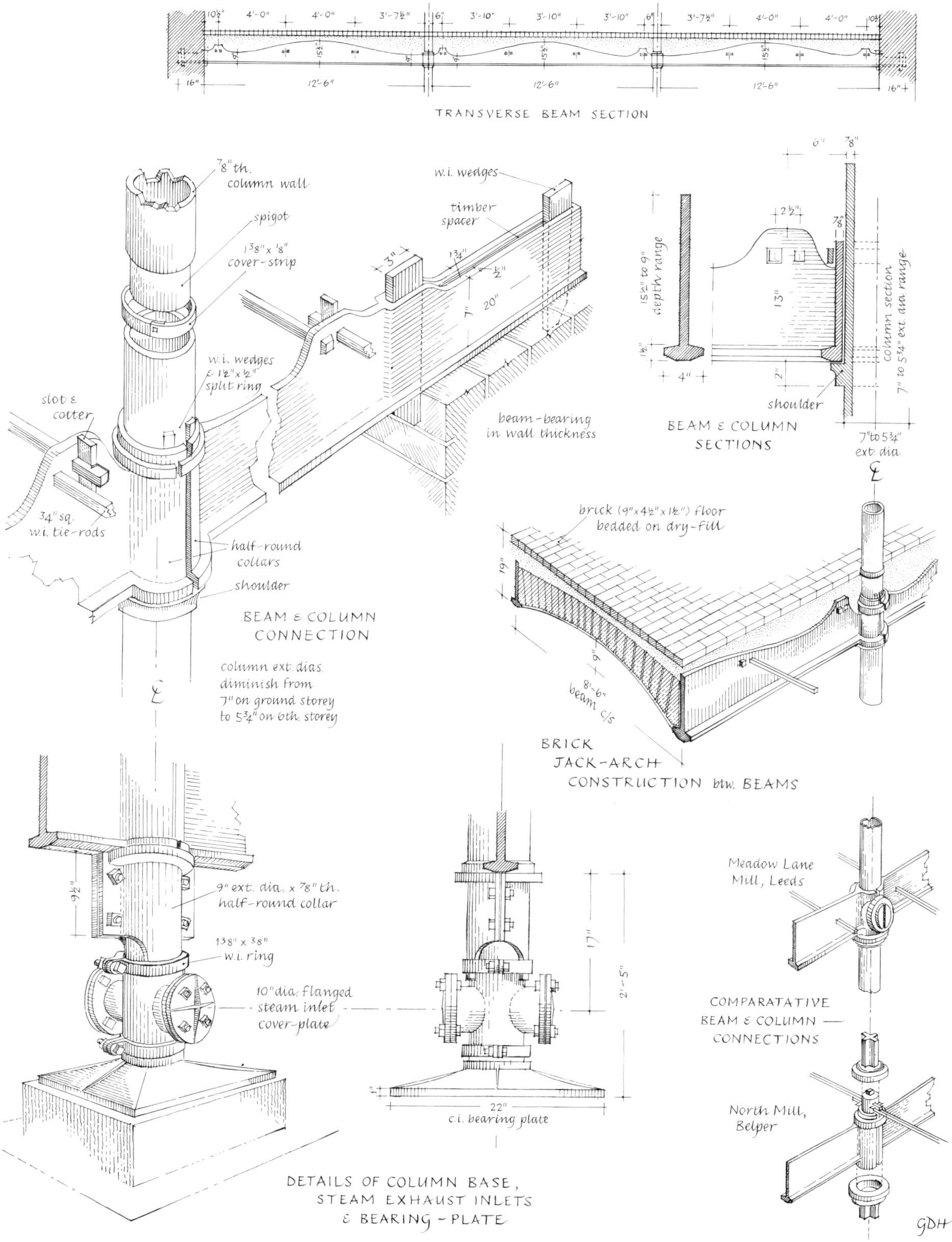

TRANSVERSE BEAM SECTION

7/8" th.
column wall

spigot

1 3/8" x 1/8"
cover-strip

w.i. wedges

timber
spacer

w.i. wedges
& 1 1/2" x 2"
split ring

slot &
cotter

3/4" sq.
w.i. tie-rods

half-round
collars

shoulder

BEAM & COLUMN
CONNECTION

column ext. dias.
diminish from
7" on ground storey
to 5 3/4" on 6th storey

beam-bearing
in wall thickness

15 1/2" to 9"
depth range

13"

4"

shoulder

BEAM & COLUMN
SECTIONS

7" to 5 3/4" ext. dia.
column section

7" to 5 3/4"
ext. dia.

brick (9"x 4 1/2" x 1 1/2") floor
bedded on dry-fill

19"

9"

beam c/s

8'-6"

BRICK
JACK-ARCH
CONSTRUCTION btw. BEAMS

9 1/2"

9" ext. dia. x 7/8" th.
half-round collar

1 3/8" x 3/8"
w.i. ring

10" dia. flanged
steam inlet
cover-plate

17"

2'-5"

22"
c.i. bearing plate

DETAILS OF COLUMN BASE,
STEAM EXHAUST INLETS
& BEARING - PLATE

Meadow Lane
Mill, Leeds

COMPARATATIVE
BEAM & COLUMN
CONNECTIONS

North Mill,
Belper

GDH

Houldsworth's Cotton Mill, Glasgow; structural details

89

A

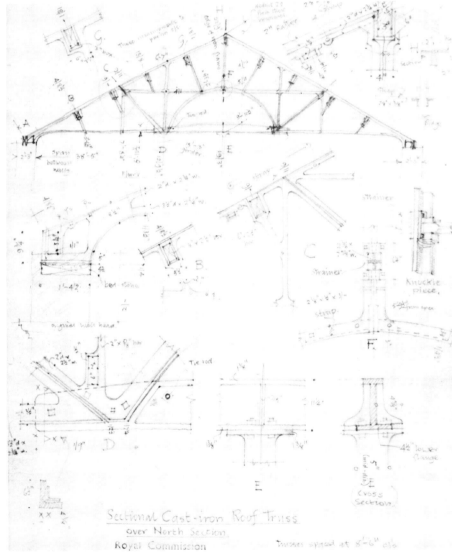

Sectional Cast-iron Roof Truss
over North section
Royal Commission

Trusses spaced at 8'-6" c/o

B

Houldsworth's Cotton Mill,
Glasgow
A. cast-iron roof-trusses
(centre columns and
beams inserted)
B. sketch details of
roof-truss

A

B

Atlantic and Pacific Mills, Paisley, Renfrewshire
  A. s façade
  B. interior of Atlantic Mill, fourth floor

Atlantic and Pacific Mills   NS 488636
Paisley, Renfrewshire
        Strathclyde, Renfrew   # 1972

Prior to its demolition in 1972, the linear range comprising the Atlantic and Pacific Mills formed part of the vast Anchor Thread Works of J & P Coats Limited. Completed to a three-stage plan between 1871 and 1883 and ultimately covering the considerable area of 532 ft by 80 ft (162·2 m by 24·4 m), the two mills were uniformly built in red brick with selected sandstone features, and conformed to a symmetrical layout incorporating a central and secondary tower _91_ A of two-bay width. The mill floors were composed of twin wooden main beams and joists, boarded and surfaced with maple and carried on cast-iron columns, which divided _91_ B them into four longitudinal aisles with corresponding ridged roofs. But the central tower, built as the last phase in order to unite the E and W mill ranges, was designed as an intervening fireproof barrier with thick walls and floors of _92_ sophisticated jack-arch and cast-iron construction. The secondary towers, central to each mill, contained the power-plant, which consisted of a horizontal compound steam-engine with a 32 ft-diameter (9·75 m) grooved fly-wheel driving a rope-race engaging with the line-shafting on each floor.

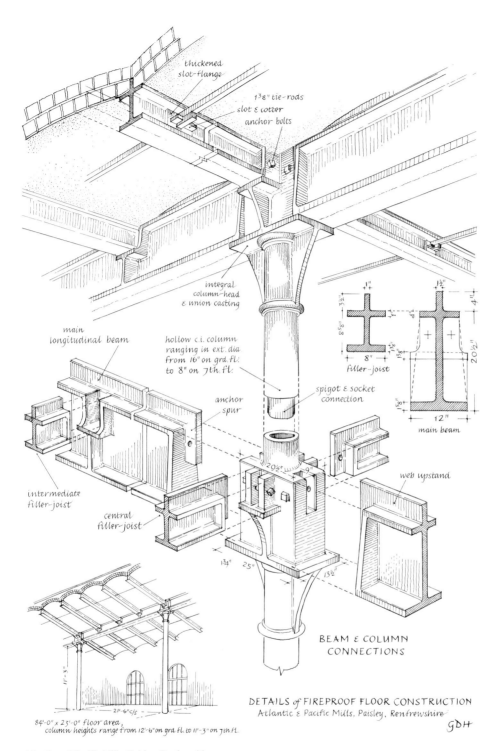

thickened
slot-flange

1⅜" tie-rods
slot & cotter
anchor bolts

integral
column-head
& union casting

main
longitudinal beam

hollow c.i. column
ranging in ext. dia
from 16" on grd. fl.
to 8" on 7th. fl.

8⅝"

filler-joist

3½"
1"

1⅝"

8"

1"

1½"

1"

20½"

4¼"

5⅝"

12"

main beam

anchor
spur

spigot & socket
connection

web upstand

intermediate
filler-joist

central
filler-joist

20½"

9"

1¾"   25"

13½"

BEAM & COLUMN
CONNECTIONS

DETAILS of FIREPROOF FLOOR CONSTRUCTION
Atlantic & Pacific Mills, Paisley, Renfrewshire
GDH

11'-3"

21'-6" c/s

84'-0" x 23'-0" floor area,
column heights range from 12'-6" on grd. fl. to 11'-3" on 7th. fl.

Atlantic and Pacific Mills, Paisley, Renfrewshire;
structural details, central tower

92

A

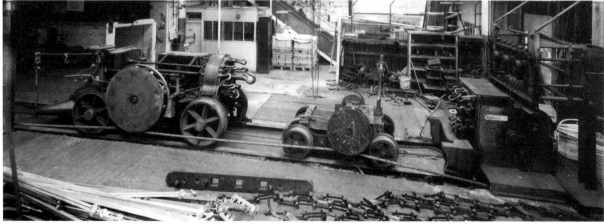

B

The Gourock Rope Work, Port Glasgow, Renfrewshire
  A. interior of central section
  B. ropewalk machinery comprising foregear,
       traveller and top-cart

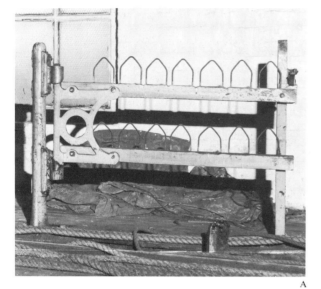

A

B

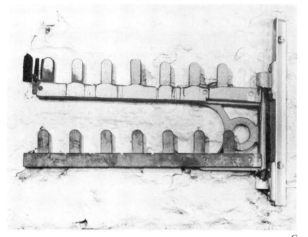

C

D

E

The Gourock Rope Work, Port Glasgow,
Renfrewshire
  A-D. gate-rests and stake-posts
  E. membership certificate of the
        Gourock, Greenock and Port Glasgow
        Ropemaker Society

A

B

C

D

The Gourock Ropework

Port Glasgow, Renfrewshire
Strathclyde, Inverclyde

NS 324743

1976

Established in 1797 as a result of a merger between the Port Glasgow Rope & Duck Company (founded 1736) and the original Gourock Company (founded 1777), this firm enjoyed a world-wide reputation in the manufacture of ropes, canvas and sailcloth. At the turn of the 19th century it became particularly well known for its special proofing process of canvas and sailcloth, usually identified by the trademark 'Gourock A1 Birkmyre Proofed'. On its closure in 1976, the works complex included a large brick multi-storeyed block, formerly a sugar refinery, and a *95 A* ropewalk. The ropewalk, which extended along the N side of the Glasgow–Greenock railway, was built partially of random rubble and brick, with a slate roof, and comprised three main sections totalling approximately one quarter mile (400 m) in length. The earlier 854 ft (260 m) single-storeyed portion was extended westwards, probably in 1840, by the addition of two successively wider units which *93 A* incorporated upper floors of jack-arch fireproof construction. The extensions were evidently planned for ropewalk machinery, designed and perfected by the com- *93 B* pany. One such machine, comprising foregear, traveller and top-cart, dating from 1859, remained *in situ* on the ground floor. At about the same time the first floor was evidently used for making ropes by the 'house machine' method, which dispensed with the need for a long ropewalk. The ropewalk had three trackways, of which the longest was capable of hauling out three-strand ropes of 191 fathoms (348·67 m), up to 20 in (0·51 m) in circumference of hemp or manilla, and 36 in (0·91 m) of coir; and the two other tracks, 172-fathom (314 m) ropes of manilla or sisal up to 24 in (0·61 m) in circumference. The several fixtures along the *94* walks included a variety of pronged gate-rests and stake-posts spaced at appropriate intervals in order to maintain the rope at a 'level lay'.

The Gourock Rope Work, Port Glasgow, Renfrewshire
   A.   ropewalk from NW
Forth and Clyde Roperie, Kirkcaldy, Fife
   B.   fixed foregear at N end
   C.   traveller
   D.   top-cart

A

B

Forth and Clyde Roperie, Kirkcaldy, Fife
A.   interior looking N
B.   ropewalk from NE

Forth and Clyde Roperie   NT 277901
Kirkcaldy, Fife
   Fife, Kirkcaldy   # 1974

This ropework was established at the s end of Kirkcaldy in 1850 by a local boat-builder and a twine manufacturer for the manufacture of soft-fibre ropes (e.g. hemp). Originally it appears to have measured 656 ft (200 m) in length from N to s, but the building was soon extended at both ends to approximately 1227 ft (374 m), and roofed uniformly with pantiles. A wider brick portion at the N end housed offices and machinery for spinning and processing the strands, and also a tarring-pit complete with a wooden-framed winding- 97 A reel. The ropewalk itself was a rubble-built range with low undulating side-walls and broken roof-line; within its long 96 A,B narrow confines—sparingly lit with small shuttered windows beneath an open timber roof—the floor accommodated three trackways and sets of rope-making equipment. The latter, which varied in date and design, comprised a fixed foregear at the N end and a mobile traveller, or bogie, 95 B-D and top-cart. In 1896 the firm assumed the name of Forth & Clyde Roperie Company Limited and subsequently used the ropewalk for the manufacture of hard-fibre ropes of about 175 fathoms (320 m) in maximum length.

A

B

Forth and Clyde Roperie, Kirkcaldy, Fife
  A.   tarring-pit and winding-reel
Cardy Net Manufactory, Lower Largo, Fife
  B.   factory interior, 1885

A

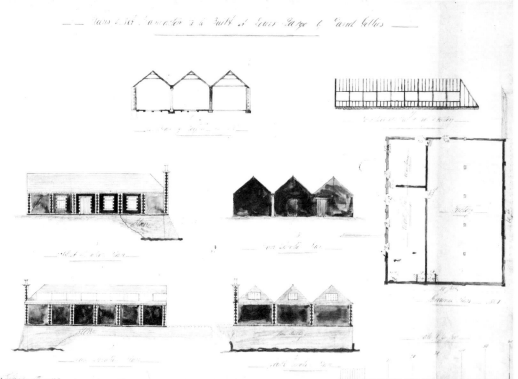

B

Cardy Net Manufactory, Lower Largo, Fife
A. view of works and proprietor's house, 1872
B. design drawings, 1867

Cardy Net Manufactory, Lower Largo, Fife; interior of warehouse

Cardy Net Manufactory NO 422026
Lower Largo, Fife
    Fife, North-east Fife 1977

Situated on the edge of the foreshore of Lower Largo, the modest-sized networks built by David Gillies in accordance with drawings dated 1867, though now disused, is otherwise well preserved. Externally it is best appreciated from a trade card engraving which shows the complex as a going concern complete with factory, formal walled garden and the proprietor's mansion. The factory building, measuring 60 ft (18·29 m) by 50 ft (15·24 m) overall, is a two-coloured brick structure panelled externally by pilasters and divided from N to s by three roof-ranges covered with slates and having ample roof-lights. Internally, the two eastern ranges contain the working area, divided by a central row of structural columns, and the third range is divided off to form a workshop with forge, a smaller warehouse and an office. At the time of survey in 1978, the warehouse and office were much as they had been left when the works closed some twenty years previously; an early photograph shows the factory interior in operation.

98 B
98 A
99
97 B

NOTES

n.1   *Inventory of Stirlingshire,* **2,** Nos. 258, 259.

n.2   *Inventory of Peeblesshire,* **2,** No. 552.

n.3   *Inventory of Stirlingshire,* **2,** No. 258.

n.4   A similar latrine-tower has been recorded at the Calderhaugh Mills, Lochwinnoch, Renfrewshire (NS 352586), SIAS, December 1983.

n.5   Fairbairn, W, *Mills and Millwork* (1861), part 1, 126; part 2.

n.6   *Inventory of Stirlingshire,* **2,** No. 264.

n.7   Hume, *Ind Archaeol Scotland,* **2,** (1977), 58.

n.8   *Inventory of Stirlingshire,* **2,** p. 316.

n.9   *Inventory of Peeblesshire,* **2,** p. 287.

n.10   The technical information in this account is based on discussions with the then weaver, Mr W B Christie. Mr J Barbour Hill, of the Science Museum, London, and Dr J A Iredale, of Bradford University, have also been consulted.

n.11   Hume, J R, 'The industrial archaeology of New Lanark', in Butt, J (ed.), *Robert Owen, Prince of Cotton Spinners* (1971), 215–49.

n.12   For a detailed account of the works' history, see Cooke, A (ed.), *Stanley. Its History and Development* (1977).

n.13   Hay, G D, *Post-Medieval Archaeology,* **8,** (1974), 92–100.

Carron Ironworks, Stirlingshire;
ship's Carronade, no. 75990, cast 1810

4 METALLURGY AND ENGINEERING

Evidence of early iron-smelting operations in Scotland is still to be found at the numerous bloomery sites widely dispersed in the once wooded areas of the Highlands.[1] Bloomeries generally survive as grass-covered mounds of slag and were a crude form of charcoal furnace. They were often no more than shallow cavities scooped out of the ground for the purpose of producing a 'bloom' or lump of malleable iron, which was then repeatedly hammered to remove impurities. These primitive methods of iron-making continued to be employed in Scotland until the 17th century, when the potential of ample charcoal supplies, allied to water-power and the presence of bog-ore in the Highlands, began to attract English and Irish ironmasters, who by then were well practised in commercial production of cast iron in charcoal-fuelled blast-furnaces.

Many of these enterprises, such as those at Glen Kinglass, Argyll (NN 082371) (c.1722), and Abernethy, Inverness-shire (NJ 0020) (c.1730),[2] were short-lived ventures, but this did not deter ironmasters from the Furness district of North Lancashire during the 1750s from setting up two new sites in *108-14* Argyll, respectively at Bonawe, by Loch Etive, and at *114-15* Furnace, by Loch Fyne. During this period most of the iron smelted in the furnace was either cast into pigs for subsequent refining as wrought iron, or tapped direct into moulds—a procedure normally confined to hand tools,

simple household ware such as pans and firebacks, and notably cannon-balls and shot. Charcoal pig-iron continued to be valued by ironmasters for special fine-quality castings until about the mid-19th century, but by the 1760s the widespread use of coke for smelting iron, presaged by the successful experiments of Abraham Darby at Coalbrookdale, had become the standard method for the commercial production of iron.

In Scotland, the first coke blast-furnaces were installed at the Carron Iron Works, Stirlingshire, the vast, rationally planned complex founded in 1759 by Dr John Roebuck in association with William Cadell and Samuel Garbett of Birmingham. In subsequent decades blowing-engines were installed to supply the powerful blast, and a mill for boring guns and cylinders; following the success of Henry Cort's puddling and rolling process, reverberatory furnaces fuelled by coke were used for reheating pig-iron and converting it into wrought iron. Apart from the historic connection with James Watt's early experiments with the steam-engine, *100* Carron's rise to fame was vested in the 'Carronade', a large-bore cannon of relatively short length and exceptional strength, and likewise the production of fine-quality castings for all kinds of engineering- and building-purposes. *101* A,B Part of the early foundry, with arched masonry openings and massive timber roof, survived in a modified state until

A

B

Carron products, Callendar House, Stirlingshire
  A.   kitchen oven
  B.   kitchen hotplate

H

A

B

Carron Ironworks, Stirlingshire
A. old part of High Foundry
    looking s
B. old part of Low Foundry,
    w side, roof structure

102 A,B
115-17
about 1970, as did also a mid-19th-century engineering-shop and a bank of four furnaces dating from about 1890. All that now remains of the complex is the red sandstone two-storeyed office-block built in 1876, which preserves in the walling the fragment of a cast-iron lintel of the first furnace of 1760, and part of a steam cylinder made by James Watt, cast with the inscription CARRON/1766. Carron

A

B

set the trend and location for the new foundries, which logically became concentrated on the principal coal-producing areas of the central Lowlands,[3] but further developments in the Scottish iron industry had to await James

Neilson's invention of the hot-blast process which he patented in 1828 and applied successfully at the Clyde Ironworks two years later. His method of pre-heating the blast before it went into the furnace resulted in a great improvement in iron output and fuel utilisation; in particular, it permitted the large deposits of low-grade coals and blackband ironstone of the Lowlands to be used for smelting. Wide application of the process, coupled with the water-cooled tuyère invented by James Condie of the Blair Ironworks, Glasgow, marked the beginning of Scotland's rise to world status by the 1850s in the output of iron and engineering products.

In the construction industry eminent engineers like Fairbairn, Hodgkinson and Tredgold had rationalised the structural merits of cast iron and wrought iron in their application to building and bridge design. Thus the middle decades of the 19th century witnessed the manufacture of ironwork for London's Crystal Palace at Fox and Henderson's Renfrew factory,[4] and James Kibble's design for the smaller but equally successful multi-domed structure in *103* C glass and iron in Glasgow's Botanic Gardens.[5] In 1855-6 another significant advance was the use of an all-cast-iron frame for the multi-storeyed warehouse at 36 Jamaica *104* Street, Glasgow, built by the ironfounder R McConnell in conjunction with John Baird.[6]

An earlier example in the architectural application of cast iron is the dome and rotunda formerly concealing the water-cistern of the neo-Classic Perth Waterworks, *105* A,B designed by Adam Anderson in 1832. Throughout the course of the 19th century, however, the most lasting testimony to the ironfounder's art rests in the multifarious uses of iron for furnishing Scotland's towns and cities with a remarkable wealth of architectural detail and incidental features, particularly in Edinburgh and Glasgow. Both wrought iron and cast iron, often in combination, were used for this purpose on a mass-produced scale for the miles of *105* C street railings, decorative balconies and all kinds of *106-7* everyday accessories and utilities.

C
Carron Ironworks, Stirlingshire
  A, B. cast-iron fragments

C. Botanic Gardens, Glasgow; conservatory (Kibble Palace, *c.* 1860)

A

Warehouse, 36 Jamaica Street,
Glasgow
    A.   view from SE
B   B.   detail of structural bay

Perth Waterworks
- A.   cast-iron dome and rotunda
- B.   view from s

Former Caledonian Railway station, Peebles
- C.   wall drinking-fountain

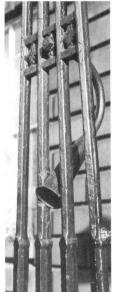

Street ironwork, Edinburgh
    A.   railings and lamp-standards, Charlotte Square
    B.   balcony and overthrow, Melville Street
    C, D. lamplighter extinguishers
Fraserburgh, Aberdeenshire
    E.   cast-iron fountain

A

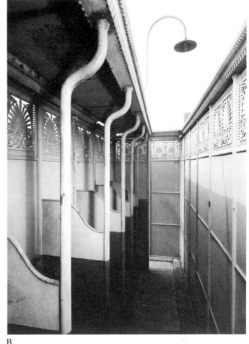

B

C

D

A-C. Cast-iron urinal, railway station,
      Melrose, Roxburghshire
D.   Bandstand, Duthie Park, Aberdeen

The period just outlined is represented here by examples drawn from two of its most significant building-types, namely the early charcoal ironworks and the mid-19th-century engineering-shops. A broader impression of the influence that metal and engineering technology had on Scotland's monuments may be obtained from the various works and artefacts covered in other sections.

Charcoal Iron-smelting Furnaces

Ironworks   NN 082371
Glen Kinglass, Argyll
    Strathclyde, Argyll and Bute   1968

The works at Glen Kinglass, which stood close to the shore of Loch Etive, were founded and run by an Irish co-partnership from 1722 to its closure about 1738, timber rights being negotiated with a number of local landowners including Sir Duncan Campbell of Lochnell. There are the remains of the furnace, measuring about 30 ft (9·1 m) square overall, as well as traces of associated buildings at a higher level above the furnace, which evidently included turf-walled sheds.[7]

Ironworks   NM 009318
Bonawe, Argyll
    Strathclyde, Argyll and Bute   ● ** 1960–75

Bonawe Ironworks, situated close to the s shore of Loch Etive by Taynuilt village, is one of the most extensive and best-preserved relics of the early iron industry in Britain.[8] It was established in 1752–3 by Richard Ford and Company as an offshoot of their works in Furness, and leases of the site and wood rights were agreed with the above-mentioned Sir Duncan Campbell and the 3rd Earl of Breadalbane for a period of 110 years. Haematite ore was brought in by sea from Lancashire and Cumberland, and a rotational system of coppicing was developed for the manufacture of charcoal, charcoal-burning stances being found in many of the natural woodlands around this part of Argyll.[9] After expiry of the original lease in 1863, a new agreement was negotiated with Alexander Kelly of Bonawe, but the furnace finally closed in 1874.

As well as the furnace and storage sheds, the company *108* A,B
erected a manager's house, workers' dwellings, and numer- *110 (H)*
ous ancillary buildings, which included a school, a church, a jetty and a truck-store, creating in effect a self-contained industrial community.

Ironworks, Bonawe, Argyll; workers' dwellings
  A. SE of furnace
  B. N of furnace

A. Ironworks, Bonawe, Argyll;
N face of furnace showing tuyère arch
after preservation

B. Ironworks, Bonawe, Argyll;
developed drawing from N

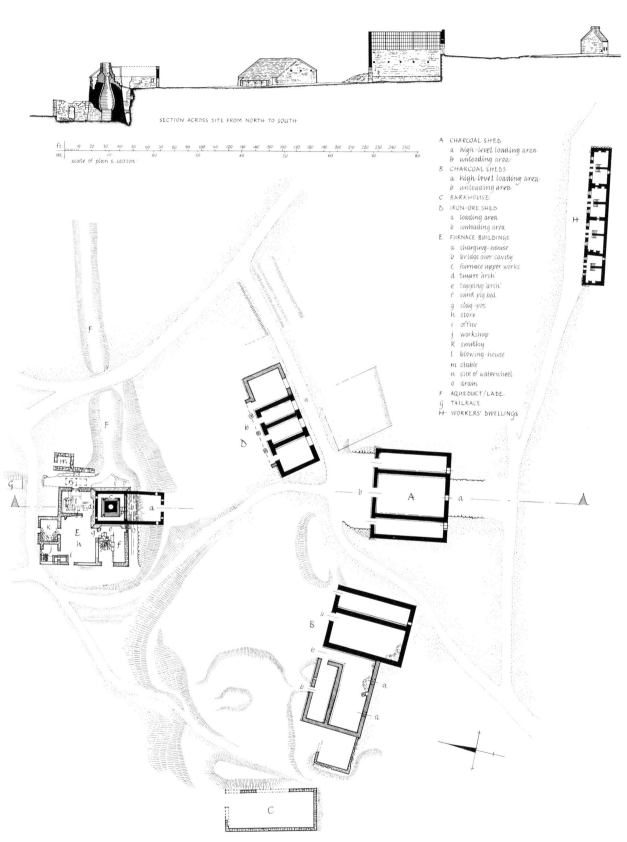

SECTION ACROSS SITE FROM NORTH TO SOUTH

scale of plan & section

A CHARCOAL SHED
  a high-level loading area
  b unloading area
B CHARCOAL SHEDS
  a high-level loading area
  b unloading area
C BARKHOUSE
D IRON-ORE SHED
  a loading area
  b unloading area
E FURNACE BUILDINGS
  a charging-house
  b bridge over cavity
  c furnace upper works
  d tuyere 'arch'
  e tapping 'arch'
  f sand pig bed
  g slag-pot
  h store
  i office
  j workshop
  K smithy
  l blowing-house
  m stable
  n site of waterwheel
  o drain
F AQUEDUCT/LADE
G TAILRACE
H WORKERS' DWELLINGS

Ironworks, Bonawe, Argyll

110

A

B

Ironworks, Bonawe, Argyll
  A.   iron-ore shed (foreground) and charcoal sheds from NE
  B.   roof-structure, E charcoal shed

At the heart of the complex are the manufactory
109 B buildings, all of which occupy bankside positions on the
110 sloping site, thus utilising the changes in level to assist what
was essentially a gravity-feed process. They are solidly built
of lime-mortared random or coursed rubble masonry,
chiefly of the local granite, but numerous features betray
their Lake District origins.

The charcoal sheds, or coal-houses, are spacious, well-
110 (A,B) ventilated barn-like structures covered with open timber

roofs of tie-beam construction carried down over the
side-ranges as catslides. Loading-doors were situated in the *111 A,B*
rear walls, and unloading-doors, at the lower ground-level,
at the front, whence the charcoal was barrowed or carried to
the charging-house. The iron-ore shed, lying along the
contours just NE of the charcoal sheds, was designed to be
filled and emptied in a similar manner once the shipments of
iron-ore had been carted up the hill from the jetty.

111

A

The blast-furnace is typical of the kind used during the later charcoal phase of the industry in Britain. The furnace openings have cast-iron lintels inscribed Bunaw. F. 1753. Apart from considerations of stability, the size and shape of the furnace were determined by the need for an adequate insulating core to reduce heat-loss and by the shaft within, whose design had to ensure a good draught and likewise prevent the friable charcoal from being crushed by an overweight of iron-ore.

The blowing-house, casting-house, store and smithy enclosing the furnace on its N and W sides are now ruinous, but the pitched roofs formerly covering these important ancillary structures can be traced by the socket-holes in the furnace walls for the roof-timbers—roofs, incidentally,

109 A
112 B

110 (E)
113

which would have given an entirely different outward appearance to the furnace compared with today. Excavations have revealed the granite base-blocks of a blowing-engine introduced at some time in the 19th century to replace the original leather bellows. Both types were powered through a camshaft worked by a low breast-shot *113(10,12)* water-wheel mounted in a pit and wheel-house along the E side. The floor of the casting-house was found to be divided by a stone kerb into a part-metalled area to the N and a bed *113(20)* of fine sand to the S.

The rear S wall is insulated from the earth bank and retaining wall by a narrow V-shaped cavity, which has a *113(27)* stone conduit running along its base and that of the casting-house—presumably for collecting seepage. At the upper level, the charging house and furnace were connected across the cavity by means of a joisted timber bridge (hence *113(23)* the alternative name bridgehouse), and by relieving arches on the side-wall. Directly beneath the bridge a long narrow chamber, carried on a joisted floor, was contrived within the cavity. Approached from the E by an external ramp, it probably served as a bothy for the furnace-keeper during *113(28)* the smelting operations, and possessed the amenity of a window and a fireplace set in the retaining wall, with horizontal flues issuing from the side-walls.

B

Ironworks, Bonawe, Argyll
  A.   cast-iron lintel above tuyère arch
  B.   furnace from NW after preservation

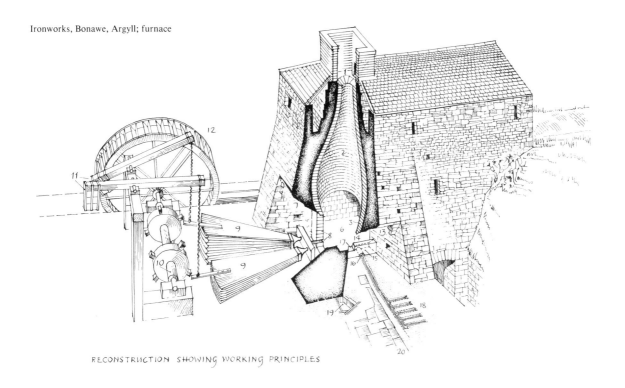

RECONSTRUCTION SHOWING WORKING PRINCIPLES

1 loading-mouth
2 furnace shaft
3 refractory lining
4 boshes
5 crucible or well
6 hearth
7 tuyere 'arch'
8 tuyere (infill over)
9 bellows
10 cam-shaft
11 weighted beams
12 waterwheel
13 tapping-arch
14 tymp-arch & infill
15 dam
16 tap hole
17 slag-notch
18 sand pig bed
19 slag-pot
20 stone kerb

21 charging-house
22 original level
23 loading bridge
24 steps up
25 gallery
26 chimney
27 insulating cavity
28 bothy
29 fireplace
30 drain

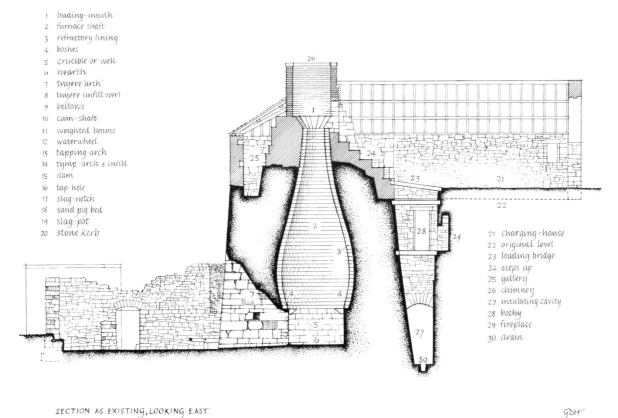

SECTION AS EXISTING, LOOKING EAST.   GDH

The principal manufactory buildings have been described approximately in the sequence in which they occur in the smelting process. Prior to this, the three ingredients—iron-ore, charcoal and limestone—underwent certain pre-treatment. Thus, the ore was washed, roasted and crushed to reduce its sulphur content and other impurities. The limestone was also broken down, and adequate stocks of charcoal had to be prepared, customarily supplied to the warehouses in 1½ cwt. (76 kg) bags and stacked there in dozens. It was also normal practice to pre-heat or season the furnace about a week in advance; the hearth area had to be relined where necessary and the apertures forming the tuyère and the tap-hole then sealed.

At the commencement of the smelting-operations the raw materials were assembled in the charging-house and measured in the correct proportions—the ore and limestone by weight, and the charcoal by volume—after which they were carried over the bridge and fed into the furnace shaft to its full height. Once the furnace was put into blast, the campaign (to use the trade term) was continuous, with recharging taking place constantly over a period lasting from about late autumn until early summer. Aided by a limestone flux for removing non-metallic impurities, the charge was heated and reduced to molten metal as it moved down the structure towards the hearth, a temperature of up to 1200°C being achieved by an upward blast of air supplied from two sets of bellows blowing alternately. Periodically liquid iron was run off through the tap-hole into a principal furrow formed in a bed of sand, called the sow, and its lesser branches the pigs (hence the term pig-iron). The slag (impurities and unreduced ore), being lighter than the molten iron, was drawn off last over the slag-dam. It has been estimated that the furnace was capable of producing about two tons of pig-iron per day, which, owing to its high carbon content, was hard and brittle and normally required further refining. For this purpose, apart from some casting and forging on a small scale, it was the policy at Bonawe to ship the rough bars of pig back to commercial plants in England.

Water for the ironworks was led from the River Awe about 1 mile (1·6 km) to the east by means of an aqueduct, turning at right angles at the furnace to drive the water-wheel. Supplementary supplies were held in two reservoirs situated on the high ground near the manager's house and adjacent to the upper terrace of workers' dwellings.

110 (F)

Ironworks

NM 025000

Craleckan, Furnace, Argyll
    Strathclyde, Argyll and Bute   ● * 1983

The Craleckan Ironworks,[10] situated at Furnace, on the shore of Loch Fyne, was established two years after Bonawe by the Duddon Furnace Company, another concern stemming from the Furness district of Lancashire. It appears to have been organised on similar lines to Bonawe, but the complex as a whole is no longer so well defined, having ceased production about 1813. Of the manufactory buildings, which occupy the customary bankside position, there are substantial remains of a former charcoal-shed,

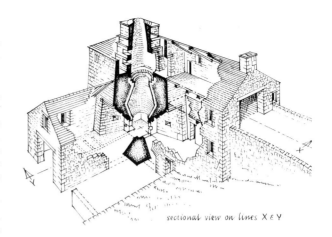

sectional view on lines X & Y

charging level
bothy level
furnace level

south elevation

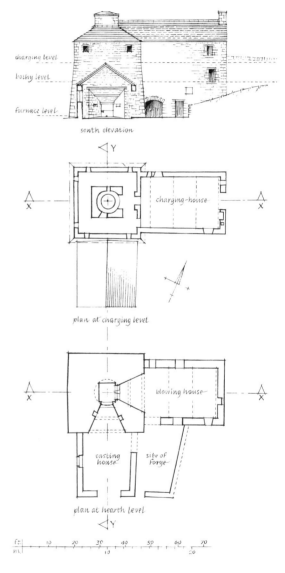

charging-house

plan at charging level

blowing house

casting house

site of forge

plan at hearth level

Ironworks, Craleckan, Argyll; furnace

A

Engineering Workshops and Foundries

With the expansion of heavy engineering during the middle decades of the 19th century, the outstanding industrial buildings to emerge were the massive engineering workshops or foundries, erected to house the diverse range of machine and production tools by then necessary for the manufacture of bulk items, whether of a general nature or in the more specialised branches of locomotive building and marine engineering.

Both in basic design and the structural use of materials, they tended to have a certain family resemblance and a common evolutionary pattern. The two main elements were a machine-hall or erecting-shop, spacious enough for manoeuvring and lifting heavy pieces of machinery in the course of assembly, and an adjacent multi-storeyed area for accommodating ancillary services such as moulding and pattern-making. Prerequisites of the machine-halls were an adequate unobstructed floor-area and height, with direct access to the multi-storeyed part, which took the form of an extension at one end, or a number of galleried aisles flanking or entirely surrounding the central space. To obtain a maximum clear floor-area, wide spans with as few point-supports as possible became the rule, and various ingenious methods of beam- and floor-suspension were devised towards this end.

Allied to an improved building technology, more spacious working-areas were progressively attained as new materials and constructional techniques became available. Traditional stonework tended to be replaced by brick, and load-bearing walls, strengthened by piers and pilasters, were used essentially as a shell to contain an internal frame composed of iron and timber. The latter, usually of Baltic

114
115 A

evidently capable of holding about 600 dozen bags of charcoal,[11] and the furnace itself, which together with its associated buildings is remarkably complete. One of the cast-iron lintels over the tuyère-opening bears an indistinct inscription, C (?G) F 1755, and the hearth area is potentially of unique technological interest in that the lining has remained undisturbed since the furnace was finally damped down. Ancillary buildings include the usual casting-house and a blowing-house, the latter, unlike the layout of its English parent furnace at Duddon Bridge and of that at Bonawe, being located beneath the charging-house. The Craleckan furnace also appears to have incorporated a forge, situated between the casting- and blowing-houses, which probably operated on a sufficient scale to be equipped with finery hearths and forging-hammers, necessary for fashioning the pig-iron into wrought iron.

Ironworks, Craleckan, Argyll
   A.   furnace from NW
Engineering-shop,
Carron Ironworks, Stirlingshire
   B.   view from SW

B

fir, or pine, was used on a prodigal scale for roofs and for double-floor construction, composed of main beams and secondary joists. Principal timber members could be as much as 14 in (356 mm) square in section and common floor-boards up to 2¼ in (57 mm) in thickness. Main internal supports consisted of cast-iron stanchions, commonly of a heavy boxed I-section, with a pierced web; anchored to bed-plates on pad foundations, they were monolithic throughout and stepped back at the upper stage to accommodate a gantry-beam. Minor components, such as beam and roof brackets are also of cast iron, while tie-rods and similar tension members were of wrought iron; the use of cast iron was also extended to door surrounds (as in the Carron example) and window frames.

For lifting-purposes the larger shops were equipped with a travelling crane running on a gantry across the upper stage of the main stanchions, and for more localised lifting, jib-cranes were attached to the stanchions, describing intersecting arcs over most of the floor-area. Externally, universal features were the commodious arched dispatch doorways, and the buildings in general evinced varying degrees of refinement such as pilastered wall surfaces and dressed stonework, though the prestigious neo-Egyptian *118-20* façade of the Randolph and Elder Works, Glasgow, was an outstanding exception. Few such concessions, however, applied to the internal structure, whose frank expression of strength and stability was consistent with the heavy concussions and moving loads which the buildings had to withstand. The five selected examples briefly described below are amplified in the accompanying drawings.

Engineering-shop   NS 880825
Carron Ironworks, Stirlingshire
Central, Falkirk   # 1960

This building,[12] distinguished for the range and quality of its castings, was part of the vast Carron complex and dates from the first half of the 19th century. Its 2 ft-thick (0·61 m) external brick walls supported king-post roof-trusses *116* A spanning 40 ft (12·19 m), the latter being used to carry a loft-floor and a suspended floor over the machine-hall, which occupied the w portion of the building. The floor hung from extensions of the king-posts secured to strap-binders and stirrup connections; the cross-beams were clamped between heavy 4 ft 6 in (1·37 m) castings which contained sockets to carry a double row of longitudinal *116* C beams, all contained within a structural floor-thickness of 12 in (0·31 m). For extra strength at mid-span, the 12 in-deep (0·31 m) roof-ties carrying the suspended floor were designed as trussed beams, the latter having pairs of *116* B 1½ in-diameter (38 mm) tension-rods slung underneath in cradle-castings, post-tensioned at the ends by means of screw bolts held in iron shoes. The machine-hall was equipped with two post-cranes fixed at the centre of the penultimate end-bays.

B

A

C

Engineering-shop, Carron Ironworks, Stirlingshire
  A. roof-structure over machine hall
  B. trussed beam and pendant post
  C. suspension point for floor above machine hall

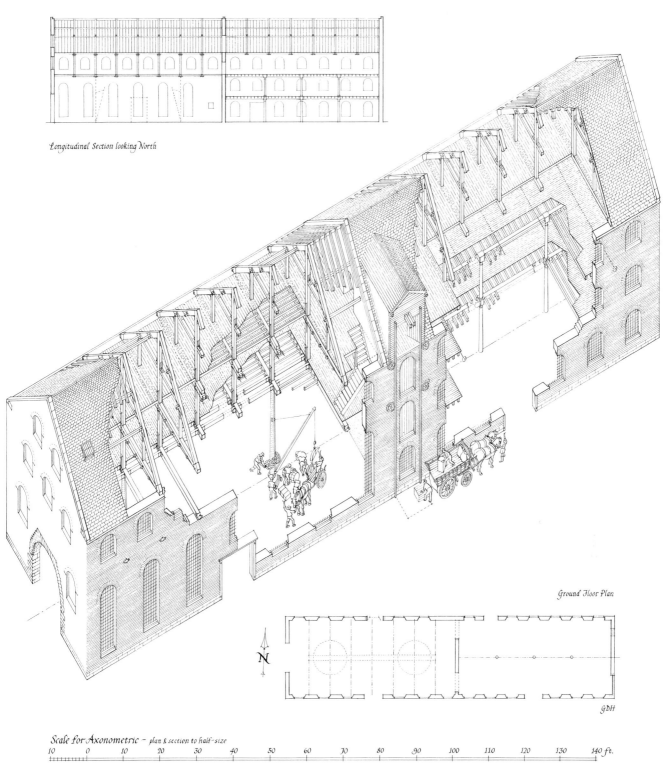

Longitudinal Section looking North

Ground Floor Plan

N

GDH

Scale for Axonometric – *plan & section to half-size*

| 10 | 0 | 10 | 20 | 30 | 40 | 50 | 60 | 70 | 80 | 90 | 100 | 110 | 120 | 130 | 140 ft. |

Engineering-shop, Carron Ironworks, Stirlingshire

117

Randolph and Elder Engineering Works, Centre Street, Glasgow; interior of central machine hall from w

Randolph and Elder Engineering Works   NS 584646
Centre Street, Glasgow
            Strathclyde, City of Glasgow   # 1969

Built on a vast scale to the design of the industrial architect William Spence between 1858 and 1860, this building was commissioned by the engineers after whom it was named for the purpose of manufacturing their patent compound marine engines. Its construction probably demonstrates the rational limits to which timber could be exploited in association with iron for erecting specialised buildings of this type.

Basically, it consisted of two 50 ft-wide (15·24 m) machine-halls, flanked by open galleries, extended at the E end into a multi-storeyed range. Within the machine-halls, which were open to the roof-structure, stability of the internal frame depended on four 8 ft-square (2·44 m) corner-piers and intervening stanchions, plus the binding-effect of the five-baulk gantry-beam traversing their upper stage. The stanchions, generously spaced at 38 ft (11·58 m)

centres in the w hall and rather less in the central hall, were of open boxed I-section with web-flange dimensions of 38 in (0·96 m) by 18 in (0·46 m) at base, tapering to a flange-head of 12 in (0·31 m); they rose to an overall height of 44 ft 9 in (13·64 m) and broke back at the upper stage to accommodate the gantry.   *120 (J,K) 121 (A)*

The latter, as well as carrying the travelling cranes, had the important function of providing a two-point intermediate support-system for the roof-structure and the suspended galleries. Details of the elaborate castings and binding-straps for the secondary supports are shown on the drawing, as also are those for the strainer-truss at the main crossing.   *120   118*
The roof-trusses, spaced at 10 ft (3·05 m) centres, were designed in the manner of girders, with upper and lower booms, tensioned by 1¼ in (32 mm) tie-rods and strengthened at all major joints by castings. The show-piece frontage encompassing the w machine-hall incorporated two massive dispatch doorways, each having a total access-area 32 ft (9·75 m) high by 30 ft (9·14 m) wide. Attributes of the pseudo-Egyptian style were the rusticated *121 B* wall surfaces, the raked pilaster profiles and a bold gorge cornice beneath the parapet.

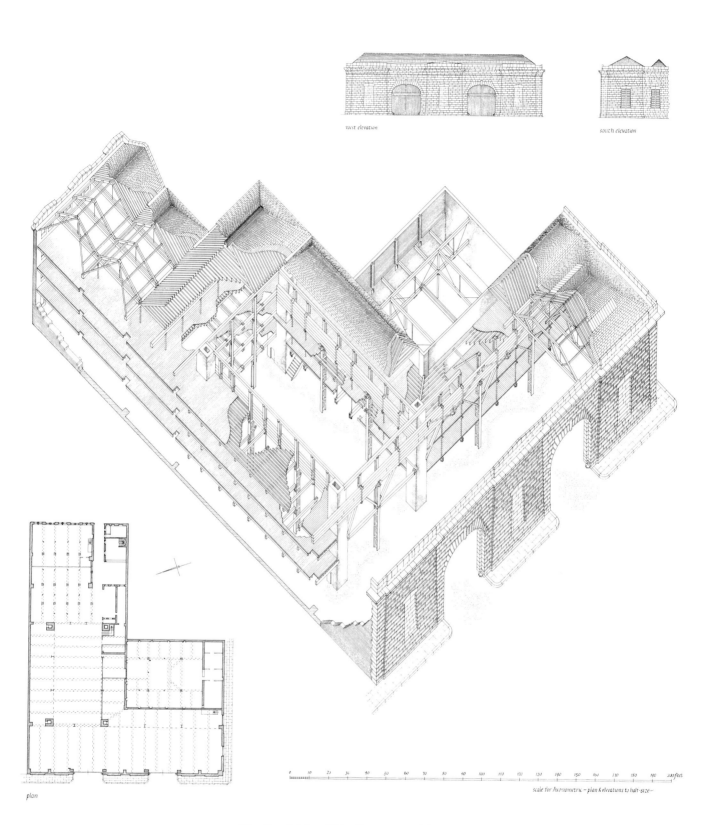

west elevation

south elevation

plan

0 10 20 30 40 50 60 70 80 90 100 110 120 130 140 150 160 170 180 190 200 feet

scale for Axonometric – plan & elevations to half-size–

The Randolph & Elder Engineering Works
Tradeston Street. Glasgow.

Randolph and Elder Engineering Works,
Centre Street (formerly Tradeston Street), Glasgow

drawing by Alan Leith

119

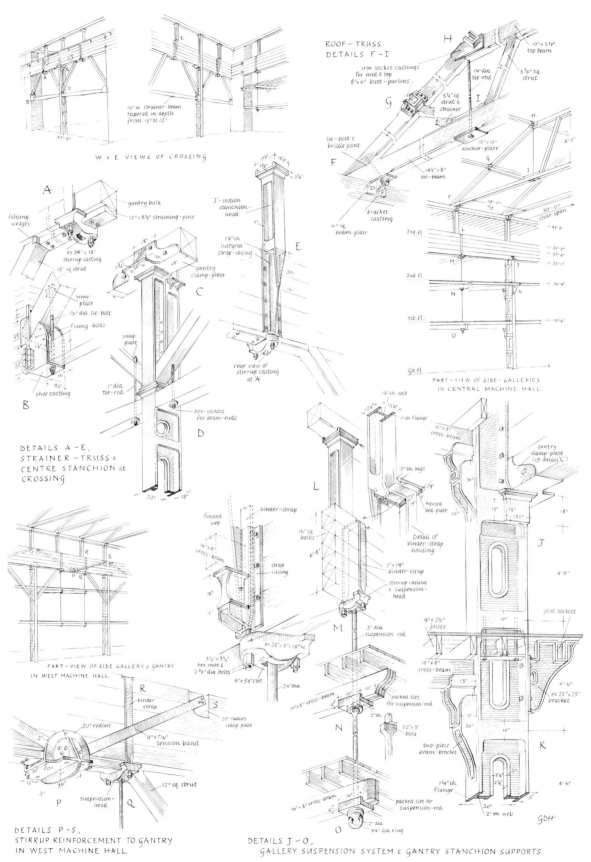

W & E VIEWS OF CROSSING

ROOF – TRUSS
DETAILS F – I

DETAILS A – E,
STRAINER – TRUSS &
CENTRE STANCHION at
CROSSING

PART – VIEW OF SIDE – GALLERIES
IN CENTRAL MACHINE HALL

PART – VIEW OF SIDE GALLERY & GANTRY
IN WEST MACHINE HALL

DETAILS P – S,
STIRRUP REINFORCEMENT TO GANTRY
IN WEST MACHINE HALL

DETAILS J – O,
GALLERY SUSPENSION SYSTEM & GANTRY STANCHION SUPPORTS

Randolph and Elder Engineering Works, Centre Street, Glasgow; structural details

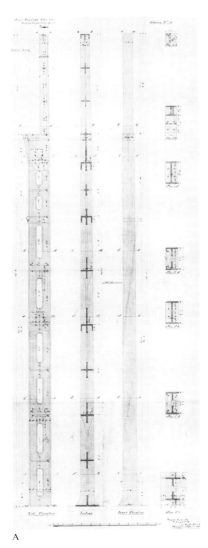

A

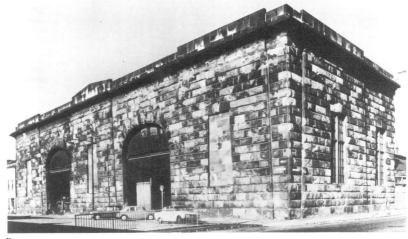

B

Randolph and Elder Engineering Works, Centre Street, Glasgow
    A.   design drawings of stanchion, 1868
    B.   principal frontage from sw

C

Linthouse Engine Works, Govan, Glasgow
    C.   interior of machine hall from w

Linthouse Engine Works

Govan, Glasgow
    Strathclyde, City of Glasgow

NS 540660

][1980

Completed in 1872, this engine-shop formed part of the 35-acre (14 ha) shipbuilding yard of Alexander Stephen and Sons established three years previously on the country estate of Linthouse, s of the River Clyde.[13] Subsequently modified, and by 1980 the only workshop of the complex not dismantled, it consisted of two parallel machine-halls with *121 C* clear spans of 53 ft (16·15 m) and an original estimated length of 240 ft (73 m) subdivided into 20 ft (6·10 m) bays by *122* stanchions and terminal brick piers. They were flanked by 33 ft-wide (10·06 m) aisles containing lofts covered by a continuation of the main roof slopes, and the s side also had

a second aisle of similar width. Apart from the use of malleable iron plate-girders for the gantries the structural techniques show no advance on those employed in the previous examples. The I-section stanchions, each said to *123* weigh 6 tons (6·1 tonnes), had web-flange dimensions of 36 in (0·91 m) by 18 in (0·46 m). Specific points were the integral castings for the brackets carrying the gantry, the tier of twin binding-beams, and the different treatment of the centre and flanking rows of stanchions at gantry level. A novel feature was the mid-point support between stanchions for the roof structure, achieved by a combination of coupled beams and a centre-post held in suspension by *124 A* tie-rods, slung between the stanchions to connect with a stirrup and cross-beam. Bracket jib-cranes with wooden *124 B* booms were fixed to alternate stanchions in both machine-halls and aisles.

121

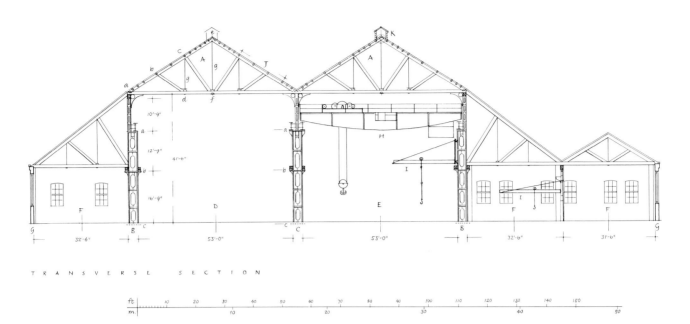

ft. | 10 | 20 | 30 | 40 | 50 | 60 | 70 | 80 | 90 | 100 | 110 | 120 | 130 | 140 | 150
m. | 10 | 20 | 30 | 40 | 50

A   principal roof trusses
     a-g on detail sheet
B   side-row stanchions
     a gantry level
     b tie-rail level
     c bed-plate level
C   centre-row stanchions
     a gantry level
     b tie-rail level
     c bed-plate level
D   north machine hall
E   south machine hall
F   pattern floors
G   brick walling
H   travelling crane
I   jib-cranes
J   glazed roof areas
K   ridge ventilators
L   terminal brick piers

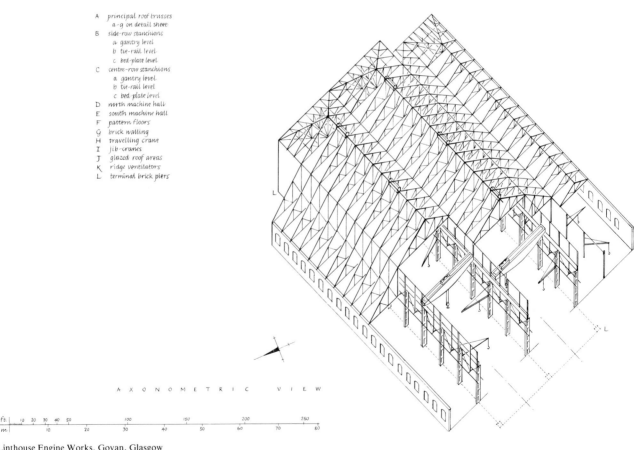

AXONOMETRIC VIEW

ft. | 10 20 30 40 50 | 100 | 150 | 200 | 250
m. | 10 | 20 | 30 | 40 | 50 | 60 | 70 | 80

Linthouse Engine Works, Govan, Glasgow

122

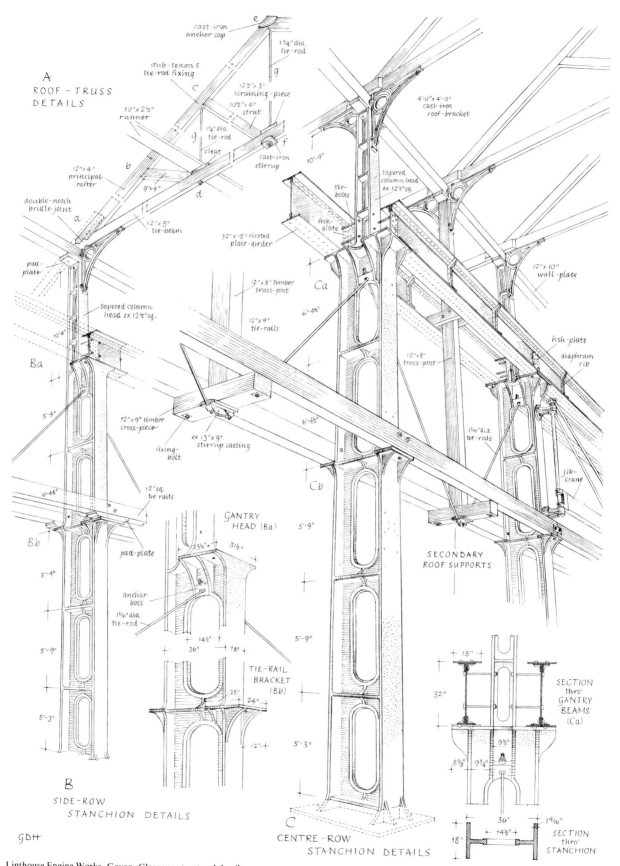

A
ROOF-TRUSS
DETAILS

cast-iron anchor cap
stub-tenon & tie-rod fixing
1¾" dia. tie-rod
12½" x 3" straining-piece
10½" x 4" strut
10" x 2½" runner
1'4" dia. tie-rod
cleat
cast-iron stirrup
12" x 4" principal rafter
double-notch bridle-joint
9" x 4"
12" x 5" tie-beam
pad-plate
tapered column head ex 12½" sq.
10'-9"

4'-0" x 4'-0" cast-iron roof-bracket
tie-bolts
tapered column head ex 12½" sq.
fish-plate
32" x 15" riveted plate-girder
12" x 8" timber truss-post
12" x 9" tie-rails
6'-4½"
12" x 10" wall-plate
Ca
12" x 8" truss-post
fish-plate
diaphragm rib

Ba
5'-4"
6'-4½"
12" x 9" timber cross-piece
fixing-bolt
ex 13" x 9" stirrup casting
12" sq. tie-rails
6'-4½"
1⅛" dia. tie-rods
jib-crane
Cb

Bb
pad-plate
5'-9"
5'-9"
5'-9"
5'-3"
GANTRY HEAD (Ba)
2½"
3½"
anchor boss
1⅛" dia. tie-rod
14½"
36"
18"
TIE-RAIL BRACKET (Bb)
.25"
24"
12"
5'-9"
SECONDARY ROOF SUPPORTS

15"
32"
SECTION thro' GANTRY BEAMS (Ca)
9½"
8⅝"
9¾"
36"
14½"
19/16"
18"
SECTION thro' STANCHION

B
SIDE-ROW STANCHION DETAILS

GDH

C
CENTRE-ROW STANCHION DETAILS

Linthouse Engine Works, Govan, Glasgow; structural details

123

B

Linthouse Engine Works, Govan, Glasgow
A. intermediate suspension point
B. bracket jib-crane

C

Fairfield Shipbuilding Yard and Engine Works, Govan, Glasgow
C. machine hall, gantry and roof

Fairfield Shipbuilding Yard and Engine Works NS 548660
Govan, Glasgow
    Strathclyde, City of Glasgow   ● 1980

After setting up a shipbuilding yard in 1863, Randolph and
Elder eventually abandoned their old works in Centre Street
in favour of an immense new engine-works at the Govan
yard. Erected in accordance with drawings dated 1869 by
Angus Kennedy, the building represents a rational step
forward both in the scale of its layout and in structural
design. Occupying the considerable area of 296 ft 6 in
(90·4 m) by 294 ft (89·6 m), it is divided into four machine-
halls running N and s and interspersed by three side-aisles,
respectively 49 ft 9 in (15·16 m) and 27 ft 6 in (8·38 m) wide.
The internal frames, divided into nine bays by cast-iron
stanchions spaced at 39 ft (11·89 m) centres, are contained
within a stout curtain wall of brick, treated with restrained
classical façades and large dispatch doorways. The boxed
I-section stanchions have web-flange dimensions of 28 in
(0·71 m) by 18 in (0·46 m), narrowing to 12 in (0·31 m) at the
flange head, and incorporate the usual bearing-point for
supporting the gantry-beam—an iron plate-girder
measuring 48 in (1·22 m) by 18 in (0·46 m) in section. The
construction departs markedly from the previous examples
in the use of a two-stage framework composed of boxed
girders and bracing-struts for stiffening the stanchions. A
third stage is repeated in timber to support the hall and aisle
roofs, which intersect with a transverse roof at each end
strengthened by a series of girder-trusses. The four
machine-halls served respectively as the fitting shop,

126

127

126 B

124 C

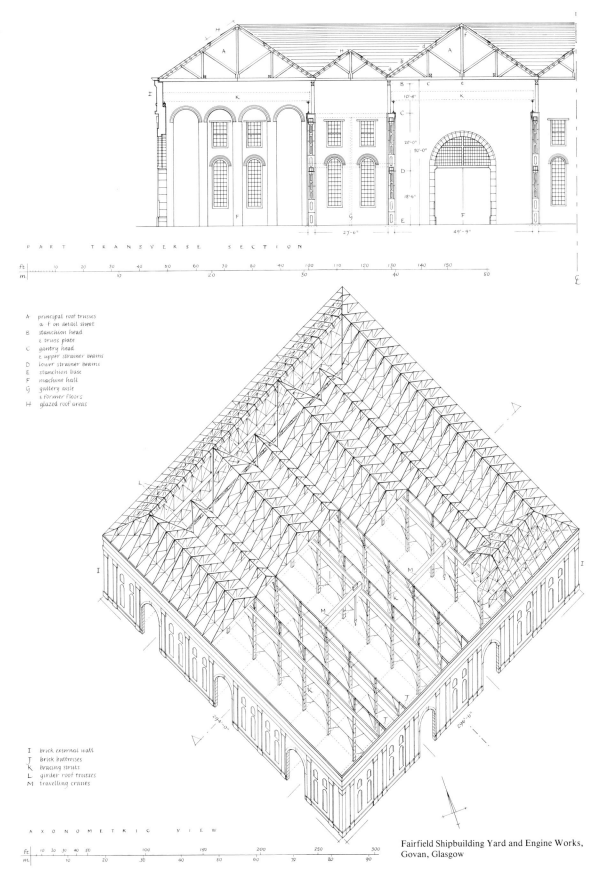

PART   TRANSVERSE   SECTION

```
ft |  10   20   30   40   50   60   70   80   90   100  110  120  130  140  150
m  |        10              20            30            40            50
```

10'-4"
20'-0"
50'-0"
18'-6"

27'-6"   49'-9"

A principal roof trusses
   a–f on detail sheet
B stanchion head
   & truss plate
C gantry head
   & upper strainer beams
D lower strainer beams
E stanchion base
F machine hall
G gallery aisle
   & former floors
H glazed roof areas

I brick external wall
J brick buttresses
K bracing struts
L girder roof trusses
M travelling cranes

A X O N O M E T R I C   V I E W

```
ft |  10 20 30 40 50        100          150          200          250          300
m  |        10        20        30        40        50        60        70        80        90
```

Fairfield Shipbuilding Yard and Engine Works,
Govan, Glasgow

125

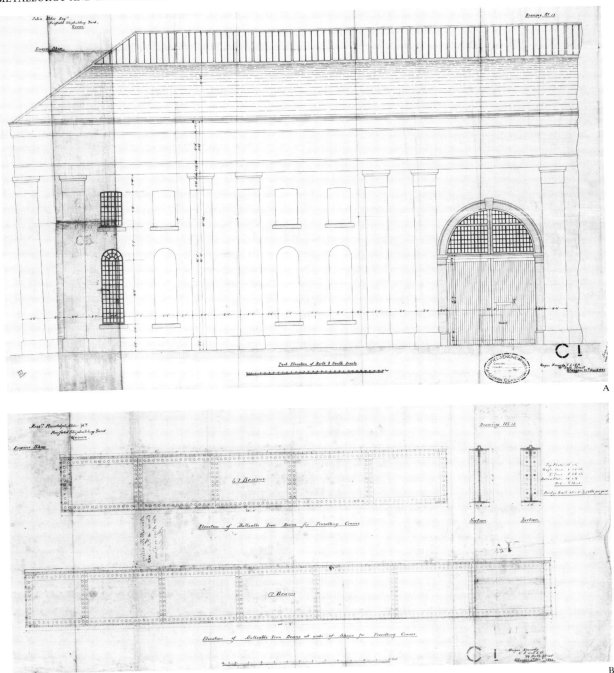

Fairfield Shipbuilding Yard and Engine Works, Govan, Glasgow;
design drawings, 1869
- A.   part elevation
- B.   gantry girder

turning shop, machine shop and boiler shop, and among the numerous uses served by the gallery floors was that of a school for apprentices.

Although the building was subsequently extended at its w end, thereby augmenting further the amount of covered space available for normal engineering duties, many of the activities connected with the shipbuilding industry were necessarily conducted out of doors or in single-storey sheds with open sides. An impression of the wide range of facilities and the vast scale on which a Clydeside shipyard operated in its prime may be obtained from the contemporary illustration of Fairfield in 1890.

128 A

126

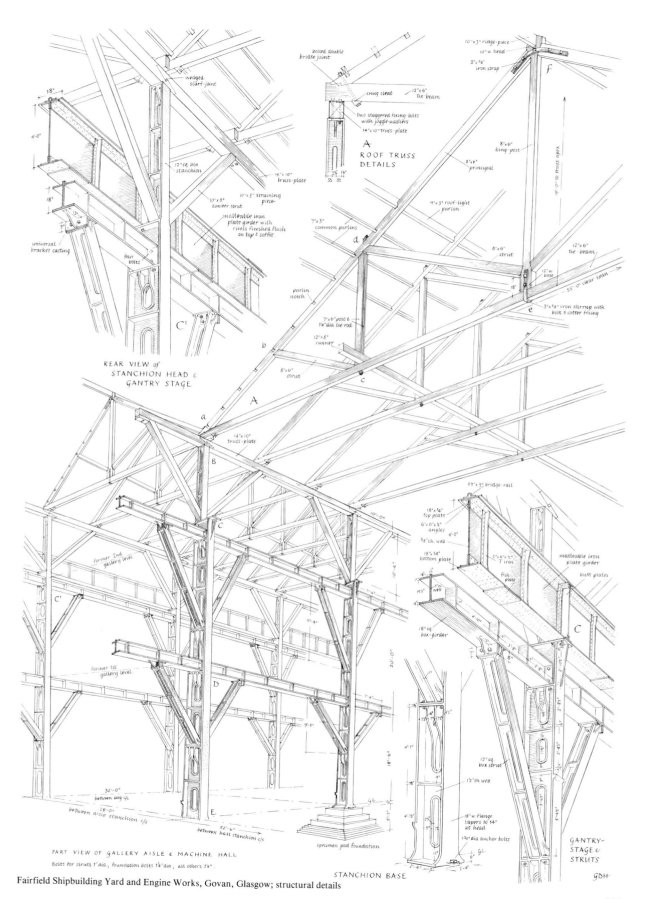

Fairfield Shipbuilding Yard and Engine Works, Govan, Glasgow; structural details

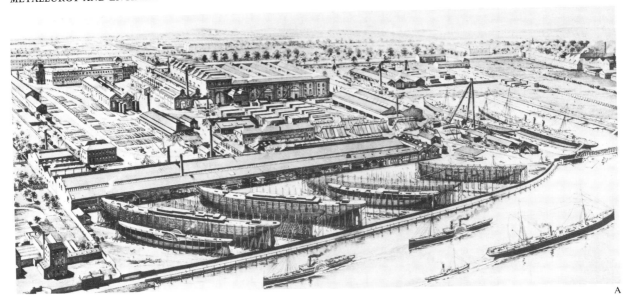

A

B

Fairfield Shipbuilding Yard and
Engine Works, Govan, Glasgow
A.   general view of works
     and shipyard, 1890
B.   key diagram to principal
     buildings and features
     A. office-block
     B. drawing-offices
     C. horse-drawn wagons
     D. electrical workshop
     E. metal stock-yard
     F. old boiler-shop
     G. old engine-works
     H. engine test-bed
     I. timber-yard
     J. old pattern-shop
     K. timber-racks
     L. joiner shops
     M. plumber shops
     N. cargo and passenger vessel
     O. stabling-yard
     P. liner
     Q. wet-basin
     R. steelworks sheds
     S. shipbuilding berths
     T. cargo vessels
     U. paddle-boat
C.   detail of roof-braces
     and girder-trusses
D.   detail of gantry girder
     and support system

C

D

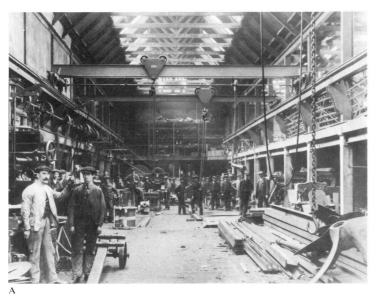

A

Foundry

Rose Street, Inverness

Highland, Inverness

NH 665456

1981

This late example is included to represent the countless
smaller foundries once active in virtually every town and
city in Scotland for serving the engineering trade, notwithstanding Glasgow's pre-eminence. Built in 1895, it was an
extension of the Northern Implement Foundry Company,
which was established in March 1872, with a labour force of
twenty, to manufacture agricultural implements. The firm
then rapidly expanded under the name of the Rose Street
Engineering Foundry Company to meet the demands of the
Highland Railway for rail- and locomotive-castings and for
bridges. Subsequently, during the two World Wars, it
became famous alike for the production of marine engines
and boom-defence equipment, and for its specialised
welding-techniques. Planned on an irregular site averaging
190 ft (58 m) by 95 ft (29 m) in area and covered with timber
roofs, it consists of a 30 ft-wide (9·14 m) central machine-
129 A hall equipped with gantry, and a gallery of similar width
enclosing it on three sides with the upper storey supported at
mid-span by a row of circular cast-iron columns. According
130 A to the design drawings, endorsed by Inverness architects
Ross and MacBeth and dated 1894, the three-arched and
130 B gabled stone frontage, as built, was modified to contain a
semicircular window in each of the gables. Internally, the
main point of structural interest is the rejection of the
129 B conventional monolithic stanchion in favour of a U-section
casting, built up in two stages—although with the modest
overall height of 21 ft (6·40 m). They are bolted together at
the head of the stouter 8 ft-high (2·44 m) lower section by
means of an intervening sleeve-casting through which runs a
rolled steel stiffening beam.

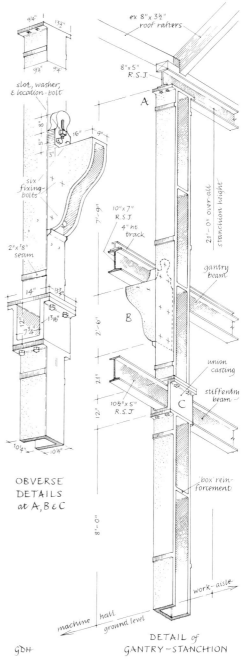

OBVERSE
DETAILS
at A, B & C

DETAIL of
GANTRY-STANCHION

B

Foundry, Rose Street, Inverness
A. central machine hall, c. 1920
B. structural details

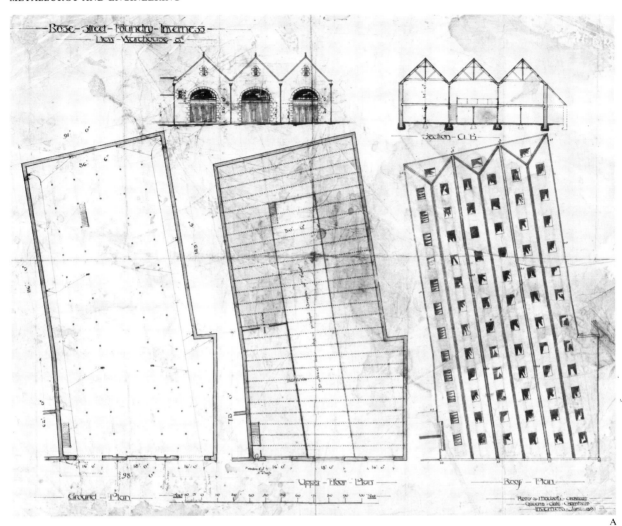

A

NOTES

n.1   E.g. *Inventory of Stirlingshire,* **1,** p. 56; **2,** pp. 444–5; *Inventory of Argyll,* **1,** No. 346.

n.2   *Inventory of Argyll,* **2,** pp. 34, 280; Butt, J, *The Industrial Archaeology of Scotland* (1967), 104–5.

n.3   Butt, J, *The Industrial Archaeology of Scotland* (1967), 110–11; Hume, *Ind Archaeol Scotland,* **1,** (1976), 160, 250.

n.4   Hitchcock, H R, *Architecture 19th and 20th Centuries* (1958), 125.

n.5   Ibid., 124, 235; Young, A M and Doak, A M (eds.), *Glasgow at a Glance* (1965), 48.

n.6   Young and Doak, op. cit., 42.

n.7   *Inventory of Argyll,* **2,** No. 358.

n.8   Ibid., No. 362; Stell, G P and Hay, G D, *Bonawe Iron Furnace* (1984).

n.9   *Inventory of Argyll,* **2,** p. 281.

n.10   *Inventory of Argyll,* **6,** forthcoming.

n.11   *Glasgow Courier,* 16 December 1809, p. 4.

n.12   *Inventory of Stirlingshire,* **2,** No. 265.

n.13   Carvel, J L, *Stephen of Linthouse* (1961), 64–6.

B

Foundry, Rose Street, Inverness
A.   design drawings, 1894
B.   E frontage, *c.* 1920

5 ENGINES AND MACHINES

Engines and machines, which are probably the most vulnerable of all industrial artefacts, constitute an essential element in the function of virtually every form of traditional industry. Some, such as the horse-engine and water-mill machinery, have already been described, while others are discussed briefly where they affect building-design and industrial processes. The following case studies, however, have been chosen as representatives of their class, or because of their rarity or significance in the field of engineering technology; at the time of survey they were among the relatively few examples to remain *in situ,* some as working units.

5,9

11,13

Beam-engine   NJ 782055
Garlogie, Aberdeenshire
    Grampian, Gordon   ● * 1980

Mills for the spinning of wool, together with a small industrial community, were well established at Garlogie by 1843 under the ownership of Alexander Hadden & Son of Aberdeen. Evidently steam-power was then being used to augment the water-powered machinery, and latterly the engine was superseded by a water-turbine. It ceased to operate in 1904, when the mills were closed and afterwards

64

Beam-engine, Garlogie, Aberdeenshire; beam and parallel motion

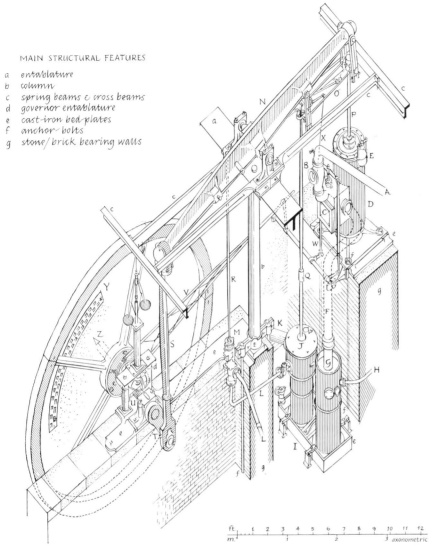

MAIN STRUCTURAL FEATURES

a entablature
b column
c spring beams & cross beams
d governor entablature
e cast-iron bed-plates
f anchor-bolts
g stone/brick bearing walls

PRINCIPAL WORKING COMPONENTS

A main steam pipe
B steam valve *
C valve chest
D cylinder
E relief valve
F steam exhaust *
G condenser
H cold water feed
I non-return valve *

J air pump
K air pump waste discharge
L return hot-feed to boiler
M boiler feed pump
N beam or great lever
O parallel motion
P piston rod
Q air pump rod
R feed pump rod

S connecting rod
T crank
U crank shaft & eccentric
V eccentric rod
W slide valve linkage
X governor/throttle valve linkage *
Y fly-wheel & barring-rack
Z to outboard bearing

* denotes missing or incomplete

Beam-engine, Garlogie,
Aberdeenshire;
axonometric drawing

partly demolished. All that now survives is the masonry-built engine-house and adjacent parts of the buildings.

The engine, although derelict, is virtually intact and enjoys the distinction of being the only Scottish example of its type to remain *in situ*. Compactly arranged within an area of 34 ft 6 in (10·52 m) by 8 ft 6 in (2·60 m), the engine is a house-built rotative beam-engine of medium size, with a double-acting cylinder, separate condenser and air pump.

The cylinder, fitted with an integral valve-chest, has a 50 in (1·27 m) stroke and an estimated 16 in–18 in (c. 430 mm) bore. Other principal features are as follows: the cast-iron beam, 16 ft 3 in (4·95 m) between the centres, with its connecting-rod and parallel motion for the piston-rod; linkages for the air pump and feed pump; and the main drive-shaft which turns a 16 ft-diameter (4·88 m) flywheel and engages with a centrifugal governor and an eccentric by

132

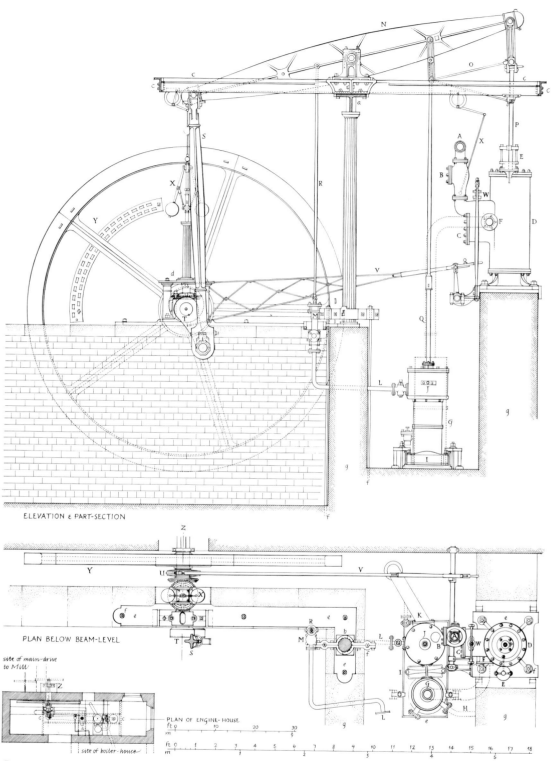

ELEVATION & PART-SECTION

PLAN BELOW BEAM-LEVEL

site of main-drive
to Mill

PLAN OF ENGINE-HOUSE

site of boiler-house

Beam-engine, Garlogie, Aberdeenshire

means of bevel gearing. The engine probably developed about 50 horsepower.

The maker is not known but, assuming that the engine dates from the late 1830s, it may possibly be ascribed to Mitchell & Neilson of Glasgow, whose known engines had similar design features.

K

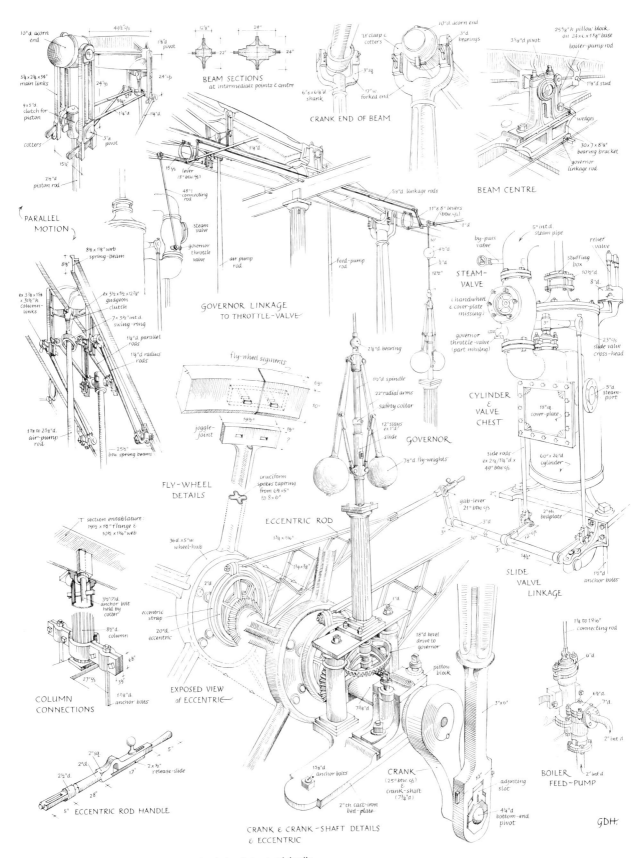

10"d acorn
end

4½"c/s

1⅛"d
pivot

5⅜ x 2⅛ x ¾"
main links

24"c/s

24"c/s

9 x 5"d
clutch for
piston

9¼"d

1¼"d.

1½"d.

3"d pivot

cotters

15½"

PARALLEL
MOTION

2½"d
piston rod

BEAM SECTIONS
at intermediate points & centre

12⅜"

22"

29"

24"

'U'clasp &
cotters

10"d acorn end

3"d bearings

3"sq

17"w.
forked end

6⅜ x 6¾"d
shank

CRANK END OF BEAM

25⅝"h pillow block
on 24 x c 15¼"base

3⅝"d pivot

boiler-pump rod

1⅛"d stud

wedges

30 x 7 x 8⅛"
bearing bracket

governor
linkage rod

BEAM CENTRE

15"r lever
(8" btw c/s)

48"d
connecting
rod

⅝"d linkage rods

11" & 8" levers
(btw c/s)

1"d

10"

4½"d

½"d

12½"

steam
valve

governor
throttle
valve

air pump
rod

feed-pump
rod

by-pass
valve

5"int d.
steam pipe

relief
valve

STEAM-
VALVE
(handwheel
& cover-plate
missing)

stuffing
box

10½"d

8"d

GOVERNOR LINKAGE
TO THROTTLE-VALVE

governor
throttle-valve
(part missing)

23"c/s
slide valve
cross-head

8⅝ x 1⅛"web
spring-beam

8⅞"

ex 3⅞ x 1⅝
x 31½"h
column-
links

ex 3½ x 1½ x 12⅞"
gudgeon
clutch

7 x 3½"int d.
swing-ring

1¼"d parallel
rods

1¼"d radius
rods

2¼"d. bearing

1½"d spindle

22"radial arms

safety collar

12"stays
ex 1"d

slide

GOVERNOR

7½"d fly-weights

CYLINDER
&
VALVE
CHEST

18"sq
cover-plate

5"d
steam-
port

60"d x 26"d
cylinder

1⅞ to 2⅜"d.
air-pump rod

25½"
btw spring beams

fly-wheel segments

6½"

10"

19½"

1½"

joggle-
joint

FLY-WHEEL
DETAILS

cruciform
spokes tapering
from 6½ x 5"
to 8 x 6"

ECCENTRIC ROD

side rods
ex 2¼/1⅜"d x
49" btw c/s

gab-lever
21" btw c/s

3"d

2"th
beadplate

SLIDE
VALVE
LINKAGE

1½"d
anchor bolts

'T' section entablature:
19½ x 1½" Flange &
10½ x 1¹/₁₆" web

36d x 5"w
wheel-hub

13¼ x 1¹/₁₆"

13¼ x ⅝"

5"

50"

3"

12¹/₁₆"

14½"

3½"/½"d
anchor bolt
held by
cotter

8½"
column

2"d

18"d bevel
drive to
governor

pillow
block

1¼ to 1⁹/₁₆"
connecting rod

6"d

6½"d.

7"d.

eccentric
strap

20"d.
eccentric

4½"

27"c/s

3½"

1⅛"d
anchor bolts

EXPOSED VIEW
of ECCENTRIC

7¾"d

3" x 6"

CRANK
(25" btw c/s
&
crank-shaft
(7¼"d)

12"

adjusting
slot

2"int d.

2"int d.

BOILER
FEED-PUMP

COLUMN
CONNECTIONS

5"

2"sq

2"d

2 x ½"
release-slide

2½"d.

17"

28"

5" ECCENTRIC ROD HANDLE

13⅛"d
anchor bolts

2"th cast-iron
bed-plate

CRANK & CRANK-SHAFT DETAILS
& ECCENTRIC

4¼"d
bottom-end
pivot

GDH.

Beam-engine, Garlogie, Aberdeenshire; mechanical and structural details

Beam-engine, Garlogie, Aberdeenshire

Water-powered Beam-engine
Wanlockhead, Dumfriesshire
    Dumfries and Galloway, Nithsdale

NS 870131

** 1970, 1983

154 B
Situated at the N end of the old lead-mining village of Wanlockhead, this engine stands above a disused mine-shaft on what was part of the Straitsteps Mine. It probably dates from about the last quarter of the 19th century and is believed to have served as an auxiliary pump for draining water from abandoned workings to the S. Technically defined as a water-bucket pumping-engine, its motive power was supplied by the weight of water fed into a box-like bucket at one end of the beam, which worked on a centre and carried the pumping-apparatus at the other; at the bottom of each stroke the water was discharged from the bucket through a sluice or flap-valve, thereby transmitting the primary load to the far end of the beam and causing it to move up and down alternately. An earlier engine, evidently conforming to the same working-principles, was recorded in operation in the parish of Canonbie, Dumfriesshire, during the 1790s, and by that time similar engines were being used extensively on coal- and metal-mines in various parts of Britain.[1] Today, *136* however, the engine at Wanlockhead is believed to be the only example of its type in Britain to remain virtually intact.

137-8
The beam, which measures 27 ft 9 in (8·46 m) in length and 25 in (0·63 m) by 11½ in (292 mm) in section, is made of two baulks of pitch-pine, strengthened by moulded wooden pad-plates at the ends and centre, and bound together by a combination of iron straps and tie-rods. Mounted on a 13 ft-high (3·96 m) dressed stone pillar, the beam is pivoted on a forged gudgeon-block set in cast-iron plummer-blocks

and split-brass bearings. The plummer-blocks are secured to their mountings by long anchor-bolts extending through the masonry to the base of the pillar; the beam itself is locked on to the gudgeon-block by means of a lower clamp-plate whose soffit is shaped and recessed to fit round the seating. At the power end the bucket-rod is attached to a crosshead-slide which moved up and down on guide-rails held in a wooden steeple-frame; the slide in its turn is connected to the beam by two link-rods and a crosshead-coupling. In general, the various iron forgings and castings are made to a high standard, and all the critical moving parts are held in brass bearings.

No trace of the bucket remains, but the stone-lined pit into which it descended, measuring 5 ft (1·52 m) in depth and 4 ft (1·22 m) by 2 ft 3 in (0·69 m) in area, preserves its drainage outlet at the bottom, and also the iron-clad wooden rails for steadying the bucket when in motion. An 8 in-diameter (203 mm) iron plate with raised rim, held loosely on the end of the bucket-rod by a large iron wedge, may have been part of the water-release valve mechanism attached to the bucket. Depending on the position of the bucket on the rod, the related lengths of the bucket-rod and steeple slide-rods (respectively 11 ft 2 in (3·40 m) and 10 ft (3·05 m) between centres) would allow an engine-stroke of approximately 7 ft (2·13 m). The other end of the beam overhangs the mine-shaft and carries the remains of a 5 in-square (127 mm) wooden pump-spear, which is connected to the beam by a shackle and crosshead-coupling.

Water for working the engine was collected in a cistern situated on the hillside above and then piped into the bucket at a level coinciding with the head of the stroke. On the evidence of a photograph taken *c.*1900, the engine was then in a state of disuse, but at that time it still retained a sheer-leg structure over the mine-shaft, used apparently in association with a nearby horse-gin for the handling of materials and pumping-apparatus.

A

B

Water-powered beam-engine,
Wanlockhead, Dumfriesshire
  A.   view from N
  B.   view from SW

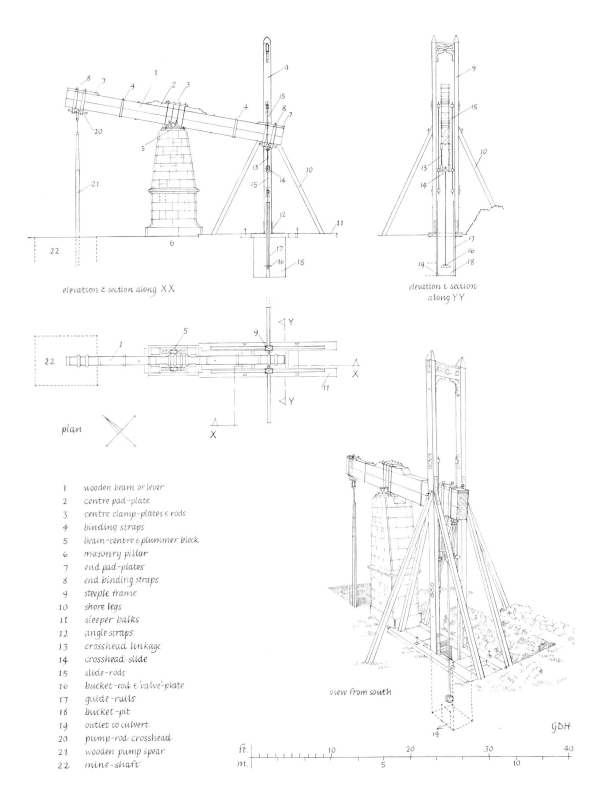

elevation & section along XX

elevation & section
along YY

plan

view from south

GDH

1	wooden beam or lever
2	centre pad-plate
3	centre clamp-plates & rods
4	binding straps
5	beam-centre & plummer block
6	masonry pillar
7	end pad-plates
8	end binding straps
9	steeple frame
10	shore legs
11	sleeper balks
12	angle straps
13	crosshead linkage
14	crosshead slide
15	slide-rods
16	bucket-rod & 'valve'-plate
17	guide-rails
18	bucket-pit
19	outlet to culvert
20	pump-rod crosshead
21	wooden pump spear
22	mine-shaft

ft. 10 20 30 40
m. 5 10

Water-powered beam-engine, Wanlockhead, Dumfriesshire

137

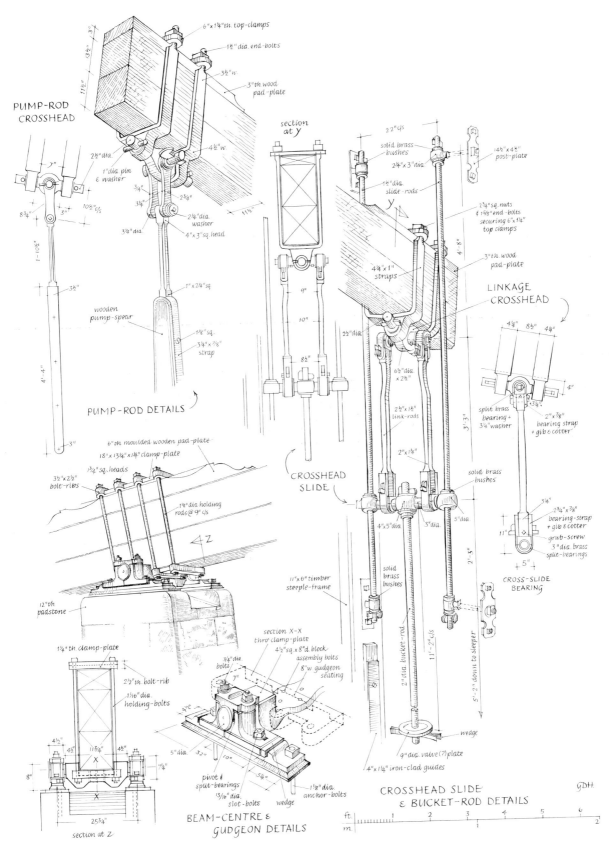

PUMP-ROD
CROSSHEAD

6"x 1¼"th. top-clamps

1½"dia. end-bolts

3½"w.

3"th. wood
pad-plate

2½"dia

7"

1"dia. pin
& washer

¾"

2¾"

2¼"dia.
washer

3¼"dia.

4"x 3"sq. head

4½"w.

11½"

8¾"

3"

10½"c/s

1-10½"

3½"

1"x 2¼"sq.

wooden
pump-spear

1⅛"sq.

3¾"x⅞"
strap

4-4"

3"

PUMP-ROD DETAILS

section
at y

9"

10"

8½"

2½"dia

2 2"c/s

solid brass
bushes

2¼"x 3"dia

1½"dia.
slide-rods

14½"x 4½"
post-plate

2¾"sq. nuts
& 1⅝" end-bolts
securing 6"x 1¼"
top clamps

4'-8"

3"th. wood
pad-plate

4¼"x 1"
straps

6½"dia.
x 2½"

2½"x 1⅞"
link-rods

2"x 1¼"

solid brass
bushes

LINKAGE
CROSSHEAD

4⅛" 8½" 4⅛"

4"

split brass
bearing +
¾"washer

2"x ⅞"
bearing strap
+ gib & cotter

3¼"

3'-3"

CROSS-SLIDE
BEARING

2¾"x ⅞"
bearing-strap
+ gib & cotter

grub-screw

3"dia. brass
split-bearings

11"

5"

6"th. moulded wooden pad-plate
18"x 13¼"x 1¼" clamp-plate

1¾"sq. heads

3½"x 2½"
bolt-ribs

1⅛"dia. holding
rods @ 9" c/s

Z

CROSSHEAD
SLIDE

5"dia

4"x 5"dia

3"dia.

solid brass
bushes

12"th
padstone

11"x 6" timber
steeple-frame

solid brass
bushes

11'-2"c/s

5'-2" down to sleeper

1¼"th. clamp-plate

2½"th. bolt-rib

1⅒"dia.
holding-bolts

11¾"

section X-X
thro' clamp-plate

4½"sq. x 8"d. block
assembly bolts

8"w gudgeon
seating

¾"dia.
bolts

2"

4½"

4½"

8"

4½"

4½"

7¼"

25¾"

section at Z

5"dia.

3¼"

10"

5½"

pivot &
split-bearings

13/16"dia.
slot-bolts

wedge

1⅛"dia.
anchor-bolts

BEAM-CENTRE &
GUDGEON DETAILS

2"dia bucket-rod

9"dia. valve(?)plate

4"x 1¼" iron-clad guides

wedge

CROSSHEAD SLIDE
& BUCKET-ROD DETAILS

GDH.

ft.   1   2   3   4   5   6
m.   1   2

Water-powered beam-engine, Wanlockhead, Dumfriesshire; mechanical details

138

Cornish Beam Pumping Engine   NT 373736
Prestongrange, East Lothian
Lothian, East Lothian   ● * 1981

154 A   Now preserved as an industrial monument, this giant
beam-engine at the former Prestongrange colliery is a
worthy tribute in Scotland to its builders, the famous
engineering firm of Harvey & Co., of Hayle, Cornwall.
140 B   Built in 1874 to pump water from a depth of 800 ft (244 m),
it is a single-acting non-rotative beam-engine of a type once
extensively used for draining mines in Britain, but notably
in Cornwall, where the majority were manufactured. In
common with other Cornish engines, its distinctive feature
is the nature of the cycle, which in essence uses high-
141 B,C   pressure steam, controlled by a system of cut-off levers and
valves, in such a way as to give a high degree of economy.

The engine forms an integral part of the engine-house,
and the massive cast-iron beam, which weighs approxi-   *141 A*
mately 30 tons (30·38 tonnes), must presumably have been
raised to its height of 27 ft (8·23 m) by means of jacks as the
work proceeded, or winched into position subsequently on
timber shores.[2*] The beam is 33 ft (10·06 m) long and 6 ft 4 in   *140 A*
(1·93 m) deep at the centre, with the fulcrum located
eccentrically at a point 18 ft (5·49 m) from the steam end,
giving the latter a stroke of 12 ft (3·66 m) and the pump-rams
one of 10 ft (3·05 m). The engine was equipped with a steam
cylinder of 70 in (1·78 m) diameter and developed a normal
working speed of three and a half strokes per minute and a
water-pumping capacity of 650 gallons (2,955 litres) per
minute. It was modified in 1895 to work larger shaft-pumps
with rods of 23 in-square (0·58 m) Oregon pine, for which
purpose an ingenious overhead strengthening truss had to
be contrived on the beam. The engine continued to be fully
operational until 1954 and is the centre-piece of a historical
site devoted to the Scottish coal industry.

Cornish Beam Pumping Engine,
Prestongrange, East Lothian;
engine-house from NE

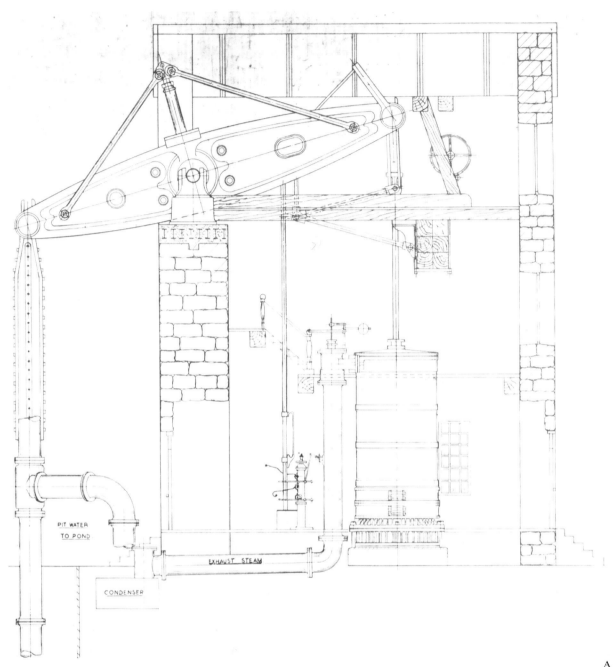

PIT WATER
TO POND

EXHAUST STEAM

CONDENSER

A

B

Cornish Beam Pumping Engine,
Prestongrange, East Lothian
   A.   sectional drawing
        (National Coal Board, 1980)
   B.   date panel over E doorway

A

B

C

Cornish Beam Pumping Engine,
Prestongrange, East Lothian
    A.   steam end of beam
    B.   steam cylinder and cut-off
          valves from above
    C.   from below

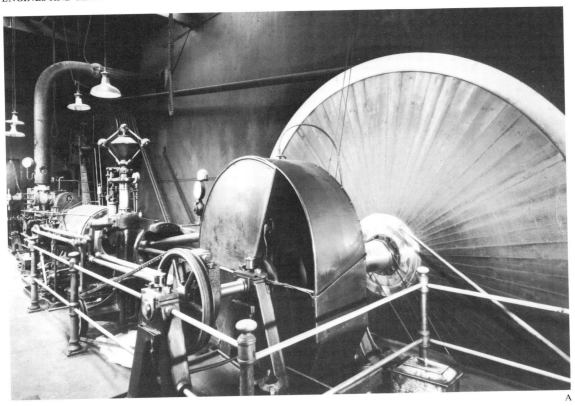

A

C

B

Horizontal Tandem Compound Engine,
South Dudhope Jute Works, Dundee
A.   general view
B.   safety cut-out valve
C.   makers' name-plate

Horizontal Tandem Compound Engine
South Dudhope Jute Works, Dundee
    Tayside, City of Dundee

NO 3930

1967

This steam-engine of advanced design initially worked 154 looms and four dressing-machines in the works of Alexander Henderson & Sons, Dundee.

A plate on the engine bore the maker's name, James
142 C Carmichael & Coy Limited, Engineers, Ward Foundry,

Dundee, and the date 1899. Of a type popular in textile mills because of its narrow layout, the engine had its high- and low-pressure cylinders arranged in line and linked by a rigid *143 A* piston-rod producing a 36 in (0·91 m) stroke. A Corliss rocking-valve, controlled by a Watt-type governor, regulated the speed of the engine very accurately, and it was equipped with a Tate patent safety cut-out. The flywheel *142 B* measured 14 ft 3 in (4·34 m) in diameter and had a six-rope drive to the machinery. The engine also powered a Lowdon *143 B,C* generator for supplying the factory with electricity and continued in operation until 1966. A year later it was dismantled for scrap.

A

C

B

Horizontal Tandem Compound Engine,
South Dudhope Jute Works, Dundee
  A.   cylinders and cut-out valve
  B.   generator
  C.   makers' name-plate

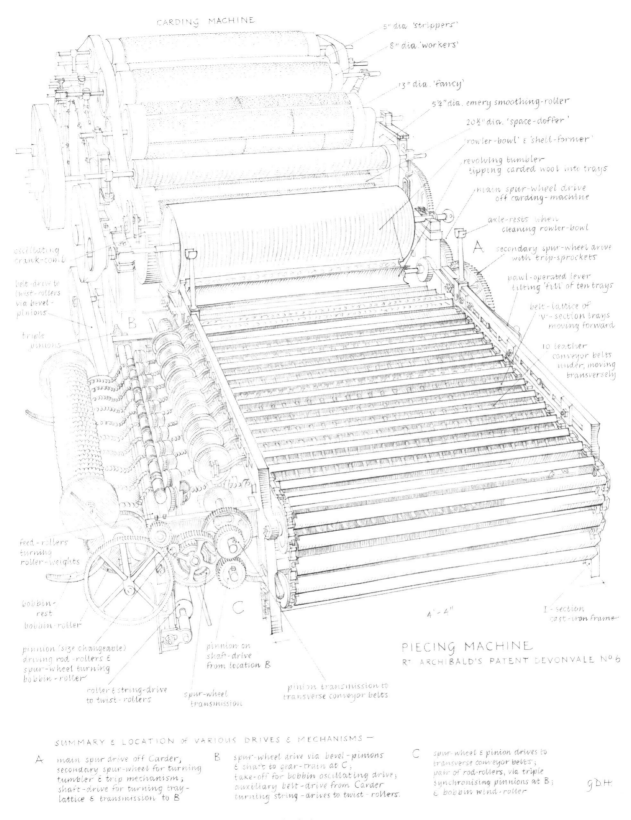

CARDING MACHINE

5" dia 'strippers'

8" dia 'workers'

13" dia 'fancy'

5½" dia. emery smoothing-roller

20½" dia. 'space-doffer'

'rowler-bowl' & 'shell-former'

revolving tumbler tipping carded wool into trays

main spur-wheel drive off carding-machine

axle-rests when cleaning rowler-bowl

A

secondary spur-wheel drive with trip-sprockets

pawl-operated lever tilting 'full' of ten trays

belt-lattice of 'v'-section trays moving forward

10 leather conveyor belts under, moving transversely

oscillating crank-comb

belt-drive to twist-rollers via bevel-pinions

triple pinions

B

feed-rollers turning roller-weights

bobbin-rest bobbin-roller

pinion ('size changeable) driving rod-rollers & spur-wheel turning bobbin-roller

roller & string-drive to twist-rollers

C

spur-wheel transmission

pinion on shaft-drive from location B

pinion transmission to transverse conveyor belts

4'-4"

I-section cast-iron frame

PIECING MACHINE
Rᵀ ARCHIBALD'S PATENT DEVONVALE Nᵒ 6

SUMMARY & LOCATION OF VARIOUS DRIVES & MECHANISMS —

A   main spur drive off Carder, secondary spur-wheel for turning tumbler & trip mechanism; shaft-drive for turning tray-lattice & transmission to B

B   spur-wheel drive via bevel-pinions & shaft to gear-train at C, take-off for bobbin oscillating drive; auxiliary belt-drive from Carder turning string-drives to twist-rollers.

C   spur-wheel & pinion drives to transverse conveyor belts; pair of rod-rollers, via triple synchronising pinions at B; & bobbin wind-roller

G.D.H.

Woollen mill, Islay, Argyll; piecing machine, carder at rear (pencil drawing)

Textile Machinery   NR 352632
Bridgend, Islay
    Strathclyde, Argyll and Bute   1979

Woollen mill, Islay, Argyll: piecing machine;
trip-mechanism

71-5 This water-powered woollen mill, which has already been described in general terms in Section 3 above, contains three specific pieces of machinery of rare and, in one instance, unique technological interest.[3] Of these, the Piecing Machine is believed to be one of only three specimens to survive in Britain, the Slubbing Billy may now be the only one left of its kind, and the two Spinning Jennies may have no more than three counterparts elsewhere in the country. Moreover, all this machinery has the added distinction of being *in situ,* and virtually still in working order.

Piecing Machine

Wool delivered by the early machines was in the form of long separate strips, and the function of the piecing machine was to join them into continuous lengths before they could be spun. In Britain its adoption in the woollen mills from about the middle of the 19th century obviated the need for this operation to be done by hand, usually by children. It was gradually superseded by the condenser, which removed the wool from the carder in a continuous form, but, as evidenced by the machine in this particular mill, its use is known to have continued in remote areas of Britain until *74 A* well into the 20th century. Technically, however, the piecing *144* machine remained an indispensable extension of the carding machine while the wool was produced in short lengths.

After being processed in the carding machine, the wool *146* was finally passed through a space doffer (a revolving drum clothed intermittently with wire sheeting) which, in conjunction with a smoothing-roller formed the wool into loose fibrous strips extending the full width of the frame; these in turn were removed by an oscillating crank-comb and then rolled to improve their strength between a rowler-bowl and former (a revolving drum with a shell-casing round its lower part). Known then as cardings, or rowans in Scotland, the separate strips of wool were cast on to the piecing machine by means of a revolving tumbler or cowper. The rowans were received in V-shaped trays which travelled slowly forward in the form of an endless lattice until ten of them each contained a rowan. An automatic trip-mechanism, *146 (A)* operated by a pawl-lever, caused the trays to be tilted simultaneously at a certain point, after which they righted themselves automatically and returned to the tumbler end.

From the trays the rowans were deposited on to a second *146 (C)* conveyor system, moving transversely to the first, in this case consisting of ten flexible leather belts equipped with thin metal fins to retain the strips of wool. At the delivery end the ten rowans were fed individually through a corresponding set of heavy press-rollers, which served to condense the rowans and to join them to the ends of the succeeding batch coming off the belts. The continuous strands, then known as rovings, were next fed through contiguous pairs of knurled twist-rollers, set at right angles to the press-rollers. Each roller was rotated in the same direction by a string-drive so that their opposing peripheral actions imparted a slight twist to the material.

Finally, after being drawn across a pair of rod-rollers on which were superimposed a series of short roller-weights to hold the material in tension, the rovings were turned on to a bobbin by means of a roller beneath. The latter turned the bobbin by friction drive, and a separate drive oscillated the bobbin sideways in order to assist the winding action. The actual piecing operation was managed by the succeeding batch of rowans being timed to fall automatically on to the ends of the first with a slight overlap, and since the ends were already tapered by the action of the carding machine, a type of scarf-joint resulted, which preserved a uniform thickness when formed in to a roving.

A patent for this make of piecing machine was granted in 1858 to 'Robert Archibald of Devon Vale, Tillicoultry, in the County of Clackmannan'.[4] The one here described is marked RT ARCHIBALD'S PATENT DEVONVALE NO. 6, and the *147 B* mark number suggests that it is one of a series incorporating subsequent improvements. It does, in fact, possess one important variation on the more normal pattern, in that its piecing action, comprising press-rollers and twist-rollers, *146 (C)* dispenses with the leather rubbers (a pair of roller aprons *147 A* which oscillated sideways to condense and piece the rowans) used in earlier models—for example, that preserved in the Science Museum, London. The precise date of the machine is open to conjecture, but its mark number and the fact that the mill was not built and fitted out with machinery until 1883 may perhaps give an approximate indication.

145

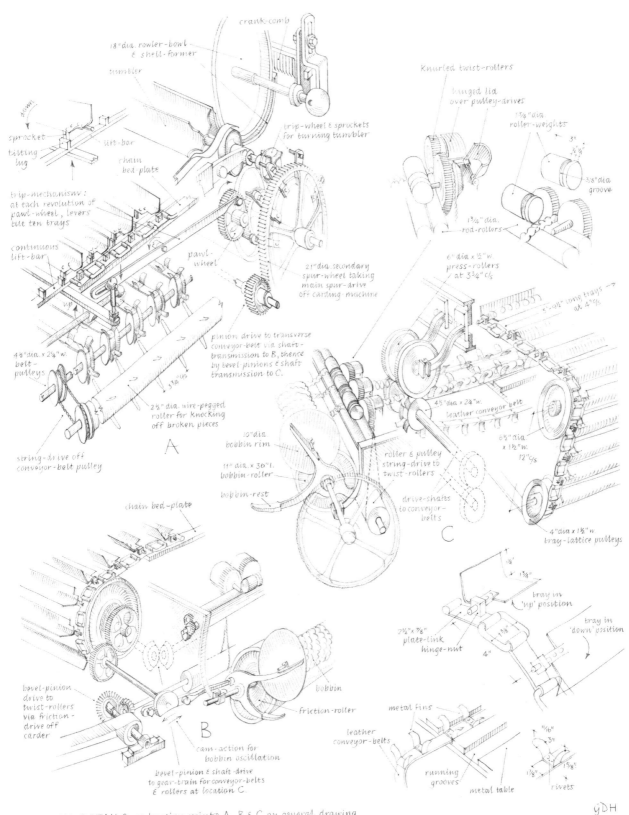

crank-comb

18"dia. rowler-bowl & shell-former

tumbler

down

sprocket tilting lug

lift-bar

chain bed-plate

trip-mechanism: at each revolution of pawl-wheel, levers tilt ten trays

continuous lift-bar

pawl-wheel

trip-wheel & sprockets for turning tumbler

21"dia. secondary spur-wheel taking main spur-drive off carding-machine

48"dia. x 24"w. belt-pulleys

5½"c/s

pinion drive to transverse conveyor-belt via shaft-transmission to B, thence by bevel-pinions & shaft transmission to C.

2½"dia. wire-pegged roller for knocking off broken pieces

string-drive off conveyor-belt pulley

A

Knurled twist-rollers

hinged lid over pulley-drives

1¾"dia. roller-weights

3"

3/8"dia. groove

1¾"dia. rod-rollers

6"dia. x ½"w. press-rollers at 3¾"c/s

5"-9½" cone-trays at 4"c/s

45"dia. x 24"w. leather conveyor belt

6½"dia. x 1½"w. 12"c/s

10"dia. bobbin rim

11"dia. x 36"l. bobbin-roller

bobbin-rest

roller & pulley string-drive to twist-rollers

drive-shafts to conveyor-belts

4"dia x 1½"w tray-lattice pulleys

C

chain bed-plate

bevel-pinion drive to twist-rollers via friction-drive off carder

B

cam-action for bobbin oscillation

bevel-pinion & shaft-drive to gear-train for conveyor-belts & rollers at location C.

bobbin

friction-roller

tray in 'up' position

tray in 'down' position

2½"x 7/8" plate-link hinge-nut

¼"

1¾"

4"

metal fins

leather conveyor-belts

running grooves

metal table

11/16"

3"

1 7/8"

1 5/8"

rivets

SKETCH DETAILS at location points A, B & C on general drawing

gDH

Woollen mill, Islay, Argyll: piecing machine; mechanical details (pencil drawing)

A

Woollen mill, Islay, Argyll;
piecing machine
    A.   piecing mechanism
    B.   maker's name-plate

B

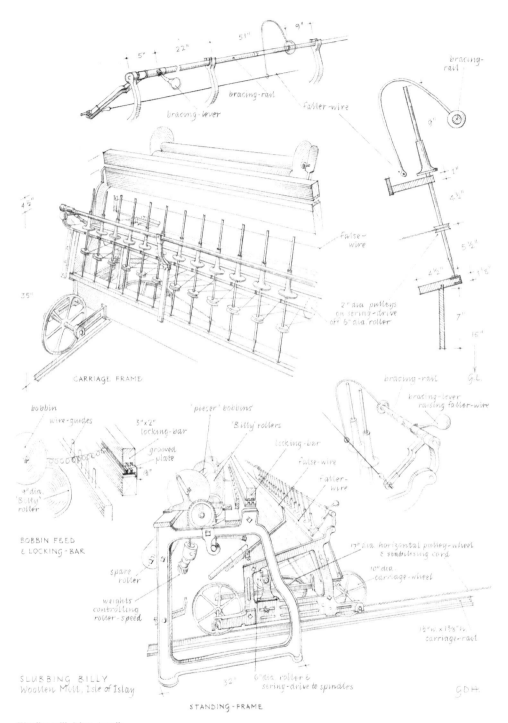

Woollen mill, Islay, Argyll:
slubbing billy; mechanical details (pencil drawing)

A

B

Woollen mill, Islay, Argyll;
slubbing billy
  A.   detail of standing frame and carriage
  B.   power-drive mechanism

Slubbing Billy

After piecing, the rovings had to be passed through a slubbing billy before they could be spun on the jenny, and during this operation the wool fibres were drawn out, or drafted, into a leaner yarn. The machine consists of a standing frame 31 ft (9·45 m) long, and a wheeled carriage-frame running on rails. The standing frame holds the billy-rollers and also a row of nine ten-strand bobbins from the piecing machine, the resultant number of strands corresponding with a row of ninety spindles on the carriage. To set up the machine, the individual strands, or slubbings, on the standing frame were passed through wire spacer-guides and a clasp, or locking-bar. The latter consists of a wooden rail running the full length of the frame, grooved on its underside to interlock with a similarly grooved bed-plate. Then on the carriage the strands were led over a false-wire, and under a faller-wire, and finally their ends were attached to spools set on spindles.

In working action the bobbins were frictionally turned at slow speed by the line of billy-rollers beneath, while the spindles on the carriage were revolved at high speed by pulleys attached by string-drives to another line of rollers— all powered from the far end. The carriage, however, was

73 A
148
149 A
149 B

L

A

B

C

Woollen mill, Islay, Argyll;
spinning jenny (102-spindle)
   A.   detail of standing frame and carriage
   B.   general view
   C.   detail of weights and roller-shaft

drawn back manually, aided by a system of stabilising ropes and pulleys at floor level to keep the two frames parallel. When in operation, the strands were slowly fed from the bobbins and through the lock, while their stretch or tension was maintained by drawing back the carriage. The purpose of the lock, which was controlled manually by a lever, was to regulate the amount of draft, and thus the thickness of the yarn being spun. So when the lock was clamped down and the carriage continued to be drawn back, the drafting and twisting process was limited to the amount of yarn extending between the lock and spool. The false-wire and faller-wires on the carriage-frame served respectively to tension the strands and to guide them on to the spools during the winding operation.

Spinning Jennies

The two spinning jennies, one of 102 spindles and the other of 118 spindles, were similar in design and operation to the slubbing billy, except that, being purely for spinning, the locking device was not necessary for the initial drafting of the yarn. The yarn was spun progressively finer by being transferred from one row of spools on the standing frame set on fixed wooden skewers, to a corresponding row on the carriage, set on fast-revolving spindles. The draft in this case was controlled by passing the yarn through a row of weighted rollers, acting on a knurled rod-roller which was intermittently driven.

150

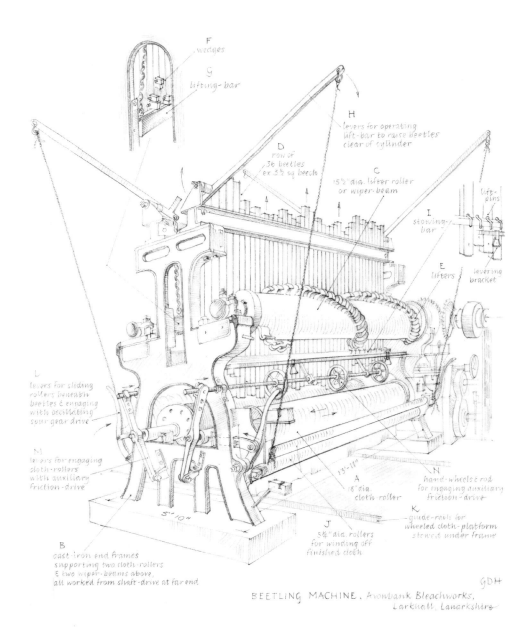

F
wedges

G
lifting-bar

H
levers for operating
lift-bar to raise beetles
clear of cylinder

D
row of
36 beetles
ex 3½ sq beech

C
15½" dia. lifter roller
or wiper-beam

I
stowing-
bar

lift-
pins

E
lifters

levering
bracket

L
levers for sliding
rollers beneath
beetles & engaging
with oscillating
sour gear drive

M
levers for engaging
cloth-rollers
with auxiliary
friction-drive

A
18" dia.
cloth roller

N
hand-wheels & rod
for engaging auxiliary
friction-drive

K
guide-rails for
wheeled cloth-platform
stowed under frame

J
5¼" dia. rollers
for winding off
finished cloth

B
cast-iron end frames
supporting two cloth-rollers
& two wiper-beams above,
all worked from shaft-drive at far end

5'·10"

13'·11"

GDH

BEETLING MACHINE, Avonbank Bleachworks,
Larkhall, Lanarkshire

Beetling Machines
Larkhall, Lanarkshire
    Strathclyde, Clydesdale

NS 753510

1980

Although comparatively late examples, these four beetling machines were among the few to survive in Scotland before being dismantled in 1981. They were part of the Avonbank Bleach & Dye Works, situated on the sw outskirts of Larkhall, and owned by D C Miller & Company. The firm imported cotton cloth off the loom from Lancashire and, after bleaching and dyeing it on the premises, specialised in the manufacture of cotton roller blinds with a unique finish widely known as 'Scotch Holland'. The latter had a distinctive patterned watermark and a hard dust-repellent sheen to its surface which was achieved by using the beetling machine. The preliminary process consisted of singeing the cloth to remove hair and fluff, washing, bleaching or dyeing it, followed by sizing and drying.

Basically, each machine consisted of twin rotating rollers (A) mounted on a cast-iron A-frame at each end (B), and above these were another pair of rollers (C) which provided the lifting action for the rams, or beetles (D), pounding the cloth. The lower, or cloth rollers operated independently so that each side of the machine processed a separate length of cloth. They rotated slowly and at the same time moved back and forth a short distance on their axis in order to ensure that the surface of the cloth was treated uniformly. The upper rollers, or wiper beams, were encircled by a broad spiral of large cogs, or lifters (E), which in the course of rotation raised the beetles consecutively by striking a wedge fixed through their shafts (*F*). Made of 3½ in-square (89 mm) beech, with rounded edges on their striking end, the row of thirty-six beetles on each side was lifted and allowed to fall individually during the working process; but when not in action the entire row could be suspended clear of the cylinder by means of a lifting bar (*G*) operated by an overhead chain and lever (*H*). Similarly, when the machine was at rest, individual beetles could be supported on a stowing bar (*I*) by means of projecting angle-hooks, or pins. The finished cloth was wound off between two free rollers (*J*) and folded into bales, mounted on a boarded platform

running on rails (*K*) beneath the frame.

The four machines were linked to a common drive traversing one end, and a system of clutch-gearing allowed them to work independently. The cloth-rollers worked off spur-gearing, engaged by a lever (*L*), which was combined with a form of helical gearing for transmitting the oscillating action. They could also be connected manually to an auxiliary friction-drive by means of a screw-rod and lever (*M* and *N*). In addition, the speed of the wiper-beams, and hence the action of the beetles, could be accelerated by engaging them with a rapid-drive mechanism.

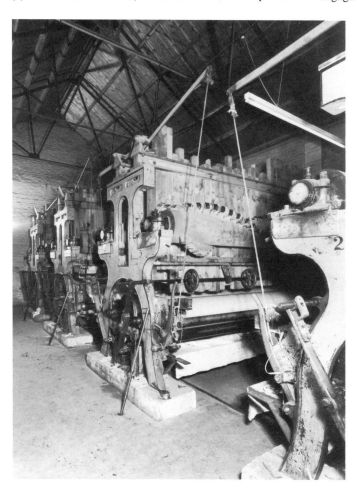

Beetling machines,
Larkhall, Lanarkshire

NOTES

n.1 *Stat. Acct.,* **14** (1790), 415. See also Downs-Rose, G and Harvey, W S, in *Industrial Archaeology, 10*, (1973), 137–47; **15** (1980), 16–19, and refs to Wanlockhead cited in Section 6 below.
n.2 The latter method was employed at the Ryhope Pumping Station, Co. Durham. See Hudson, K, *World Industrial Archaeology* (1979), illustration 195.
n.3 *Inventory of Argyll,* **5,** No. 440. This account is based on technical information kindly supplied by Mr W B Christie, Mr J B Hill, Dr K R Gilbert and Dr J A Iredale. See also Iredale, J A, in *Industrial Archaeology,* **4,** (1967), 51–6.
n.4 Letters Patent, AD 1858–, No. 73, filed in the Great Seal Patent Office on 16 July 1858.

6 EXTRACTIVE, CHEMICAL AND
RELATED INDUSTRIES

Coal has long been the major fuel of industrial Scotland, and groups of coalfields in the Midland Valley of central Scotland have at different times supplied the needs of an enormously wide range of industries. Notwithstanding the crucial historical importance of the Scottish coal industry, however, many aspects of its archaeology and upstanding physical remains are still comparatively unrecorded. For its part, this Commission can claim to have done little more than touch upon the subject: old coal-workings were noted in the course of surveys in Stirlingshire and Peeblesshire,[1] whilst, more recently, photographic records have been made of the Lady Victoria Colliery, Newtongrange,

A

B

A. Coal-bing, Gilmerton, Edinburgh
B. Lady Victoria Colliery, Newtongrange, Midlothian

153

Midlothian (1890–4; NT 333637) and of the relatively modern Cardowan Colliery (1924–83; NS 566683), the last operational deep mine in Lanarkshire. However, particular attention has been paid to the monumental show-piece of *139-41* the industry, the great pumping-engine and engine-house at *154* A the former Prestongrange Colliery in East Lothian.[2]*

The manufacture of marine salt was closely related to *163-4* coal-mining activities, most notably on the Ayrshire coast and around the shores of the Forth Estuary.[3]* After the

middle of the 18th century the lime-burning industry, like coke-smelted iron, also began to consume coal at a lavish *164-6* rate. The main centres of the industry were in the Lothians and Fife, where workable coal and limestone deposits coincided, and where there was a heavy demand for lime for improved agricultural, building and industrial purposes.[4] But throughout the country there were localised outcrops of limestone worked on a commercial basis in the later 18th and 19th centuries, and in the west Highlands, for example,

A. Prestongrange Colliery, East Lothian, *c.* 1910

B. Lead-mines, Wanlockhead, Dumfriesshire; view by ?Clerk of Eldin, *c.* 1775

154

the Commission has recorded the remains of fairly extensive workings on the island of Lismore, at one time an important centre of lime production for the surrounding seaboard region.[5]

Coal and blackband ironstone, made usable after 1828 by Neilson's 'hot-blast' smelting-process, were the great twin mineral bases of 19th-century Scottish industry. But, perhaps as a by-product of early searches for gold and silver, lead was one of the most anciently known of Scotland's mineral resources, even though most surviving remains of the lead-mining industry date from the 18th and 19th centuries. The evidence for the extensive lead-workings around Strontian, and to a lesser extent in Gleann Dubh, Morvern, and on the island of Islay, has been fully described in the course of the Commission's Argyll survey.[6] The most substantial remains of lead-mining and lead-smelting activities in Scotland are, however, to be found in and around the villages of Wanlockhead and Leadhills, tucked away in the Lowther Hills on the Dumfriesshire-

154 B

Lanarkshire border, and the water-bucket pumping-engine at Wanlockhead, described in the previous section, is undoubtedly the most interesting mechanical relic associated with the industry in Scotland.[7]

136-8

An abundance of stone has always been one of Scotland's great natural assets, and in some parts of the country the quarrying of building-stone assumed vast industrial proportions in the 18th and 19th centuries. Although the Commission has recorded none of the major sandstone, granite and flagstone quarries out of which modern Scotland has been built, numerous old quarry-workings have been described in the course of the county surveys, and particular importance attaches to those sites in, for example, Roxburghshire and Argyll, from which medieval building-stone is likely to have been derived.[8] Parts of the Argyll seaboard and its offshore islands constitute the historic centre of the Scottish slate industry, and the extensive remains of the principal slate-quarries at Ball- achulish and Easdale have been described in detail, while

155
156 A

Slate-quarries,
Ballachulish, Argyll;
East Laroch quarry
from SE

155

A

the later workings that dominate the remarkable little slate island of Belnahua (NM 7112) have also been examined and noted.[9] Evidence of small-scale marble workings has been encountered in Argyll, and the main quarry on Iona (NM 268217) still retains a gas engine and cutting-frame.[10] *156 B,C*

Argyll and Stirlingshire are also among the areas where the specialised activity of millstone-quarrying is known to have *156 D* been pursued, often attested in the shape of incomplete stones wrought from outcrops of rock considered suitable for the purpose.[11]

Clayworks and the fireclay industry, though not long established, were, as a review of the industry by the SIAS has shown, more widespread and important in the 19th century than is generally thought. The demand for field

B

C

A. Slate-quarries and
   workers' dwellings,
   Easdale, Argyll
B, C. Marble-quarry,
   Iona, Argyll; view from
   N and cutting-frame

D. Millstone-quarry,
   Barrnacarry, Argyll

D

drainage-tiles, a by-product of agricultural improvement, gave further impetus to the smaller establishments in outlying rural areas, of which the brick- and tile-works at *167-70* Blackpots was an outstanding vernacular specimen. *171-4* Although Scottish potteries made limited use of local clays, especially as a means of production, close proximity to the coalfields and transport-routes of central Scotland was the main requirement of this industry; the crucial factor was that some fifteen tons of coal were usually required to make *172* one ton of pottery in a bottle-kiln.[12]

Because of the need to fuse silica and soda at high temperatures, glass-making was one of a whole range of chemical manufactures that looked to coal as a staple fuel. With its local coalfield, its strong and active promotion by the Erskines of Mar, and its ready access to urban markets, the glass-work at Alloa, Clackmannanshire, was from its *174-5* foundation in 1750 well placed to become the major centre of the bottle-making industry in eastern Scotland.[13]

Probably the most widespread of the coal-based chemical service industries was the production of gas from the redistillation of coal tar. Until recently Scotland possessed a remarkably good series of small town gasworks, including *176-80* those recorded at Inveraray, Argyll, and at Biggar, *157* Lanarkshire (NT 038376), which in its preserved state will continue to serve as a physical reminder of the early stages and development of the industry.[14]* The provision of stone or brick gasometer-houses with wooden and slated roofs and adequate ventilation was a mistaken safety requirement

A

Gasworks, Biggar, Lanarkshire
   A.   view from E
   B.   hand-fired retorts

B

A

B

Edinburgh and Leith Gasworks
A. two-unit gasometer-house and counterweight turrets (see p. 182, n. 39)
B. s end of five-unit gasometer-house

of the early gas industry, prior to the advent of open all-metal holders with telescopic sections. Stone gasometer-houses of this type, among the last remaining examples in *158-9* Britain, have been recorded in detail at Musselburgh and Leith (NT 274765).

By a process patented by James Young in 1850 oil was produced from the distillation of a rich type of bituminous or 'cannel' coal at Bathgate, in West Lothian. Supplies of this mineral were soon exhausted, but the discovery of oil-shale at Broxburn in 1858 ensured that the Scottish oil industry remained centred in the region of West Lothian, where such typical oil-works communities as Oakbank *160* (NT 079664) were established, and where the massive shale *161* bings are its greatest monument.

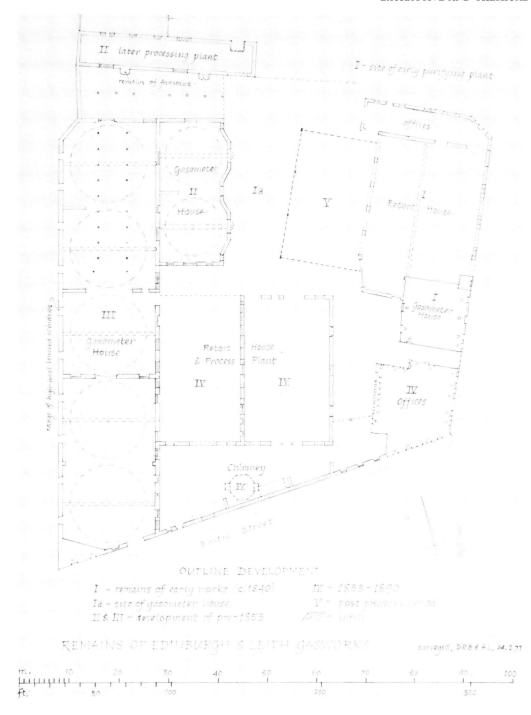

II later processing plant

I - site of early purifying plant

remains of foresians

offices

Gasometer

Ia

II
House

Y

Retort House

I
Gasometer
House

III

Gasometer
House

Retort
& Process

House
Plant

IV
Offices

IV

IV

Chimney

IV

Baltic Street

OUTLINE DEVELOPMENT

I - remains of early works (c.1840)   IV - 1853-1890
Ia - site of gasometer house   Y - post gasworks period
II & III - development of pre-1853   //// - infill

REMAINS OF EDINBURGH & LEITH GASWORKS   surveyed, DRB & AL, 24.2.77

m.   10   20   30   40   50   60   70   80   90   100
ft.   50   100   200   300

Shale-oil works, Oakbank, West Lothian; A. general view, c. 1930   B. village and bing, c. 1930

Paper-making was—and is—among the chemical industries that were largely independent of indigenous minerals. Its main requirements were 'a plentiful supply of fresh running water, a good market for the paper and a ready supply of raw material',[15] the sources of cellulose being successively rags, esparto grass and wood-pulp. The Edinburgh area remained pre-eminent in Scotland, but paper-making establishments were to a lesser extent attracted to the hinterlands of flourishing cities such as Aberdeen, and, like the mills at Inverurie, were in a good position to take early advantage of the timber resources of Scotland and Scandinavia when technological advances in the 1880s made possible the use of wood-pulp.

The manufacture of gunpowder, a chemical mixture of saltpetre, sulphur and carbon, required an abundant supply of charcoal (the bulkiest and sole native ingredient) reliable water-power for the mills and relatively easy access, preferably by water-borne transport. It was linked to the demands of quarrying, mining and munitions, and the locational requirements drew the industry to those districts which had earlier attracted the charcoal ironmasters. Indeed, part of the ironworks at Craleckan was subsequently converted to this purpose in the 19th century to serve a large granite-quarry nearby, while the gunpowder-works at Melfort[16] had been established by the proprietors of Bonawe Iron Furnace. A riparian layout similar to that at Melfort can also be seen at Clachaig in Glen Lean (NS 122814). This, the former Clyde Powder Mills is the largest and most complete of a group of ruinous gunpowder-works in Cowal, which are shortly to be surveyed.

A

B

C

Shale-bings, West Lothian
  A, B. West Calder
  C.   Broxburn

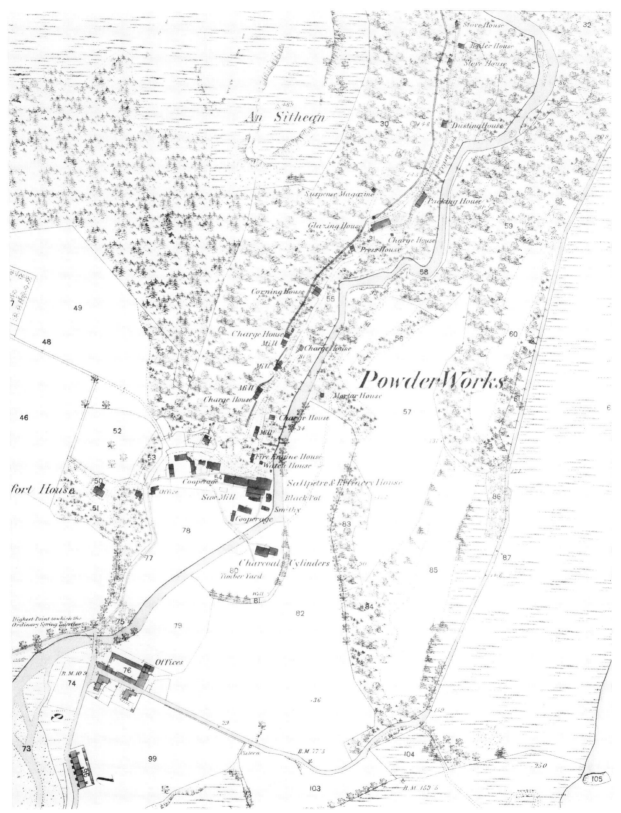

Gunpowder works, Melfort, Argyll; OS 1:2,500 map (1871), sheet CXXII, 13

A

Because of the risks of explosion in the manufacturing process, remoteness from centres of population was desirable in this phase of gunpowder manufacture. The most geographically remote chemical industry in Scotland, however, was the manufacture of kelp, the calcined ashes of seaweed used as a source of alkali. Orkney and the Western Isles were the main areas of production, which reached a peak of prosperity during the period of the Napoleonic Wars but which declined rapidly thereafter.[17] During the course of its survey of Argyll, the Commission found much evidence of kelp-making activity around the shores of the island of Tiree, the most conspicuous surviving remains *163* A,B being simple drystone kilns of an open-ended rectilinear type.[18]

B

A. Kelp-burning, Kenavara, Tiree, Argyll
   (Erskine Beveridge, 1903)
B. Kelp-burning kiln, Tiree, Argyll

Salt-work   NR 971511
Cock of Arran, Island of Arran
        Strathclyde, Cunninghame   * 1979

Coal was discovered and mined at this remote site on the NE coast of Arran in the early 18th century, and salt was manufactured here intermittently between 1710 and 1735.[19] Some of the workmen were imported from Bo'ness on the River Forth, where the Hamilton family, owners of Arran, possessed major coal and salt undertakings. Coal was again temporarily worked at the Cock of Arran in the 1770s, and although the possibility of reopening the salt-pan was considered, there is no evidence of any manufacture of salt at that period. The site has thus lain comparatively undeveloped, and the roofless and ruinous buildings here probably constitute the earliest and most complete surviving remains of a Scottish salt-work. It is probably a typical small-scale version of the numerous contemporary establishments around the River Forth, the principal centre of the marine salt industry in Scotland.

The semicircular-ended building (*A*) is the pan-house or *164* boiling-house which occupies a shore-side position for a *163* B

C. Salt-work, Cock of Arran; pan-house and fore-house

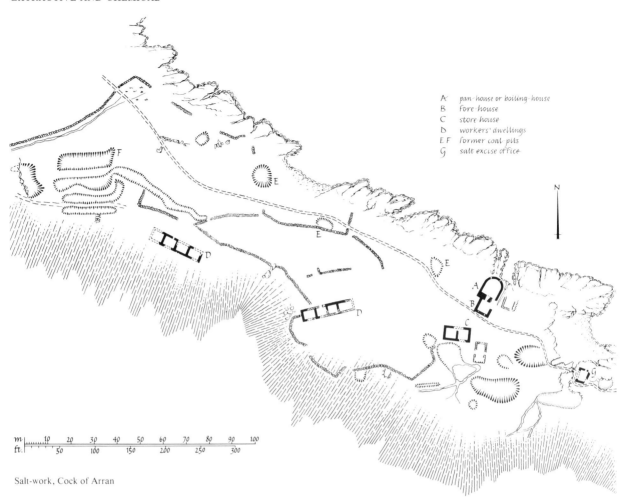

A   pan-house or boiling-house
B   fore-house
C   store house
D   workers' dwellings
E F former coal-pits
G   salt excise office

N

m | 10 20 30 40 50 60 70 80 90 100
ft. | 50   100   150   200   250   300

Salt-work, Cock of Arran

convenient regular supply of sea-water. The interior of the building measures 26 ft 3 in (8·00 m) by 23 ft (7·01 m) and retains the vaulted furnace-area and stone piers on which the pan was mounted. According to contemporary accounts, a Scottish pan was usually made of iron plates and measured 18 ft (5·49 m) in length by 9 ft (2·74 m) in width and 1 ft 6 in (0·46 m) in depth.[20] The furnace was stoked and emptied in the adjacent fore-house (B) which, on an upper floor, may also have had a bothy for the salters. The nearby bicameral building (C) is a storehouse or girnal known to have been built in 1712, and the two ranges marked (D) appear to be the remains of workers', probably colliers', dwellings. Sunken areas (E) and (F) represent the flooded mouths of some of the coal-pits, and it has been plausibly suggested[21] that building (G) may have accommodated salt Excise officers.

Limeworks

Murrayshall and Craigend, Cambusbarron, Stirlingshire
    Central, Stirling   * 1982, 1984

Abundant limestone deposits in the area to the sw of Stirling have been extensively wrought by opencast and

mining operations at Murrayshall and Craigend, and, according to an account written in 1841, 'the stones, brought out in carts, are prepared and burned in kilns close at hand'.[22] In 1860 Murrayshall Limeworks was described as having 'three kilns in good working order' whilst Craigend had 'three kilns in good working order and one in ruins', the coal in each case coming from Bannockburn. Both limeworks were disused by 1896–9, when the name Murrayshall Limeworks was being applied to a post-1860 establishment further N.[23]

All the surviving stone-built kilns occupy the customary bankside positions for ease of loading at the kiln head. Murrayshall I (NS 773908) has a continuous NW frontage about 18 ft (5·5 m) high built of coursed rubble masonry and partly buttressed. It has a bank of three circular charging-holes, or pots, and at the base of each there are three segmental draw-arches, or vents, one in front and one in each side, reached by taller segmental-arched access-tunnels. Each draw-arch was equipped with two draw-holes, or eyes, for running off the quicklime. The heavily overgrown bank of four kilns at Craigend (NS 761905) is of similar construction, scale and layout with front draw-arches and much higher tunnel-mouths occupying alternate positions in the main NE frontage. The impressive 182 ft-long (55·47 m) N frontage of the kilns at Murrayshall II

165 A

165 B

166

A. Murrayshall Limeworks,
Cambusbarron,
Stirlingshire;
front of kiln-block

B. Craigend Limeworks, Cambusbarron, Stirlingshire;
access tunnels and draw-arch

(NS 770930) has front openings of uniform height refined with rusticated red sandstone voussoirs. The range was evidently erected in two phases, the earlier w half being built in coursed rubble with arches of red sandstone, and the other in squared random rubble with grey sandstone dressings. It incorporates six kilns of two different types: the four w kilns are of the three-draw variety with circular charging-holes of inverted cone shape; the two E kilns are of a larger four-draw type, each with a pair of front draw-arches and a round-ended rectangular charging-hole. All draw-arches have single draw-hole points. The wall-head is reinforced by a prominent row of oval iron wall-ties, and the kiln-pots are lined with header-course brickwork. The works evidently enjoyed the commercial advantage of being connected with the neighbouring Forth & Clyde Junction Railway to the N by means of a tramway which it shared with Hayford Mills, situated a short distance to the E.

166 C

165

M

NORTH ELEVATION OF KILN-BLOCK

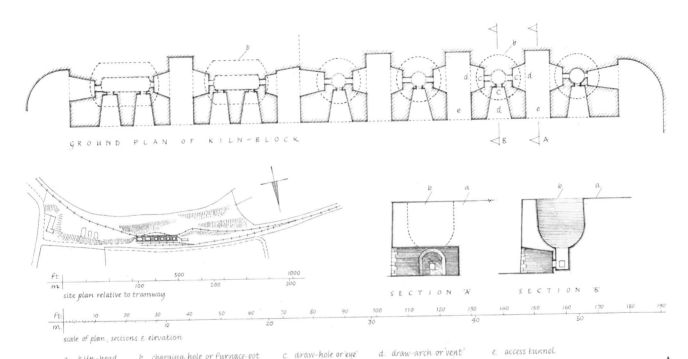

GROUND PLAN OF KILN-BLOCK

ft.
m.
site plan relative to tramway

| | 500 | 1000 |
| 100 | 200 | 300 |

SECTION 'A'   SECTION 'B'

ft.
m.
scale of plan, sections & elevation

a. kiln-head   b. charging-hole or furnace-pot   c. draw-hole or 'eye'   d. draw-arch or 'vent'   e. access tunnel

A

B

C

Murrayshall II Limeworks,
Cambusbarron, Stirlingshire
   A.   survey drawings
   B.   front of kiln-block
   C.   charging-hole

166

A

B

Blackpots Brick and Tile Works
Whitehills, Banffshire
    Grampian, Banff and Buchan

NJ 660657

1971

This small clayworks, which was demolished by 1978, stood on the coast at Knock Head, about 3 km w of Banff. It was established on the farm of Blackpots by one Dr Saunders a few years before 1788, at which date it was extended by his son.[24] The works assumed its final layout in about 1840 when the manufacture of drainage tiles commenced.[25] The production of pantiles and bricks ceased in the early 20th century and in 1946 respectively.[26] At the date of survey in 1971 the works produced only field drainage-tiles and employed eleven men in the summer season, the same number as in 1840.

Blue gault clay was dug manually at a quarry on the E side of the headland, and was transported to the works in hand-operated bogies on a narrow-gauge railway. There it was gravity-fed into the machine-shed and passed through

167 B

167 D

C

D

Blackpots Brick and Tile Works,
Whitehills, Banffshire
  A.   works and harbour
  B.   bogie and quarry
  C.   wire cutting-machine
  D.   machine-shed

Blackpots Brick and Tile Works,
Whitehills, Banffshire
    A, C, D. survey drawings of machine-shed
        and drying-shed
    B.   wall-louvres
    E.   drying-racks
    F.   three-tier barrow
    G.   kiln barrow

two sets of diesel-powered (originally steam-powered) pug-mills and a plunger which removed the stones; a twin-piston extruder forced the mixed clay through two pipe-dies, and the moulded sections were cut by hand-operated wire cutting-machines. The green clay pipes were then carried in three-tier barrows to the racks of the adjacent drying-shed, a fine pantile-roofed and louvred structure measuring 234 ft (71·32 m) in length by 28 ft 6 in (8·68 m) in width overall. It was laid out on a three-aisled plan with four parallel rows of simple box-framed drying-racks. Each rack was about 6 ft 6 in (1·98 m) high and 8 ft 3 in (2·52 m) long, a dimension which was determined by the load-bearing capacity of the wooden shelves and which in turn governed the bay module of the whole building.[27*] There were two tiers of louvres, or passes, in each bay; they were made up of ledged boards and were hopper hung, being pivoted on strap-hinges and secured in the open position by rough props. Over the years the simple post-and-lintel construction of the building had settled

168 F
168 A.B

168 E

unevenly, giving the roof an irregular but pleasing undulating profile. A timber wall-plate composed of scarf-jointed sections was carried on masonry piers placed at the angles and midway along the side-walls; intermediate support was provided by timber posts demarcating each bay. Set on stone bases, the posts were notched to receive raking struts and spiked to the soffit of the wall-plate.

The air-dried tiles were then transferred to the kiln which had a capacity for some forty tons of ware and was fired about sixteen times each season. Although largely rebuilt as recently as 1953, the kiln was a modified version of the traditional 'Scotch' up-draught type; it was equipped with low-level furnace-holes staggered opposite one another in alternate bays along the side-walls, which were flanked by 9 ft-wide (2·74 m) stoking-aisles.[28*] The kiln yard was adjoined on the SE by a house and the manager's office. To the NW, and still surviving, there is a small harbour with a rubble-built pier, which was used for importing coal and exporting some of the clay-ware products.

169
170

169 C

167 A

A

B

C

Blackpots Brick and Tile Works,
Whitehills, Banffshire; kiln
A. exterior
B. interior
C. stoking-aisle

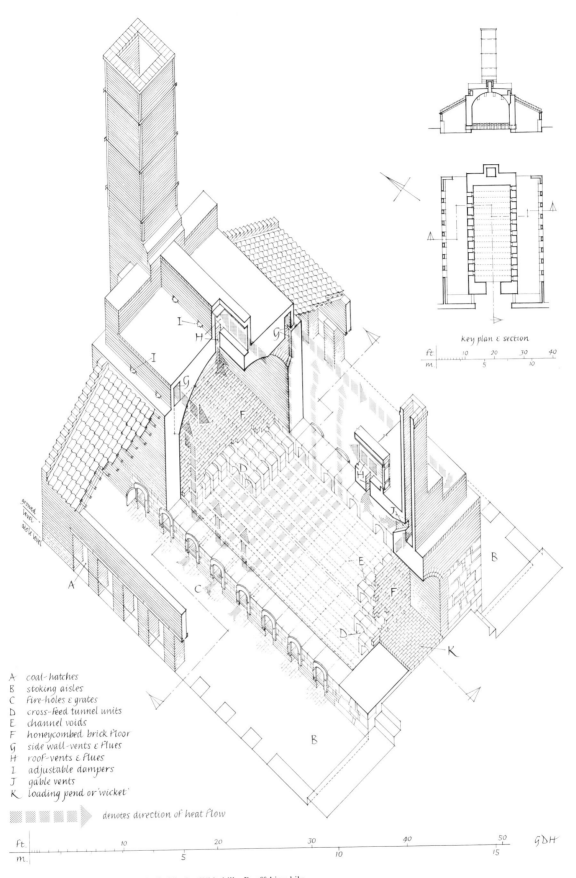

key plan & section

ft. 10 20 30 40
m. 5 10

A coal-hatches
B stoking aisles
C fire-holes & grates
D cross-feed tunnel units
E channel voids
F honeycombed brick floor
G side wall-vents & flues
H roof-vents & flues
I adjustable dampers
J gable vents
K loading pend or 'wicket'

▓▓▓▓ ▒▒▒▒ ░░░░ ▷ denotes direction of heat flow

ft. 10 20 30 40 50
m. 5 10 15

GDH

Blackpots Brick and Tile Works, Whitehills, Banffshire; kiln

Pottery, Portobello, Edinburgh
A.   general view from sw
B.   pan-mill

Pottery   NT 304742
Portobello, Edinburgh
Lothian, City of Edinburgh   ][1972

Portobello was one of the principal centres of the ceramic industry on the s bank of the River Forth, and at their closure in 1972 these premises of the Thistle Pottery of A W Buchan & Company Ltd, formerly known as the Portobello or Waverley Pottery, probably constituted the last complete industrial pottery in Scotland. First established in about 1770, the pottery came into the ownership of the Buchan family in 1867.[29]* It was substantially rebuilt and extended after 1879, partly covering the area of an infilled 18th-century harbour which was originally built to serve Rathbone's Midlothian Pottery nearby.[30] At the date of survey it manufactured a decorated and buff-glazed stoneware using ball-clay and china-clay imported from Devon and Cornwall.

Much of the plant and machinery was of comparatively recent date but included a steam-powered pan-mill for *171* B crushing faulty or impure ware. It had a cast-iron pan 7 ft (2·13 m) in diameter which was driven by an upright shaft and overhead gearing; it was rotated beneath a pair of solid iron-rimmed sandstone wheels 3 ft 6 in (1·07 m) in diameter and 1 ft (0·31 m) wide. The earliest identifiable feature of structural interest was a timber king-post roof-structure of about 1800; this was incorporated in a two-storeyed brick building which had a two-bay arcaded and gabled frontage to Harbour Road.

Three coal-fired bottle-kilns of traditional design were installed in 1903, 1906 and 1909, and, although replaced by an electric furnace in 1956, the two latest kilns still survived at the closure of the works. At that time only the 1909 kiln *173* A was accessible for detailed inspection and measurement. *172*

171

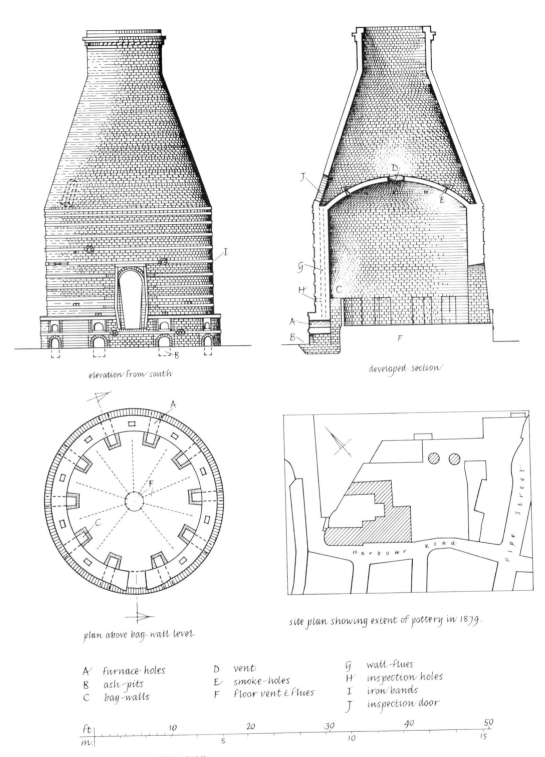

elevation from south

developed section

plan above bag-wall level

site plan showing extent of pottery in 1879.

A	furnace-holes	D	vent	G	wall-flues
B	ash-pits	E	smoke-holes	H	inspection holes
C	bag-walls	F	floor vent & flues	I	iron bands
				J	inspection door

ft | 10 | 20 | 30 | 40 | 50
m. | 5 | 10 | 15

Pottery, Portobello, Edinburgh; 1909 bottle-kiln

A. Pottery, Portobello, Edinburgh;
   1909 kiln, preserved

B. Pottery, Dunmore, Stirlingshire; kiln

Constructed of a yellowish-coloured brick laid in an English garden-wall bond, the circular kiln stands to a height of 39 ft (11·89 m). It has an angular bottle profile, slightly narrower in the neck than its neighbour, and the drip-course at the top is ornamented with a dentil-band. At the base the kiln measures 23 ft 3 in (7·09 m) in diameter over walls 3 ft (0·91 m) thick. Ten arched furnace-holes with associated ash-pits are formed in the perimeter of the kiln and correspond with dwarf 'bag-walls' inside. In the initial firing-process a circular vent in the saucer-domed roof of the kiln-chamber was left open, thus creating an up-draught; the damper was then closed and a down-draught was induced through a circular aperture in the centre of the kiln floor, passing beneath a tunnelled floor, upwards through mural flues and emerging around the outer rim of the dome. Each firing consumed about 13–14 tons (c.13·72 tonnes) of coal, and, including a cooling period, lasted for about two and a half days. The kiln had a capacity for about 130 piles of saggars.

Pottery NS 872883
Dunmore, Stirlingshire
   Central, Falkirk # 1976

This small pottery manufactured tiles and domestic ware from the local red clay of Dunmore Moss and from the superior clays of Devon and Cornwall. It originated in the early 19th century, but most of the surviving remains appear to date from the period after about 1860, when the pottery was acquired by Peter Gardiner of Alloa.[31] The remains include the ruins of a brick-built bottle-kiln about 16 ft 9 in (5·11 m) in diameter, which was badly damaged in a gale in January 1974 and subsequently demolished.[32] There is a range of single-storeyed and pantile-roofed workers' cottages in a nearby field, and the manager's house stands a short distance to the SE of the kiln. A room in the E wing of this house has a decorative tiled interior, the tiles at one time covering the ceiling and much of the walls, as well as the fireplace and doorway. The tiles are of a highly colourful faience type, typical of Dunmore ware, and one of the ceiling plaques is dated 1887. There was a decoratively tiled *174 A* lavatory in an outbuilding SE of the house, and it is believed *174 B* that both these schemes were carried out in honour of a visit to the pottery by the Prince of Wales, later Edward VII.[33*]

173

A

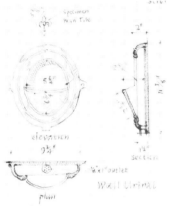

B

D

Pottery, Dunmore, Stirlingshire; manager's house
- A.   ceiling plaques
- B.   wall-urinal (pencil drawing)

Glass-cones, Alloa Glass-work, Clackmannanshire
- C.   south cone
- D.   cone and furnace, Diderot, 1772

Glass-cones   NS 880924
Alloa Glass-work, Clackmannanshire
   Central, Clackmannanshire   # 1968

At the date of survey in 1968 there were two large brick-built cones within the precinct of the Alloa Glass-work close to the N shore of the River Forth. The cones dated from about 1825, when the work was taken over and extended by the Edinburgh, Glasgow and Alloa Glass Company.[34]* The s cone, probably the slightly older of the two, was the main subject of the survey and was demolished in 1972; the other is one of the few left standing in the United Kingdom.

The demolished cone stood to an overall height of 79 ft (24·08 m) above ground level; it was set on an octagonal and arcaded stone base 20 ft (6·10 m) high and 65 ft (19·81 m) across opposing faces. The bricks were of local manufacture, and for the first 11 ft (3·35 m) above the stone base were laid in alternate courses of headers and stretchers (English bond), the remainder being in an English garden-wall bond.

The base was constructed of coursed sandstone rubble masonry and incorporated eight semicircular arches with dressed voussoirs. The cone had been used in association with a succession of gas-furnaces, and there was no clear indication of the original coal-fired pot-furnace or 174 D annealing-oven.[35]

C

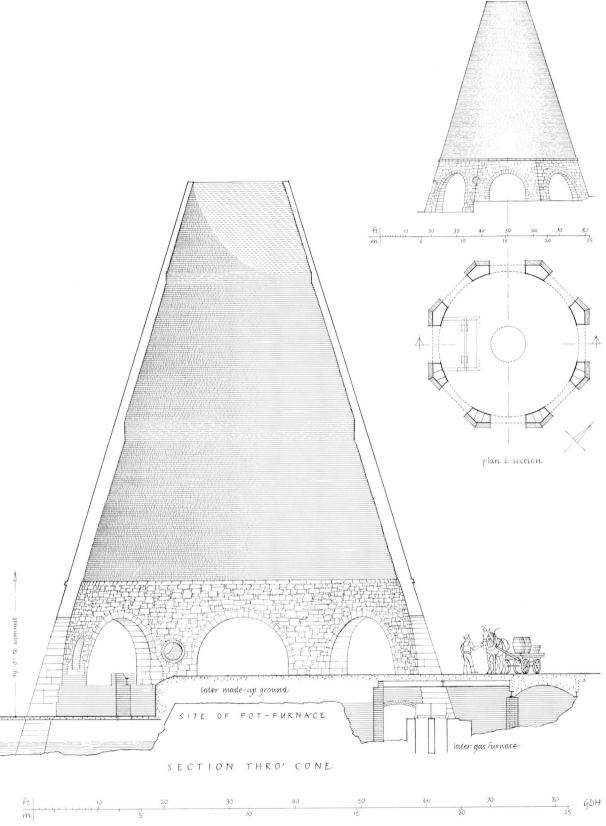

ft. 10 20 30 40 50 60 70 80
m. 5 10 15 20 25

plan & section

70'-0" to summit

later made-up ground

SITE OF POT-FURNACE

later gas furnace

SECTION THRO' CONE

ft. 10 20 30 40 50 60 70 80 GDH
m. 5 10 15 20 25

Alloa Glass-work, Clackmannanshire; south cone

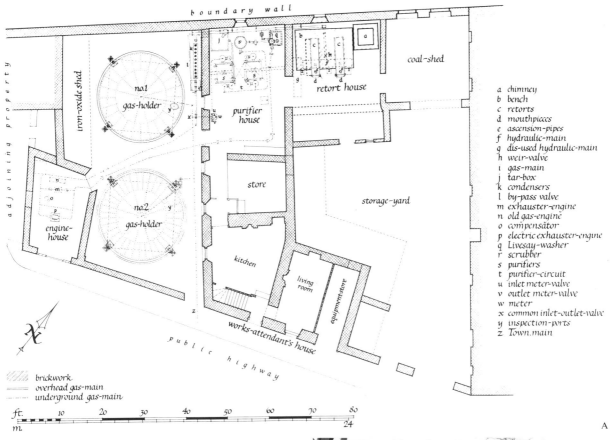

boundary wall

adjoining property

iron-oxide shed

no.1 gas-holder

purifier house

store

no.2 gas-holder

engine-house

kitchen

living room

equipment-store

works-attendant's house

retort house

coal-shed

storage-yard

public highway

a chimney
b bench
c retorts
d mouthpieces
e ascension-pipes
f hydraulic-main
g dis-used hydraulic-main
h weir-valve
i gas-main
j tar-box
k condensers
l by-pass valve
m exhauster-engine
n old gas-engine
o compensator
p electric exhauster-engine
q Livesay-washer
r scrubber
s purifiers
t purifier-circuit
u inlet meter-valve
v outlet meter-valve
w meter
x common inlet-outlet-valve
y inspection-ports
z Town.main

brickwork
overhead gas-main
underground gas-main

ft. 10 20 30 40 50 60 70 80
m. 24

A

Gasworks

Inveraray, Argyll
    Strathclyde, Argyll and Bute

NN 094083

1965

At the date of its closure in 1964 this small gasworks preserved much of its early layout, plant and character. It was established in 1841 by the 7th Duke of Argyll to serve the burgh of Inveraray, and continued to produce coal gas by original processes until converted to a more efficient exhauster gas system in 1949.[36] The retort-house stood against the N boundary-wall flanked by the coal-shed and purifier-house; its SE wall had been extended some 8 ft (2·44 m) farther out, and the bench incorporated a hydraulic main and three hand-fired retorts[37]* that required periodic renewal. The chimney stood in its original position in the N corner, and the roof of the retort-house was of a fireproof type—the roof-trusses and battens being of iron, and the slates affixed to the battens with copper wire. In the original arrangement, gas was introduced into the purifier-house directly after being cooled in the bank of condensers, and the purifier-house still retained a number of original fittings, including two lime-purifiers and a tar box. In the later system an exhauster-engine placed in the engine-house drew the gas from the condensers and fed it back under pressure to the scrubber and washer in the purifier-house, and thence through the purifiers. The two gasholders were original installations, although gasholder no. 2 had been partly rebuilt. Each measured 20 ft (6·10 m) in diameter and

177 B
177 A
176 B
177 C
178 A

Gasworks, Inveraray, Argyll
A.   layout of plant
B.   condensers

B

A

B

Gasworks, Inveraray, Argyll
  A.   retort-house; detail of
       fireproof roof
  B.   retort-house; hand-fired
       retorts, ascension pipes and
       hydraulic main
  C.   purifier-house; tar-box,
       scrubber, washer and purifiers

C

D. Stone gasometer-house,
Musselburgh Gasworks,
East Lothian

Gasworks, Inveraray, Argyll
  A.   gasholders from SE
  B, C. no. 1 gasholder; balancing mechanism

had columnar posts with pulley-wheels at their heads,
178 B,C originally designed to receive the controlling counterpoise
weights.

Stone Gasometer-house   NT 348733
Musselburgh Gasworks
    Lothian, East Lothian   1969

This circular stone-built structure was erected in about 1831
for the gas company serving Musselburgh and Portobello,
which was established in that year;[38] it survived until 1970,
being one of the last remaining examples of its type.[39*] It
measured 42 ft 6 in (12·95 m) in diameter over walls of
sandstone ashlar masonry 2 ft (0·61 m) in thickness. A
single-storeyed structure, possibly an early retort-house and
purifier-house, had formerly abutted the N face of the
building. Ventilation for the gasholder was provided by
four tall louvred windows with pointed arched heads, and

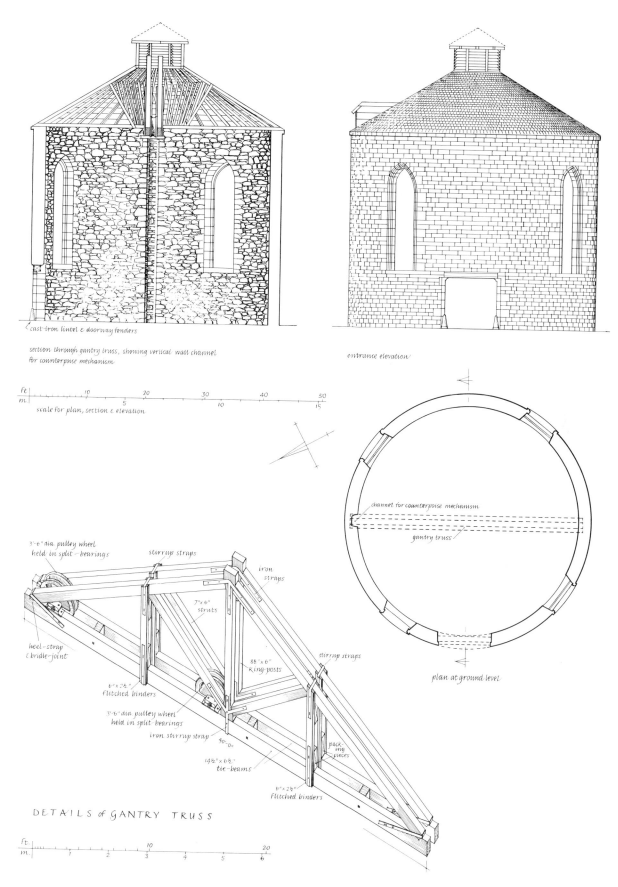

cast-iron lintel & doorway fenders

section through gantry truss, showing vertical wall channel
for counterpoise mechanism

entrance elevation

ft
m

| 10 | 20 | 30 | 40 | 50 |

5 | 10 | 15

scale for plan, section & elevation

channel for counterpoise mechanism

gantry truss

plan at ground level

3'-6" dia pulley wheel
held in split-bearings

stirrup straps

iron
straps

7" x 6"
struts

heel-strap
& bridle-joint

8½" x 6"
king-posts

stirrup straps

6" x 2½"
flitched binders

3'-6" dia pulley wheel
held in split-bearings

iron stirrup strap 40'-0"

14½" x 6½"
tie-beams

packing
pieces

6" x 2½"
flitched binders

DETAILS of GANTRY TRUSS

ft.
m

| 10 | 20 |

1 | 2 | 3 | 4 | 5 | 6

Stone gasometer-house, Musselburgh Gasworks, East Lothian

179

A

Stone gasometer-house, Musselburgh Gasworks,
East Lothian
    A.   single-lift gasholder, Accum, 1815
    B.   gantry truss and roof

B

the slated conical roof was surmounted by an octagonal
louvred cupola. The internal gas containers had long been
absent, but the empty masonry shell still preserved a few
structural details, including a channel for a counterpoise
weighted frame. The principal feature of interest was a
substantial double-frame king-post gantry-truss with stir-
ruped main joints. Two iron pulley-wheels were held
between the pair of flitched tie-beams. Descriptions of early
single-lift gasholders of this type show that a chain attached _180_ A
to an eye-bolt at the top of the internal vessel was drawn
over the two wheels and affixed at the other end to a
counterpoise weight, almost equal to the weight of the
vessel.[40] The radial roof-structure otherwise comprised a _180_ B
system of common rafters and ties held together by iron
rings.

A

B

Acid-producing tower,
Inverurie Paper Mills,
Aberdeenshire
  A. view from SE
  B. view, *c.* 1910
  C. design drawing of
      acid-producing tower,
      ?Ekman, *c.* 1890

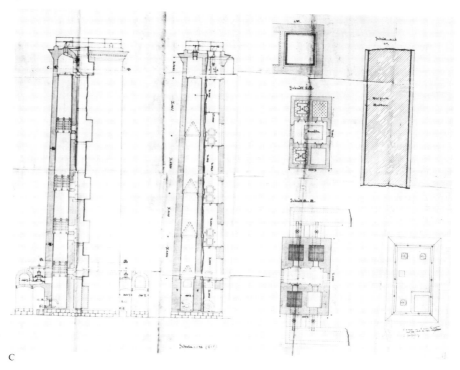

C

Acid-producing Tower   NJ 781192

Inverurie Paper Mills, Aberdeenshire
      Grampian, Gordon   1980

The paper mills of Thomas Tait & Sons Ltd., Inverurie, stand on the w bank of the River Don, and were first established in 1852.[41] This tall rectangular tower dates from about 1890, and reflects an important early stage in the use of wood-pulp as a raw material in the paper-making process. The process was first exploited commercially in Sweden by C D Ekman, who may have supplied or influenced the design of the Inverurie tower. It was designed to produce calcium bisulphate, an acid liquor in which wood chips were boiled for pulping under pressure.[42] From a tank at the top of the tower, water or milk of lime trickled down square lead-lined vertical shafts over a series of inverted V-shaped racks, which held lumps of limestone; at the base of the tower sulphur dioxide was blown in from pyrites burners which were specially constructed to keep down the combustion temperature, thus preventing the formation of sulphur trioxide and sulphuric acid.

The tower rises to a height of 92 ft (28·04 m) and has a slightly tapering profile in the central section. The lowest 23 ft (7·01 m) is constructed of coursed granite masonry, the remainder being of brick laid in English garden-wall bond. On plan at ground level it measures 27 ft 6 in (8·38 m) by 19 ft (5·79 m) overall. An original corbelled cornice encircling the top of the tower has been removed.

The interior was not accessible at the date of visit, but it is known that all original plant and fittings were removed before 1950 except, perhaps, the two horizontal egg-end cylinders standing near the base of the tower, which may have been part of the pulping plant. The top of the tower now houses two water-tanks for the mills.

181

NOTES

n.1   *Inventory of Stirlingshire,* **2,** No. 564; *Inventory of Peeblesshire,* **2,** No. 657. For a list of old coal- and other mines, see the *Catalogue of Plans of Abandoned Mines,* **5** (Scotland) (HMSO, 1931).

n.2   The beam and part of the pump-rod of the pumping-engine still survive in the engine-house at Devon Colliery, Sauchie, Clackmannanshire (1865; NS 897958).

n.3   Adams, I H, *Scottish Geographical Magazine,* **81,** no. 3 (December 1965), 153–62; Duckham, B F, *A History of the Scottish Coal Industry,* **1,** 1700–1815 (1970), 15–16, 25–6; Whatley, C A, *'That Important and Necessary Article' The Salt Industry and its Trade in Fife and Tayside c. 1570–1850* (1984). Probably the most substantial remains surviving from the later phases of the industry are those of the former salt-work on Preston Island in the River Forth (NT 007852), which operated from 1800 until about 1840, Adams, op. cit., 160; SIAS survey March 1983.

n.4   Skinner, B C, *The Lime Industry of the Lothians* (1969); Skinner, B C, *Post-Medieval Archaeology,* **9,** (1975), 225–30. For an estimate of the consumption of coal by this industry, see Duckham, op. cit., 25.

n.5   *Inventory of Argyll,* **2,** Nos. 348, 365, 366.

n.6   *Inventory of Argyll,* **3,** Nos. 387, 392; ibid., **5,** No. 436. See also *Inventory of Peeblesshire,* **2,** Nos. 656, 658, 661; *Inventory of Selkirkshire,* No. 197; and for other non-ferrous metals (e.g. copper), *Inventory of Stirlingshire,* **2,** Nos. 561–3.

n.7   Smout, T C, *TDGAS,* 3rd series, **39** (1960–1), 144–58; idem. (ed.), 'Journal of Henry Kalmeter's travels in Scotland 1719–1720', *Scottish Industrial History, A Miscellany* (SHS, 1978), 1–52 at 26–34; various authors in *TDGAS,* 3rd series, **54** (1959), 75–146, 156–76; and Harvey, W S and Downs-Rose, G, *Industrial Archaeology,* **15,** no. 1 (Spring 1980), 11–29.

n.8   *Inventory of Roxburghshire,* **1,** Nos. 502, 532, 566; ibid., **2,** Nos. 621, 622, 975; *Inventory of Argyll,* **2,** Nos. 349, 351, 354; ibid., **3,** Nos. 380, 383.

n.9   *Inventory of Argyll,* **2,** Nos. 350, 356; Belnahua has been the subject of an SIAS survey, and for its history see Tucker, D G, *Business History,* **19** (1977), 18–36.

n.10   *Inventory of Argyll,* **4,** No. 16, and Viner, D J, *Industrial Archaeology Review,* **1,** (1976), 18–27. See also *Inventory of Argyll,* **2,** No. 355; ibid., **3,** No. 378.

n.11   *Inventory of Stirlingshire,* **2,** Nos. 567–8; *Inventory of Argyll,* **1,** Nos. 369–73; ibid., **2,** Nos. 351–2; ibid., **5,** Nos. 429, 433; and for a general survey, see Tucker, D G, *PSAS,* **114** (1984), 539–56.

n.12   Denholm, P C, *SAF,* **8** (1977), 37–51 at 37.

n.13   Carvel, J L, *The Alloa Glass Works* (1953).

n.14   Commission surveys also include a domestic gas-producer of a petrol-driven type patented in 1913, which is contained in a brick outhouse at Newton House, Millerhill, Midlothian (NT 332697); it supplied gas-light for the house. The Commissioners are indebted to Dr R F Bud of the Science Museum for the identification of the patent.

n.15   Thomson, A G, *The Paper Industry in Scotland 1590–1861* (1974), 111 and chap. 5.

n.16   *Inventory of Argyll,* **2,** No. 363.

n.17   Rymer, L, *Scottish Geographical Magazine,* **90,** no. 3 (December 1974), 142–52; Thomson, W P L, *Kelp-Making in Orkney* (1983).

n.18   *Inventory of Argyll,* **3,** No. 381.

n.19   Whatley, C A, *Industrial Archaeology Review,* **6,** no. 2 (Spring 1982), 89–101.

n.20   Smout, 'Kalmeter', op. cit., 41, cited by Whatley, 'Arran', op. cit., 92. See also St Fond, B Faujas de, *A Journey Through England and Scotland to the Hebrides in 1784* (revised edition, 1907), **1,** 175–6, cited by Duckham, op. cit., 318.

n.21   Whatley, 'Arran', op. cit., 97.

n.22   *NSA,* **8** (Stirlingshire), 331.

n.23   OS Name Book, Stirlingshire, No. 27, p. 106. OS 6-inch map, sheets 17 NW and SW (2nd edition).

n.24   SRO, Seafield Muniments (GD 248), 984/2/17; *Stat Acct.,* **20** (1798), 358.

n.25   *NSA,* **13** (Banffshire), 237–8; cf. layout of 1829 shown in SRO, RHP 8840.

n.26   Information from the Works Manager, Mr Lawrence.

n.27   Cf. the module of 5 ft (1·52 m) observed in Danish drying-sheds by Rasmussen, J and Meyer, O, *Gamle Teglvaerker* [Old Tileworks] (1968), 23.

n.28   The ruins of a double-banked kiln of similar type were noted at the former Tochieneal Brickworks, Lintmill, near Cullen, Banffshire (NJ 521648).

n.29   Fleming, J A, *Scottish Pottery* (1923), 180; and cf. Baird, W, *Annals of Duddingston and Portobello* (1898), 440, where the pottery is said to have been originally built in about 1876. For the other Portobello potteries, see also McVeigh, P, *Scottish East Coast Potteries 1750–1840* (1979), 110–28.

n.30   Plan of Pipe Street at Harbour Green 1879. Original in the possession of A W Buchan & Co.; copy in NMRS. See also Baird, op. cit., 304–5, 441, and Graham, A, in *PSAS,* **101** (1968–9), 265–6.

n.31   Fleming, op. cit., 200–3.

n.32   Measured survey by Mr Kenneth MacKay drawn out and dated June 1974; copy in NMRS.

n.33   Fleming, op. cit., 201, attributes the visit, perhaps mistakenly, to 1871. It is known that Queen Victoria purchased items from the Dunmore stand at the Edinburgh International Exhibition in 1886 (Information from Mr R A Hill, Huntly House Museum, Edinburgh).

n.34   Carvel, op. cit., 13, 15. Wood's Town Plan of Alloa (1825) shows the circular outlines of two cones in the glass-work.

n.35   Gillispie, C C (ed.), *A Diderot Pictorial Encyclopaedia of Trades and Industry* (1959), **2,** pl. 234, fig. 2, shows a section through a glass-cone of this type (from Diderot, D, *L'Encyclopédie, ou Dictionnaire Raisonné des Sciences, des Arts et des Metiérs* (1772), vol. x, Verrerie Angloise, pl. III). See also Douglas, R W and Frank, S, *A History of Glassmaking* (1972), 106, and Bremner, D, *The Industries of Scotland* (1869, and 1969 reprint), 377–82.

n.36   Information from Mr Neil Livingstone, who operated the plant during the last twenty years of its existence.

n.37   Hand-fired horizontal retorts are still to be seen at the preserved gasworks in Biggar, and have been recorded in those at e.g. Girvan, Kirkconnel, Millport, Moffat and Newton Stewart.

n.38   *NSA,* **1** (Edinburgh), 303.

n.39   At the former Edinburgh and Leith Gasworks in Baltic Street, Leith (NT 273764) the remains of three stone gasometer-houses and the site of a fourth have been recorded. These include the masonry shells of a two-gasholder unit with splayed bays and corbelled turrets (containing the recesses for the counterweights), and of a huge w range designed to accommodate five gasholders. It measures internally 276 ft (84·1 m) in length by 60 ft 6 in (18·5 m) transversely, and the wall-head is 56 ft 6 in (17·3 m) above ground level. Double rows of I-section girders set in the timber king-post roof carry the pulley-wheels of the original gas-containers and counterweights.

n.40   Accum, F C, *A Practical Treatise on Gas-light* (1815), 103–4 and pl. VII; Peckston, T S, *The Theory and Practice of Gas-lighting* (1815–19), 220 ff.

n.41   Information from the works manager; cf. Thomson, op. cit., 211.

n.42   Information on the design and operation of the tower has been supplied by Dr W A Campbell, Department of Inorganic Chemistry, University of Newcastle upon Tyne.

7 COMMUNICATIONS

The rugged and difficult terrain of much of Scotland has posed a considerable challenge to the transport engineer throughout the centuries. The earliest engineered roads in the country were those built by the Romans for military purposes, and their remains have been described in many of the county *Inventories* of southern and central Scotland, the record being considerably assisted in recent years by aerial photography.[1] Many of these roads are known to have continued in use in the Middle Ages, but the medieval and later network also included other overland routes, sometimes mere droving-tracks, of the kind encountered by the Commission in the Border counties and in the central and western Highlands.[2] The comparatively well-preserved remains of medieval roads and streets are sometimes found within the vicinity of major buildings,[3] but arched masonry bridges of single or multiple spans constitute the most substantial monuments in the country's early road-system. *183* Such bridges depended on local patronage for their construction, and, as the history of the Old Bridge of Earn *202-3* amply testifies, the powerful waters which they cross have added much to the problems and costs of maintenance. Evidence of their vulnerability and the need for detailed recording is all too clear, and accounts of numerous early bridges have appeared in most published *Inventories*.[4]

Stirling Old Bridge (*c.* 1500)

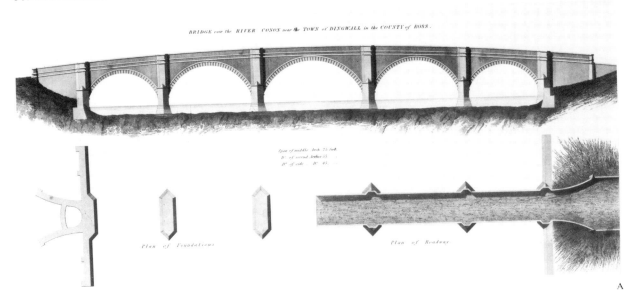

BRIDGE over the RIVER CONON near the TOWN of DINGWALL in the COUNTY of ROSS.

Span of middle Arch 75 feet.
D.° of second Arches 65
D.° of side D.° 45

Plan of Foundations

Plan of Roadway

A

B

Conon Bridge, Ross and Cromarty
(Thomas Telford, c. 1812)
   A.   design drawings
   B.   view from SE

C. Toll-house, Conon Bridge, Ross and Cromarty

Parts of the well-known military and civil ('Parliamentary') road-building programmes in the Scottish Highlands have been described in the course of surveys in Stirlingshire and Argyll, whilst 18th- and 19th-century roads and bridges of all kinds have been recorded in *184* systematic surveys and in anticipation of their removal or adaptation to modern requirements.[5] These have included structures affected by the reconstruction of the A9 highway, as well as elements of the turnpike-roads such as toll-houses, milestones and wayside-markers.[6]

Masonry and timber, sometimes in combination,[7] have long served as the principal bridge-building materials, and a handful of minor road- and foot-bridges of timber trestle construction, such as those at Garve, Ross and Cromarty *185* (NH 397613) and Broomhill, Inverness-shire (NH 996223), still remain in use. The early 19th century saw the first use of cast iron in Scottish bridge construction, and a bridge at Duich on Islay, which had already stood 'several years' by 1808, may be claimed as the earliest cast-iron bridge in Scotland, though no longer extant.[8] The oldest surviving cast-iron arch bridges, which date from 1815 and 1813 respectively,[9]* are Telford's celebrated road bridge across *204-6*

A

B

Wooden bridges
  A.   Broomhill, Inverness-shire
       (1894)
  B.   Garve, Ross and Cromarty
       (late 19th century)

A

Duchess Bridge, Langholm, Dumfriesshire
A. arch-rib and spandrel detail,
    NE abutment
B. SW approach

B

the River Spey at Craigellachie, and the Duchess Bridge at 186
Langholm, Dumfriesshire (NY 355852), a less renowned 187 A,B
footbridge of similar construction. Structural members of
cast iron were thereafter employed, sometimes in conjunction with wrought iron, in various types of 19th-century
bridges, including suspension bridges and parallel girder 207-9
bridges such as Balmoral Bridge.

In Britain the suspension principle was pioneered in the
Scottish Borders, and Scotland has continued to produce
many variations in the design and size of suspension
bridges, culminating in the 5,980 ft (1822·7 m) span of the
Forth Road Bridge completed in 1964.[10] Captain Samuel
Brown's Union Suspension Bridge (1820) over the River
Tweed at Hutton, Berwickshire (NT 933510), was the first 187 C,D
road bridge of this type, the chains being made up of
wrought-iron rods and hangers joined together with a
system of link-pins, flat links and cast-iron saddle pieces.
The design of the derelict footbridge over the Aberdeenshire
Dee at Cults displays the influence of Brown's patented 209-11
techniques, whilst other groups of bridges recorded by the
Commission appear to be of hybrid stayed suspension and
cantilever types. The road bridge at Haughs of Drimmie, 212-14

186

A

B

Duchess Bridge, Langholm, Dumfriesshire
  A.   transverse ribs
  B.   dovetailed connection between arch-ribs
         and transverse ribs

C

Union Suspension Bridge, Hutton,
Berwickshire
  C.   detail of linkage unit, including
         later suspension system
  D.   view from NE

D

187

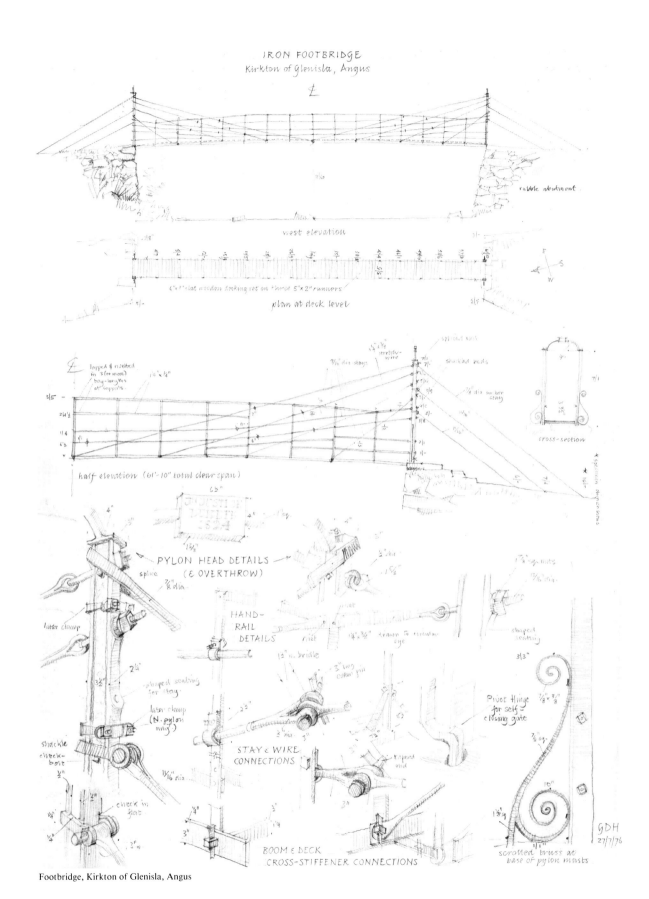

IRON FOOTBRIDGE
Kirkton of Glenisla, Angus

Footbridge, Kirkton of Glenisla, Angus

for example, follows the pattern of an earlier footbridge of 1824 at Kirkton of Glenisla, Angus (NO 212603) and is almost certainly by Justice & Co. of Dundee. The two Ness Island footbridges in Inverness (NH 661436 and 664439), like the Bridge of Oich at Aberchalder, Inverness-shire (NH 337036), are attributable to James Dredge of Bath; in his unusual patented design the main cables are made up of multiple parallel wrought-iron rods which diminish in number towards the span centres and anchor-points.

188

189 A

189 B-D

189 E-F

Footbridge, Kirkton of Glenisla, Angus
    A.   view from N

Ness Island Footbridge,
Island Bank Road, Inverness
    B.   head of pylon
    C.   linkage unit
    D.   view from SE
Bridge of Oich, Inverness-shire
(c. 1850)
    E.   linkage unit
    F.   main suspension cable

A

B

A. Harbour, Lybster, Caithness,
   from N
B. Harbour, Dunbeath, Caithness,
   from NW

Much of Scotland's long coastline has been suited to the establishment of harbours, and some sea lochs and river estuaries have provided almost ideal conditions for the development of major ports, docks and ship-building (latterly oil-rig-building) yards. The remains of small boat-landings and anchorages have been noted in close association with medieval castles occupying riverine or seaboard sites, and many later harbours and piers serving a variety of purposes have come within the Commission's purview: most of them were designed to serve the needs of the fishing industry; many acted as outlets for local industrial products such as lime, slate, bricks and tiles, or grain; and some were intended simply as transit points for ferries or even pleasure-craft.[11] Several ancillary features connected with wharf and dockside practices have also been noted in passing.

The benefits of sea-borne commerce and the fishing industry were, however, occasionally offset by the considerable hazards of coastal navigation. Some well-placed circular church-towers, such as those of Portpatrick, Wigtownshire, and Cockburnspath, Berwickshire, may have served as sea-marks,[12] but the first purpose-built beacon or lighthouse was that erected on the Isle of May in the Forth Estuary in 1636, a description of which is included in the Fife *Inventory*.[13] Southerness Lighthouse, on the Solway coast near the mouth of the River Nith, is another of the small number of lighthouses established as a result of local and private enterprise before the formation of the Northern Lighthouse Board in 1786. The lighthouse at the Mull of Kintyre (1788) was among the first four lighthouses erected by the Commissioners of Northern Lighthouses;[14] this and other Argyll lighthouses, especially those of

190

190
216-17
24-5
167-9
191
214-15

A

B

C

A. Hydraulic crane,
   Victoria Dock, Leith (1903)
B. Steam-crane,
   Victoria Dock, Dundee (1874)
C. Hydraulic bow-truss swing-bridge,
   Leith Harbour (c. 1896)
D. Two-leaf swing-bridge,
   East Dock, Leith (c. 1810)

D

191

Navigation aids, Ayr Harbour
  A. leading-light
  B. fix-light and signal-gun (c. 1920)
Union Canal
  C. vertical lift bridge, Gilmour Park,
       Edinburgh

Ardnamurchan, Skerryvore and Rinns of Islay, represent superb tributes to the determination of the Northern Lighthouse Board and to the skills of their engineers and work-forces.[15] The construction of Skerryvore Lighthouse on a reef about 11 nautical miles (20·4 km) sw of Tiree was a particularly noteworthy achievement, the building-operations having been conducted from a workyard and harbour (complete with its own hydraulic scouring-system) at Hynish, on Tiree.[16] Minor navigational aids have also been noted on the quayside of Ayr harbour.

For the transport of bulk cargoes, canals provided new links in a long-established and natural waterway system formed by the great river estuaries and navigable lochs that penetrated far inland. But, as has been pointed out elsewhere,[17] Scotland did not acquire, or need, a dense network of canals comparable with those of Midland and Northern England. The Forth-Clyde isthmus was an exception, however, and the special commercial and industrial requirements of the central Lowlands provided the impetus for two of the country's most important canal projects. The Forth and Clyde Canal, also known at one time as 'the Great Canal', as well as being the earliest British ship-canal, is the oldest and longest of the Scottish canals;[18*] about a quarter of its length was recorded in the course of the Commission's survey of Stirlingshire, while the same survey also embraced the western section of the comparatively youthful Union Canal, projected and built between 1818 and 1822.[19] This waterway ran from Port Hopetoun in Edinburgh over a distance of 31½ miles (50·7 km) to Port Downie at Camelon, Stirlingshire, where a ladder of locks formerly connected it with the Forth and Clyde Canal. Its western section boasts one of the canal's most impressive aqueducts[20] and a 700 yd-long (640 m) tunnel, the oldest in Scotland.

192 A,B

218-21

192 C
193

A

B

C

D

Union Canal;
No. 1 bridge, Viewforth,
Edinburgh (*c.* 1900)
  A, C. keystones
  B. E side
Avon Aqueduct, Stirlingshire
  D. view from SE
  E. aerial view

E

Caledonian Canal, Inverness-shire;
locks at Banavie
(Neptune's Staircase)
    A.   aerial view from s
    B.   lock-gates

A

B

Sections of the Union Canal are maintained in navigable use for pleasure-craft, but most Scottish barge canals are redundant, in many cases infilled and awaiting archaeological rediscovery, like, for example, the short Campbeltown Coal Canal, Kintyre, Argyll.[21] However, the two major ship canals, the Caledonian and the Crinan, remain busily operational, and recording of their canalside features has to anticipate the effects of constant maintenance and occasional modernisation. The construction of the Caledonian Canal (1803–22) through the Great Glen from Loch Eil to the Beauly Firth, Inverness-shire, represented a considerable engineering achievement by any standards, and at Banavie, near the southern entrance to the canal, eight of its twenty-nine locks form an impressive rise known as 'Neptune's Staircase'.[22] The building of the Crinan Canal,

194

195

Crinan Canal, Argyll: lock chambers and basins, Dunardry; aerial view from w

Crinan Canal, Argyll;
roller bridge, Dunardry
  A. in open position
  B. winch mechanism

Crinan Canal, Argyll;
automatic offlet, Ardrishaig
  C. detail of mechanism
  D. pump-house and discharge

Argyll (1794–1801), although only 9 miles (14·48 km) in overall length, was no less of a technical triumph over difficult terrain which was often too rocky or too soft;[23] the rise and fall in its short route across the relatively narrow neck of land that separates Loch Gilp and Loch Crinan necessitated no fewer than fifteen locks. A swing-bridge of 1871 still operates in a picturesque setting at Oakfield (NR 856879), and above the chamber of lock 11 at Dunardry (NR 819912) there is a hand-operated roller cantilever bridge which was installed there in 1900. The embankment of the original course of the canal across Oakfield Moss can be seen between NR 853894 and 850895; this line was breached and abandoned after flood damage in January 1805, and the waterway now skirts the hillside to the s. Overflows serve each of the canal's three reaches, but a more rapid discharge of water from the eastern reach at Ardrishaig is provided by an automatic offlet, or 'water waster' (NR 854870), designed in 1892 and built in 1895.

196 A,B

196 C,D

A

B

Some of the earliest railways of central Scotland provided links with the canal system. Within Stirlingshire, for example, the Commission encountered the remains of a horse-drawn colliery wagon-way which joined the Forth and Clyde Canal near Kelvinhead.[24] A dock on the Union Canal was the original terminus of the Slamannan Railway, which was authorised in 1835 and built between 1836 and 1840, one of the earliest public railways in Scotland. The terminal yard still retains some of the massive stone blocks used for carrying the bolted chairs for iron rails before the introduction of wooden sleepers.[25]

The canals themselves, however, were soon threatened or superseded by the railways, and in 1848 the Union Canal was acquired by the Edinburgh and Glasgow Railway. Three of the five railway viaducts described in the Stirlingshire *Inventory*[26] were on this company's main line, which was opened in 1842 and became part of the burgeoning North British Railway in 1865. The original eastern terminus of this railway was at Haymarket Station, recorded in detail prior to its partial demolition and modernisation. In 1846 the line was extended to what was originally known as Edinburgh General Station,[27*] later renamed Waverley and massively extended between 1892 and 1902 following the completion of the Forth Bridge in 1890. One of the minor showpieces of this monument to the NBR was a booking-hall with mosaic floor and timber-

Waverley Station, Edinburgh; booking-hall (1892–1902)
  A. general view
  B. detail of mosaic floor

222-4

199
200 A
197

Central Station, Glasgow
   A.   station-hall and concourse, *c.* 1920 (p. 238, n. 28)
Queen Street Station, Glasgow
   B.   arched roof of train-shed
   C.   detail of structural support

A

B

A, B. Forth Railway Bridge under construction 1887

panelled booking-office, recorded before their removal in 1970. Queen Street Station in Glasgow was the western terminus of the NBR and its parent company; a steep, tunnelled approach and a fine overall arched roof are its *198* B,C most distinguished features. The roof, which was designed by James Carswell, was built between 1878 and 1880, and now, following the demolition of St Enoch Station, remains *224-5* the last of its size and type in Scotland.[28*]

Scotland possesses some of the internationally renowned feats of Victorian railway engineering such as the Forth Bridge, the Tay Bridge and Ballochmyle Viaduct, Ayrshire. *201* A However, even the most humble works of architecture and engineering inherited from railway companies operating before the amalgamation of 1923 display considerable character and variety, some dressed in castellated or baronial style or some, like the weatherboarded station-buildings of the Highland and Great North of Scotland Railways, contributing to the vernacular building traditions *200* B-D of the regions that they served. The various physical obstacles in the path of the railway engineers in the Scottish Highlands were not tackled and overcome until the last decades of the 19th century. Their endeavours were awarded with spectacular scenic views, whether looking at or from the railways, and some of the practical difficulties have had beneficial side-effects; the wooden trestle viaduct at Aultnaslanach, for example, now the only surviving *228-9* structure of its type on a main-line railway in Scotland, possibly in Britain, has been retained because its foundations are better suited to the surrounding boggy ground than those of a heavier bridge of metal or masonry.

A. Forth Railway Bridge; general view, *c.* 1900

B, C, D. Railway station, Taynuilt, Argyll (1879)

A

B

A. Railway viaduct, Ballochmyle, Ayrshire (1846–8; see also frontispiece)
B. Airship construction shed, Inchinnan, Renfrewshire (1916); view, c. 1919

Finally, this section would not be complete without some reference to the early monuments of aviation history, one of the major aspects of the modern transport revolution that is also now recognised as a branch of industrial archaeology. The British aircraft industry and military aircraft services grew from infancy to manhood under pressure of wartime conditions between 1914 and 1918, and parts of Scotland, especially along its North Sea coastline, provided suitable 235-7 locations for aircraft stations to combat potential aerial and naval threats. Bases were established for squadrons of airships (both the rigid and the smaller non-rigid types)[29] and seaplanes, as well as more conventional aircraft. In addition, an Admiralty airship-construction shed was 201 B erected at William Beardmore's Inchinnan Works, Renfrewshire (NS 475685), where the rigid airships R24, R27,

R34, and R36 were subsequently built. Shortly after the epic trans-Atlantic flight of the R34 from East Fortune in July 1919, the Scottish stations were closed down, and by the end of 1923 all the airship sheds, which during their short existence were doubtless prominent landmarks, had been dismantled. Fortunately, other Scottish examples of early aviation architecture have suffered a less destructive fate. The flying-boat hangar at Stannergate near Dundee is 232-4 probably the earliest of its type to survive in the United Kingdom, while two groups of First World War aircraft hangars at Montrose airfield are probably the last to remain 230-2 in their original condition. In 1982 the surviving two of the more impressive and slightly later group were dismantled for museum purposes.

201

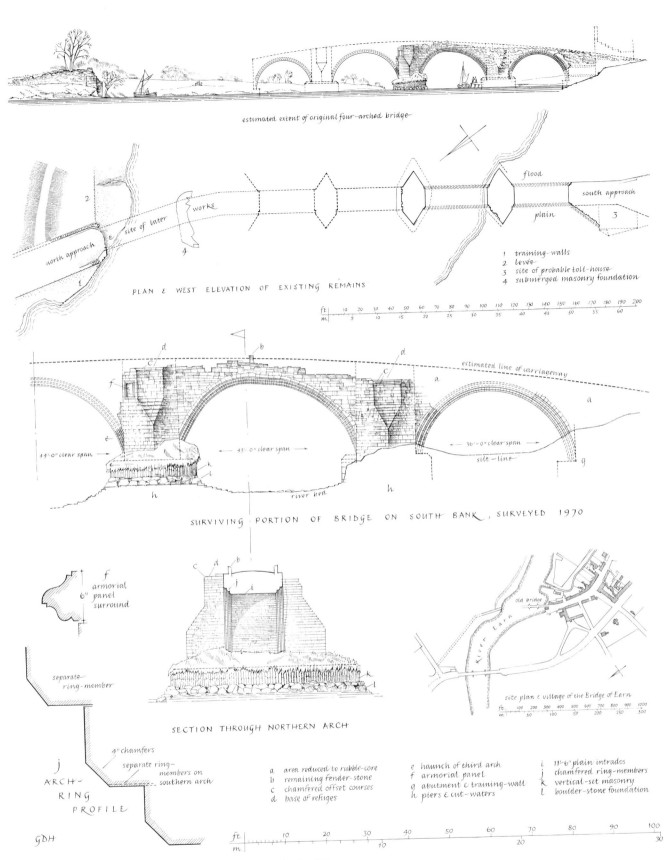

estimated extent of original four-arched bridge

1 training-walls
2 levée
3 site of probable toll-house
4 submerged masonry foundation

north approach
site of later works
flood
plain
south approach

PLAN & WEST ELEVATION OF EXISTING REMAINS

ft. 10 20 30 40 50 60 70 80 90 100 110 120 130 140 150 160 170 180 190 200
m 5 10 15 20 25 30 35 40 45 50 55 60

estimated line of carriageway

44'-0" clear span
43'-0" clear span
36'-0" clear span
silt-line
river bed

SURVIVING PORTION OF BRIDGE ON SOUTH BANK, SURVEYED 1970

f armorial panel surround
6"

separate ring-member

4" chamfers
separate ring-members on southern arch

j ARCH-RING PROFILE

GDH

SECTION THROUGH NORTHERN ARCH

a area reduced to rubble-core
b remaining fender-stone
c chamfered offset courses
d base of refuges

e haunch of third arch
f armorial panel
g abutment & training-wall
h piers & cut-waters

i 11'-6" plain intrados
j chamfered ring-members
k vertical-set masonry
l boulder-stone foundation

old bridge
River Earn
site plan & village of the Bridge of Earn

ft. 100 200 300 400 500 600 700 800 900 1000
m 50 100 150 200 250 300

ft. 10 20 30 40 50 60 70 80 90 100
m 10 20 30

Old bridge, Bridge of Earn, Perthshire; survey and reconstruction drawings

202

A

Old bridge, Bridge of Earn,
Perthshire
A. view by D O Hill, 1821
B. remains of bridge
on s bank

B

Old Bridge NO 132185

Bridge of Earn, Perthshire
Tayside, Perth and Kinross # 1970

The old bridge at Bridge of Earn[30] was an important late 15th- or early 16th-century stone arched bridge spanning the River Earn at its lowest crossing-point, a few miles upstream from its confluence with the River Tay. In its original form, the bridge was probably comparable with the existing four-arched structure at Stirling, but a fifth arch was added in about 1766 because of river erosion on the N bank. Measuring some 305 ft (93 m) overall between the abutments of the N and s approaches, it was finally abandoned and partly dismantled after 1822 upon the completion of a new bridge some 180 m upstream. At the date of survey in 1970, the surviving remains of the old bridge consisted of two complete arches and piers on the s approach (demolished in 1976) together with vestiges of the approach road and abutment on the N bank, the portions on each side of the river being separated by a distance of 195 ft (59·44 m).

183

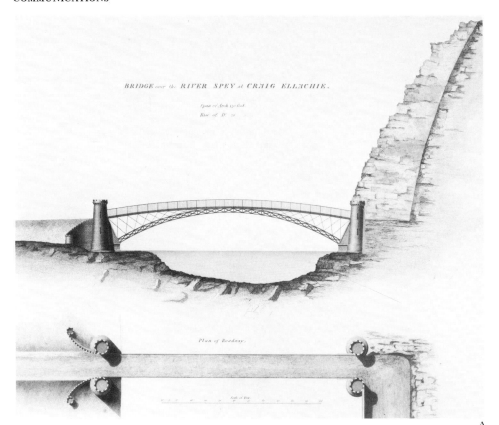

Old bridge, Craigellachie,
Banffshire
  A.   design drawings
  B.   view from NE

A

B

Old Bridge
Craigellachie, Banffshire
    Grampian, Moray

NJ 285451

● * 1980

Thomas Telford's bridge at Craigellachie, erected in
1814–15 across the River Spey, and its sister bridge built two
years earlier across the Dornoch Firth at Bonar, Sutherland,
together represent his two major works in Scotland that
employed the structural use of cast iron. They were basically
identical in design and shared the distinction of being
prototypes for his several large arch-bridges subsequently
built in Britain. The ironwork for both bridges was cast by
William Hazeldine in his foundry at Plas Kynaston in North
Wales and was probably erected on site by his foreman
William Stuttle. Prior to its reconstruction above the
arch-ribs in 1963, the Craigellachie bridge bore the
inscription 1814/CAST AT PLAS KYNASTON/RUABON DENBIGH-
SHIRE, cast in bold relief at one end of the parapet skirting.

Built in the form of a segmental arch with a rise of 20 ft
9 in (6·33 m), and a width of 15 ft 1 in (4·60 m), it spans 151 ft
6 in (46·18 m) between granite abutments topped with twin
turrets and raked at an angle radial with the arch. Its four
longitudinal ribs are made up of seven castings, each pierced
with latticed subdivisions and bolted together through
transverse ribs, also pierced with openings to lessen the
weight. For lateral stability the ribs were further stiffened
by latticed cross-plates extending over the full width of the
arch extrados, and by a series of stout horizontal tie-bars
fixed at intervals between the ribs along their lower edge.
Rows of diagonal struts, set within the arch spandrels,
provided longitudinal bracing and direct support to the
road-bearers, also stiffened transversely by tie-bars fixed to
their intersections, and by two pairs of diagonal sway-
braces on each side of the crown. In general, the various
members were connected by bolted flanges, or by a system
of joggle-and-socket joints cast on the frames and evidently
held together simply by iron pins or wedges and the
compressive forces acting upon them.

204

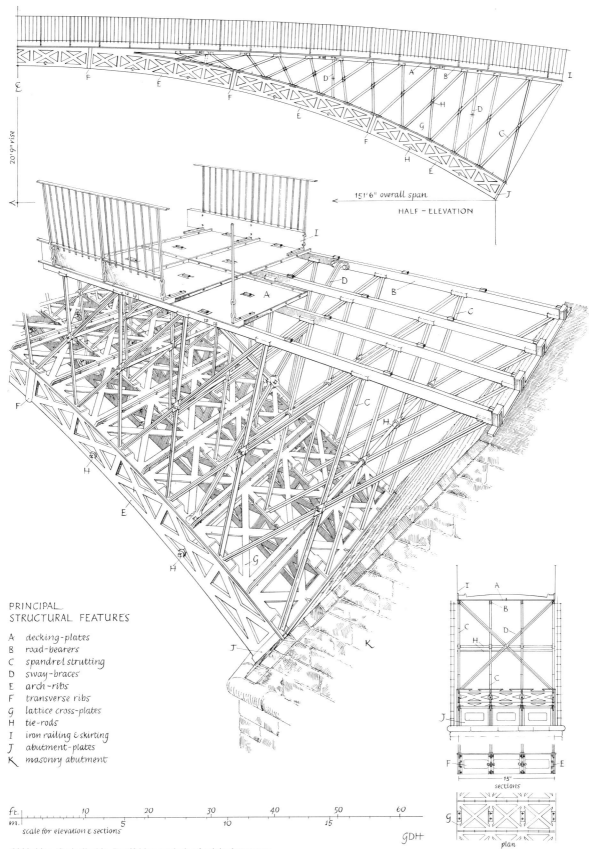

20'9" rise

151'6" overall span

HALF – ELEVATION

PRINCIPAL
STRUCTURAL FEATURES

A   decking-plates
B   road-bearers
C   spandrel strutting
D   sway-braces
E   arch-ribs
F   transverse ribs
G   lattice cross-plates
H   tie-rods
I   iron railing & skirting
J   abutment-plates
K   masonry abutment

ft.   10   20   30   40   50   60
m.   5   10   15
scale for elevation & sections

15'
sections

plan

GDH

Old bridge, Craigellachie, Banffshire; analysis of original structure

205

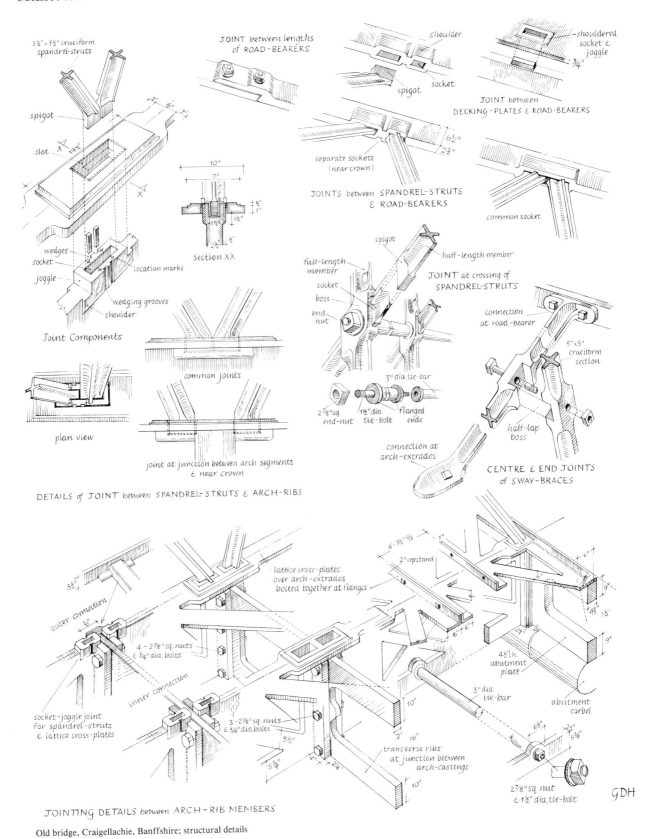

Old bridge, Craigellachie, Banffshire; structural details

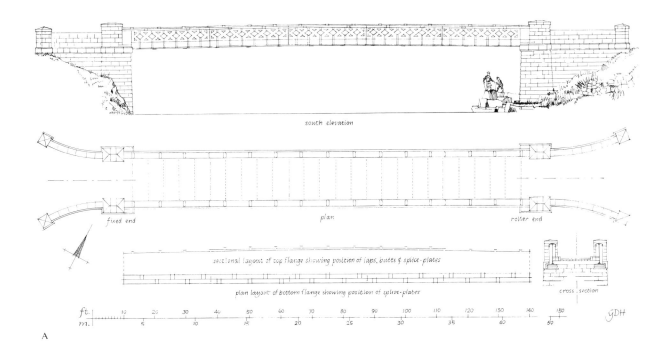

south elevation

fixed end   plan   roller end

sectional layout of top flange showing position of laps, butts & splice-plates

plan layout of bottom flange showing position of splice-plates

cross section

ft.   10   20   30   40   50   60   70   80   90   100   110   120   130   140   150
m.   5   10   15   20   25   30   35   40   50

GDH

A

Balmoral Bridge, Crathie,
Aberdeenshire
  A.   survey drawings
  B.   view from SE

B

Balmoral Bridge

NO 262949

Crathie, Aberdeenshire
     Grampian, Kincardine and Deeside   ● 1981

Designed by I K Brunel, with ironwork by R Brotherhood of Chippenham, the plate-girder bridge spanning the River Dee near the entrance to Balmoral Castle is possibly the earliest of its type of construction in Scotland.[31] Commissioned by the Royal Family as part of the improvements to the Balmoral estate, it did not meet with their wholehearted approval on its completion in 1857, owing to its severely plain appearance and marked elasticity under passing traffic. But in engineering terms it is a distinguished work, incorporating roller-bearings and one of Brunel's novel girder sections devised to resist buckling and compressive strains; and it has the refinements of a gently cambered profile and cut-out diaper-patterned web-plates.

207

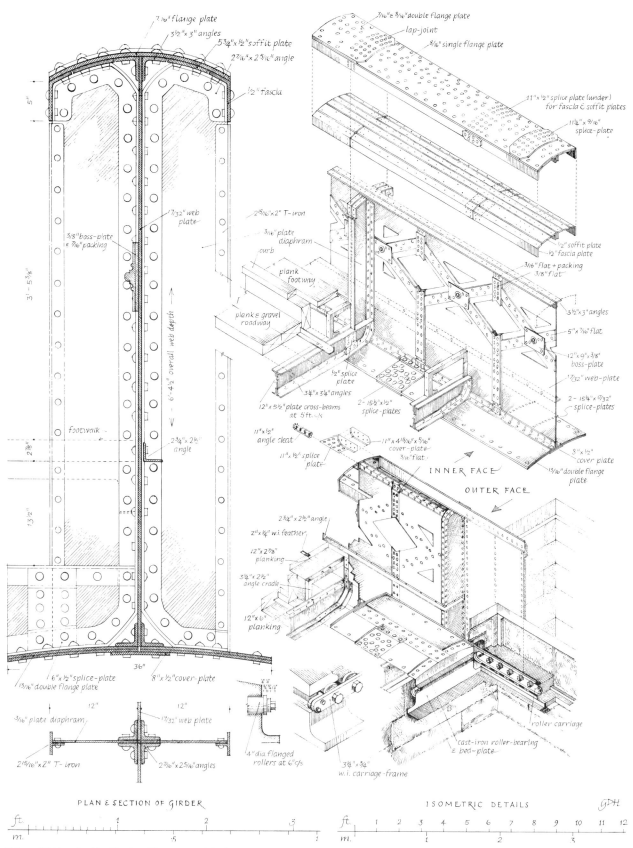

7/16" flange plate

3½" x 3" angles

5¾" x ½" soffit plate

2⅞₆" x 2⅝₆" angle

½" fascia

7/16" & 8/16" double flange plate

lap-joint

8/16" single flange plate

11" x ½" splice plate (under)
for fascia & soffit plates

11¼" x 9/16"
splice-plate

5"

3/8" boss-plate
& 7/16" packing

17/32" web
plate

2⅝₆" x 2" T-iron

3/16" plate
diaphram

curb

plank
footway

plank & gravel
roadway

½" soffit plate
½" fascia plate

3/16" flat + packing
3/8" flat

3½" x 3" angles

5" x 7/16" flat

12" x 9" x 3/8"
boss-plate

17/32" web-plate

2 - 15¾" x 9/32"
splice-plates

3' - 5⅜"

6' - 4½" overall web depth

½" splice
plate

3¼" x 3¼" angles

12" x 5½" plate cross-beams
at 5 ft. c/s

2 - 15½" x ½"
splice-plates

INNER FACE

OUTER FACE

5" x ½"
cover plate

13/16" double flange
plate

footwalk

2¾" x 2½"
angle

11" x ½"
angle cleat

11" x ½" splice
plate

11" x 4⅝₆" x 5/16"
cover-plate

3/16" flat

2⅞"

13'2"

2¾" x 2½" angle

2" x ¼" w.i. feather

12" x 2⅞"
planking

3¼" x 2½"
angle cradle

12" x 6"
planking

roller carriage

cast-iron roller-bearing
& bed-plate

36"

6" x ½" splice-plate

13/16" double flange plate

8" x ½" cover-plate

3/16" plate diaphram

12"

12"

17/32" web plate

2⅝₆" x 2" T-iron

2⅞₆" x 2⅝₆" angles

4" dia flanged
rollers at 6" c/s

3¼" x 3¼"
w.i. carriage-frame

PLAN & SECTION OF GIRDER

ft.
1   2   3

m.
·5   1

ISOMETRIC DETAILS

GDH

ft.   1   2   3   4   5   6   7   8   9   10   11   12

m.   1   2   3

Balmoral Bridge, Crathie, Aberdeenshire; structural details

208

Flanked by curved approaches, the bridge rests on *207* 18 ft-high (5·49 m) abutments built of coursed rock-faced blocks of local granite. The two principal girders, which *208* also form the parapets, are each 130 ft (39·62 m) by 6 ft 6 in (1·98 m) deep and have a clear span of 124 ft (37·80 m) between bearers. Spaced 15 ft (4·57 m) apart, the webs are connected transversely at 5 ft (1·52 m) intervals by 12 in-deep (0·31 m) plate cross-beams, which are decked with longitudinal pine planking and originally accommodated raised narrow side-walks and a 10 ft-wide (3·05 m) carriageway, surfaced with gravel. The boxed ends of the girders are mounted on cast-iron bed-plates averaging 3 ft (0·91 m) square, which are fixed inertly onto the w abutment but ride on rollers on the other to permit free longitudinal movement. The roller-bearings consist of upper and lower bed-plates with a wrought-iron framework between them containing a set of five rollers of 4 in (102 mm) diameter.

The girder components include a cambered upper flange with fascia-plates, a broader lower flange slightly dished downwards, and a vertical web-plate interconnecting them, the whole being stiffened transversely by diaphragm plates dividing the girders into five-bay units. Built up entirely of rolled wrought-iron members, the girders consist of flat plates butt-jointed together in short regular lengths and strengthened by a complex system of bracing-strips, angle-irons and cover-plates, all carefully chain-riveted to form a rigid structure. The ½ in-thick (12·7 mm) plates forming the upper flange are doubled in thickness over the three central sections, while those of the lower flange are of two layers throughout, totalling 13/16 in (20·6 mm), and are disposed so as to break joint on either side of the web-plate. Web- and diaphragm-plates, respectively of 17/32 in (13·5 mm) and 3/16 in (4·8 mm) in thickness, are stiffened with cross-bracing and angle-irons, lapped or spliced where necessary and levelled off with packing-strips. In general, the principal butt-joints are connected with single or double splice-plates and close-riveted in one or more rows on either side.

Three of the four original makers' plates remain on the bridge affixed to the parapet fascia, inscribed R. BROTHERHOOD/CHIPPENHAM/WILTS. 1856. In his initial cal-

culations, Brunel assumed that the bridge would be capable of supporting a load of 86 tons (87·38 tonnes) 'or about 1200 people'; it continues to serve the needs of present-day traffic, though the wooden decking was renewed in 1971.

St Devenick Bridge
Cults, Aberdeenshire
      Grampian, Kincardine and Deeside

NJ 897026

●][1971

This suspension footbridge was built in 1837 by Dr George Morison, minister of Banchory-Devenick parish, for those who lived in the detached portion of the parish N of the River Dee and who attended the church and school on the s bank of the river.[32*] Although the N portion of the parish was transferred to Peterculter in 1891, the bridge was reconstructed by public subscription after flood damage in October 1920. However, the s approaches have since been destroyed, and for some years the bridge has lain disused and under threat of demolition.

The bridge was designed by John Smith, architect (1781–1852), who had worked with Samuel Brown, the pioneer of British suspension bridges, on the Wellington Bridge, Aberdeen, in 1829–31.[33] The Cults bridge followed *211* the Brown suspension system in having a pair of single chains made up of wrought-iron rods and hangers joined together by iron link-pins and flat links. The main rods are *210 B,C* 1¾ in (44·5 mm) in diameter and range in length between 6 ft 4 in (1·93 m) and 6 ft 8 in (2·03 m). Thirty-five hanger-rods and their corresponding number of cast-iron cross-beams carry the slatted wooden deck. It has a timber balustrade (dismantled, together with the decking, in 1984), and is *210 A* reinforced underneath by a system of diagonally set wooden braces. The pylons are in the form of hollow cast-iron columns and entablatures of Greek Doric Order. They are set on masonry piers which, like the anchor-block abutments, are of coursed granite and have a battered profile with a cordon-moulding at the head. The clear span between the pylons is 186 ft (56·69 m) and the original overall length 316 ft 11 in (96·60 m), subsequently extended by the construction of another pier 23 ft 6 in (7·16 m) to the s.[34]

St Devenick Bridge, Cults, Aberdeenshire; view from NW

B

C

St Devenick Bridge, Cults, Aberdeenshire
A.   partly dismantled, 1984
B.   detail of suspension system
C.   linkage unit

A

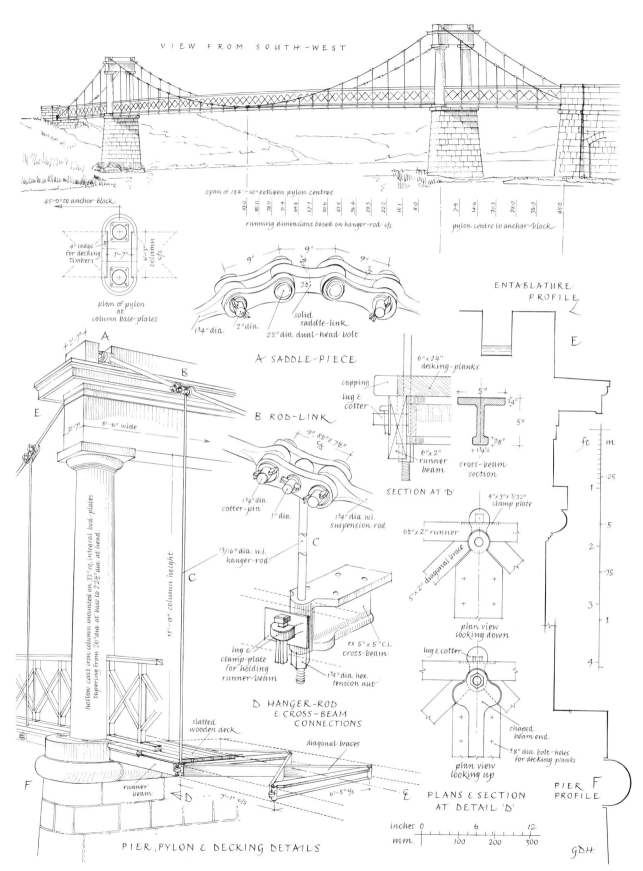

VIEW FROM SOUTH-WEST

45'-0" to anchor block

4" ledge
for decking
timbers

3'-7"

6'-3" column c/s

plan of pylon
at
column base-plates

span of 184'-10" between pylon centres

93.0 85.11 78.11 71.9 64.8 57.7 50.6 43.5 36.4 29.3 22.2 15.1 8.0 7.9 14.6 21.3 28.0 35.0 45.0

running dimensions based on hanger-rod c/s   pylon centre to anchor block

9"   9"   9"

2½"

1¾" dia.   2" dia.

solid
saddle-link
2½" dia. dual-head bolt

A SADDLE-PIECE

ENTABLATURE
PROFILE

6" × 2½"
decking-planks

capping

lug &
cotter

5"

¾"

5"

7/8"

1¾"

cross-beam
section

E

B ROD-LINK

9" 8½" 7½"
c/s

1¾" dia.
cotter-pin

1" dia.

1¾" dia. w.i.
suspension rod

6" × 2"
runner
beam

SECTION AT 'D'

4" × 3" × 3/32"
clamp plate

6½" × 2" runner

5" × 2" diagonal brace

plan view
looking down

A

B

E

2'-7"

21'-7"   8'-6" wide

hollow cast-iron column mounted on 3'3" sq. integral bed-plates
tapering from 2'6"dia. at base to 2'2½"dia. at head

11'-0" column height

13/16" dia. w.i.
hanger-rod

C

C

C

lug &
clamp-plate
for holding
runner-beam

ex 5" × 5" c.i.
cross-beam

1¾" dia. hex.
tension nut

D HANGER-ROD
& CROSS-BEAM
CONNECTIONS

lug & cotter

shaped
beam end

3/8" dia. bolt-holes
for decking planks

plan view
looking up

PLANS & SECTION
AT DETAIL 'D'

ft.   m

1

·25

2

·5

·75

3

1

4

slatted
wooden deck

diagonal braces

F

runner
beam

7'-1" c/s

6'-5" c/s

PIER, PYLON & DECKING DETAILS

PIER F
PROFILE

inches 0   6   12

mm   100   200   300

GDH.

St Devenick Bridge, Cults, Aberdeenshire

211

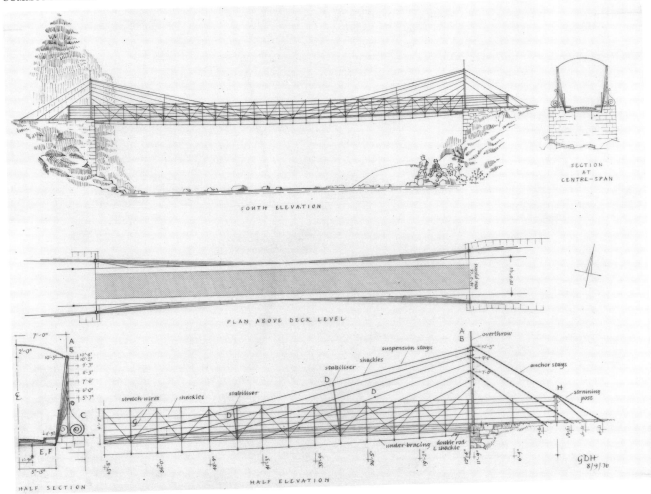

SOUTH ELEVATION

SECTION AT CENTRE-SPAN

PLAN ABOVE DECK LEVEL

HALF SECTION

HALF ELEVATION

A

B

Bridge, Haughs of Drimmie, Perthshire
A.   drawings
B.   view from SE

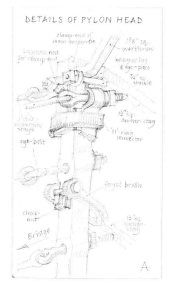
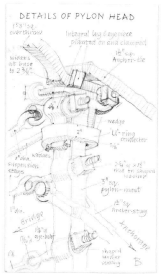
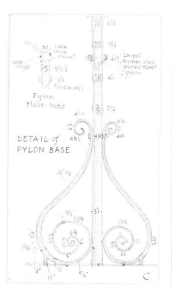
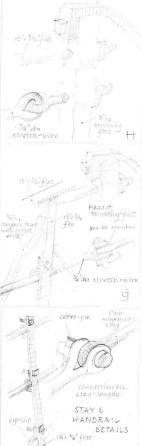

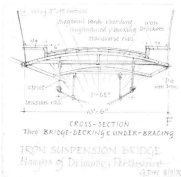
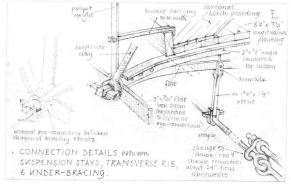

A

Bridge, Haughs of Drimmie, Perthshire
  A. sketch details
  B. underside

B

Bridge

NO 170502

Haughs of Drimmie, Perthshire
    Tayside, Perth and Kinross

● 1976

This attractive bridge, which serves Glenericht Lodge, crosses the River Ericht about 4·8 km N of Blairgowrie. Built in about 1830, it is one of a small group of wrought-iron-framed bridges of suspension type. It was probably designed by John Justice (Junior) of Dundee, and represents a large and modified version of John Justice's footbridge of 1824 at Kirkton of Glenisla, Angus (NO 213603).[35] The Drimmie bridge has a main clear span of 105 ft (32 m), the pylon-masts are 3 in (76 mm) square and 10 ft 3 in (3·13 m) high above stone abutments, and the wooden deck is 10 ft 6 in (3·20 m) wide overall.

The design is that of a complex 'basket' or multi-stayed suspension type. Each pair of pylons is held in position by three 1½ in-square (38 mm) anchor-stays, and suspended from them over the bridge are seven wrought-iron rod-stays with intermediate stabilisers, all secured to the pylons by bolts and bridle-pieces. The pylon-masts themselves have

188-9

213

B

Southerness Lighthouse,
Kirkcudbrightshire
   A.   view from sw
A   B.   light-chamber and balcony

213 (H,G)

213 (E,F)

213 B

scrolled ironwork at the bases and are inclined outwards towards the heads, where they are joined by curved segmental overthrows. The stretch-wires of the parapet handrails are held independently from straining-posts at the bridge approaches. The frame of the wooden deck comprises a series of transverse ribs, each made up of a cambered upper angle-member and a flat iron tie riveted together at the ends. Together with the eyed ends of the main suspension stays and alternate uprights of the handrails, they are secured by cotters to a continuous flat iron boom 3 in by 7/16 in (76 mm by 11 mm) in section. A system of underbracing, anchored into the abutments, reinforces the deck frame; it takes the form of a suspended 'cradle' or truss and comprises two 1 1/16 in-diameter (27 mm) suspension rods spaced 3 ft 6 in (1·07 m) apart and braced by short square-section struts notched into the transverse ribs above.

Lighthouse
Southerness, Kirkcudbrightshire
    Dumfries and Galloway, Nithsdale

NX 977542

● 1978, 1984

Originally built by Dumfries Town Council in 1748–9 and later heightened and altered, this square tower is the third most ancient and second oldest surviving purpose-built lighthouse in Scotland.[36] It was intended to serve as a guide to navigation in the difficult waters of the Nith Estuary and the inner Solway Firth, where there are treacherous sand-bars. The original beacon-tower was heightened in the 1780s, and was provided with an oil light and reflectors at about the time that its operation and maintenance were taken over by the Nith Navigation Commission upon its inception in 1811. It was further heightened and the light-system improved in 1842–3. Faced with increasing financial burdens, the Nith Navigation Commission was obliged to extinguish the light in 1867, but with the revival of water-borne trade in the late 19th century the lighthouse was restored and brought back into active use in 1894. The red sandstone upperworks of the tower date from this last period, and the brass frame of the last lantern used in the tower is mounted on a concrete plinth nearby. According to local information, the light was last operated in 1936. The tower stands on a low rubble-built platform on the tidal foreshore; it is square on plan, measuring at base 14 ft 6 in (4·42 m) over walls 2 ft 6 in (0·76 m) thick and in its final form stands to an overall height of more than 59 ft (18 m).

214

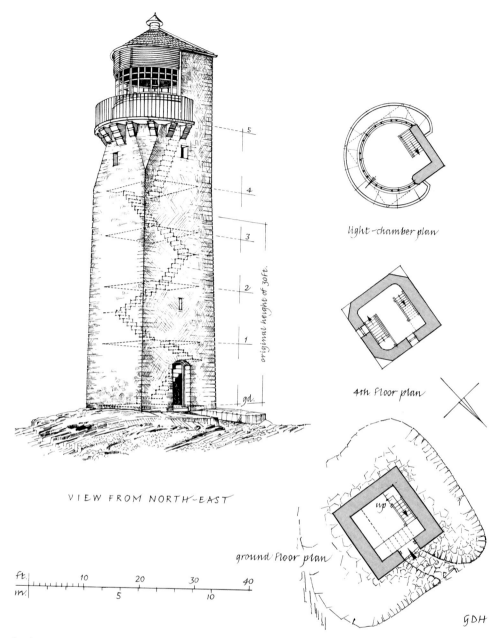

VIEW FROM NORTH-EAST

5

4

3

2

1

gd.

original height of 30ft.

light-chamber plan

4th floor plan

ground floor plan

up

GDH

ft. 10 20 30 40
m. 5 10

Southerness Lighthouse, Kirkcudbrightshire

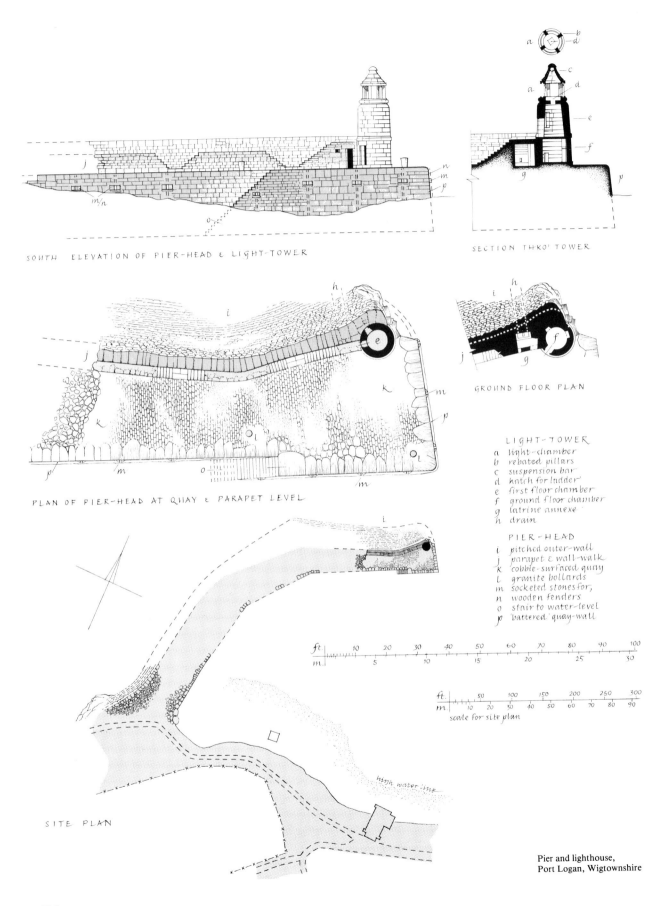

SOUTH ELEVATION OF PIER-HEAD & LIGHT-TOWER

SECTION THRO' TOWER

PLAN OF PIER-HEAD AT QUAY & PARAPET LEVEL

GROUND FLOOR PLAN

LIGHT-TOWER
a light-chamber
b rebated pillars
c suspension bar
d hatch for ladder
e first floor chamber
f ground floor chamber
g latrine annexe
h drain

PIER-HEAD
i pitched outer-wall
j parapet & wall-walk
k cobble-surfaced quay
l granite bollards
m socketed stones for,
n wooden fenders
o stair to water-level
p 'battered' quay-wall

SITE PLAN

high water line

| ft. | 10 | 20 | 30 | 40 | 50 | 60 | 70 | 80 | 90 | 100 |
| m. | | 5 | | 10 | | 15 | | 20 | | 25 | 30 |

| ft. | | 50 | 100 | 150 | 200 | 250 | 300 |
| m. | | 10 | 20 | 30 | 40 | 50 | 60 | 70 | 80 | 90 |

scale for site plan

Pier and lighthouse,
Port Logan, Wigtownshire

216

Pier and lighthouse, Port Logan, Wigtownshire

Pier and Lighthouse

Port Logan, Wigtownshire

　　　Dumfries and Galloway, Wigtown

NX 094405

●][1983

The ruins of this jetty extend in a broad arm some 185 m across the sw horn of Port Logan Bay, terminating at the seaward end in a more complete pier-head and small stone-built lighthouse tower. Efforts on the part of the McDouall proprietors to develop Port Nessock or Port Logan into a harbour were first recorded in 1682, but the existing remains correspond with the chief proposals made by John Rennie, engineer, in a report of 1813, and carried into effect between 1818 and 1820 largely at the expense of Colonel Andrew McDouall of Logan, who hoped thereby to benefit from the Irish cattle trade.[37]

The pier-head is protected by a pitched sea-wall rising to a parapet backed by a stepped wall-walk, and the inner quayside, which has a stair to water-level, has been faced with widely spaced wooden fenders clasped in position by socketed stones. This surviving portion is impressively constructed of coursed sandstone rubble masonry employing large stone blocks, and the slabbed and cobbled paving incorporates two granite bollards. The parapet terminates in a sturdy circular light-tower with a latrine annexe built under the adjacent forestair to the first-floor entry. The tower, which is ashlar built throughout, measures 11 ft 2 in (3·40 m) in overall diameter and 32 ft 2 in (9·80 m) in height. The turret has a stone-slabbed conical roof of concave profile carried on four plain square monolithic pillars, rebated presumably to receive a frame for glazed panels. An iron bar is fixed to the apex of the roof for holding the lamp, but otherwise there is no surviving evidence of the actual method of lighting. The light-chamber was evidently reached by a ladder from the first floor; the ground floor contains a small fireplace and a shelved recess.

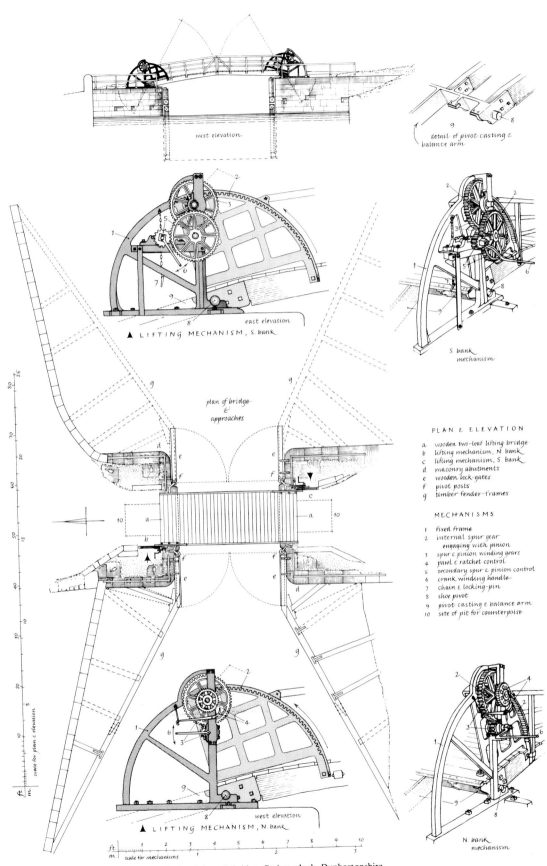

west elevation

detail of pivot casting & balance arm

LIFTING MECHANISM, S. bank

east elevation

S bank mechanism

plan of bridge & approaches

PLAN & ELEVATION

a   wooden two-leaf lifting bridge
b   lifting mechanism, N. bank
c   lifting mechanism, S. bank
d   masonry abutments
e   wooden lock-gates
f   pivot posts
g   timber fender-frames

MECHANISMS

1   fixed frame
2   internal spur gear
     engaging with pinion
3   spur & pinion winding gears
4   pawl & ratchet control
5   secondary spur & pinion control
6   crank winding handle
7   chain & locking-pin
8   shoe pivot
9   pivot casting & balance arm
10 site of pit for counterpoise

scale for plan & elevation

LIFTING MECHANISM, N. bank

scale for mechanisms

N bank mechanism

Forth and Clyde Canal; bascule bridge, Craigmarloch, Dunbartonshire

A

C

Forth and Clyde Canal;
bascule bridge, Craigmarloch, Dunbartonshire
  A, B. details of mechanism on s and n banks
  C.   view from w

B

Forth and Clyde Canal

1981–5

The oldest and longest of Scotland's major canals, the Forth and Clyde waterway linked Grangemouth in the east with Bowling in the west. It had a branch into Glasgow at Port Dundas, where it was joined to the Monkland Canal, and there were short side-cuts at Dalderse and Netherwood Lime Works. The section between Grangemouth and Stockingfield, the junction with the Glasgow branch, was completed between 1768 and 1775, but the western section to Bowling, and the final stage of the Port Dundas extension were not opened until 1790 and 1791 respectively. The canal was closed for navigation at the end of 1962.[38]

Nine of its 38¾ miles (14·48 km of 62·36 km) run through the former county of Stirlingshire, and a descriptive account of this stretch, prepared at a time when the canal was still in use, was included in the Commission's Stirlingshire *Inventory*.[39] Since the abandonment of the waterway, the threat of dilapidation or modernisation of canalside buildings and features has made further detailed recording even more necessary and urgent. Although modified with later decking and handrails, the bridge at Craigmarloch (NS 737773), for example, was until recently *218-19* one of the last surviving bridges on the canal to retain significant elements of its original design. It has been a two-part bascule bridge manually operated by spur gearing of slightly differing design on each bank, in conjunction with counterweights encased in pits within the abutments. Framed wooden fenders and gates flank the water-borne approaches to the narrow 21 ft-wide (6·40 m) opening.

The ruins of stables-blocks associated with the canal are *220 A,B* to be found also at Craigmarloch (NS 737775); like those at Shirva, Dunbartonshire (NS 691752), and elsewhere along the canal, these have had two-storeyed and hipped-roof main blocks with advanced and pedimented central bays. Their functionally handsome appearance echoes the more elegant treatment accorded the classical Canal Office of *220 C* c.1812 which stands, now dilapidated, on the North Speirs Wharf, Port Dundas (NS 588666).[40] By far the most impressive features, however, are the flight of five locks at Maryhill (NS 563690), with intervening oval basins, and the associated four-arched Kelvin aqueduct (NS 561689), all *221* built 1787–90 by Robert Whitworth.

B

A

WEST ELEVATION

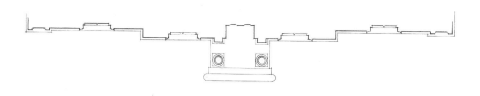

PLAN PROFILE

C

Forth and Clyde Canal;
stables, Cadder, Lanarkshire
A.   canal-side frontage
B.   interior
C.   offices, Port Dundas, Glasgow

A

B

Forth and Clyde Canal; Kelvin Aqueduct, Glasgow
    A.   view from SE
    B.   view from W showing locks and basins

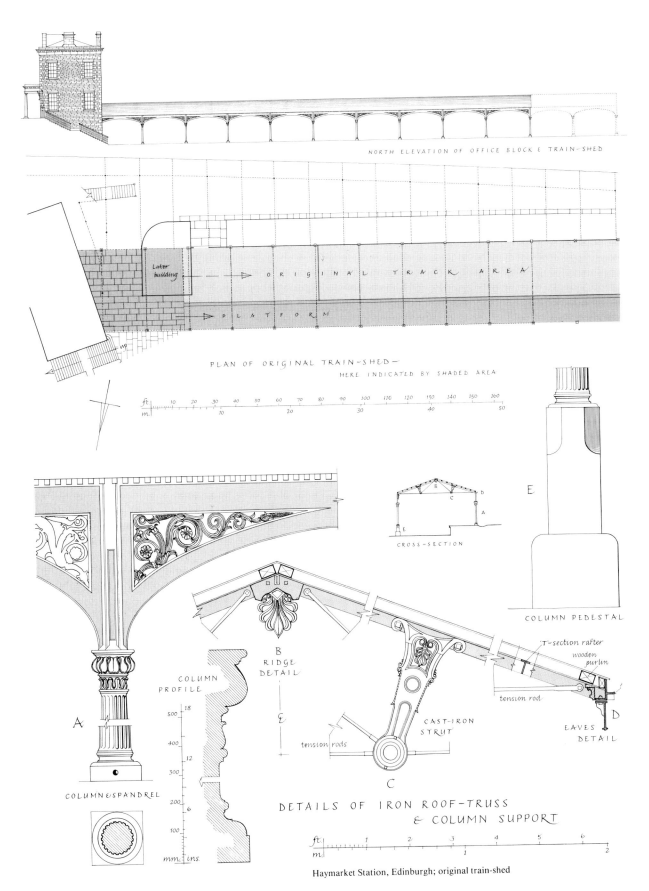

NORTH ELEVATION OF OFFICE BLOCK & TRAIN-SHED

Later building

ORIGINAL TRACK AREA

PLATFORM

up

PLAN OF ORIGINAL TRAIN-SHED —
HERE INDICATED BY SHADED AREA

ft 10 20 30 40 50 60 70 80 90 100 110 120 130 140 150 160
m. 10 20 30 40 50

CROSS-SECTION

COLUMN PEDESTAL

COLUMN & SPANDREL

A

COLUMN PROFILE

B RIDGE DETAIL

tension rods

CAST-IRON STRUT

C

'T'-section rafter
wooden purlin

tension rod

EAVES DETAIL

D

500 18
400 12
300
200 6
100
mm. ins.

DETAILS OF IRON ROOF-TRUSS
& COLUMN SUPPORT

ft 1 2 3 4 5 6
m. 1 2

Haymarket Station, Edinburgh; original train-shed

222

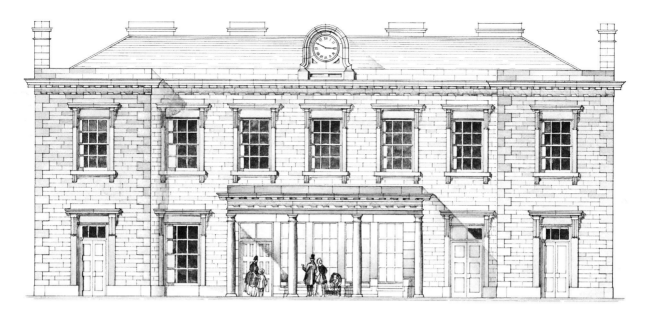

E A S T   E L E V A T I O N

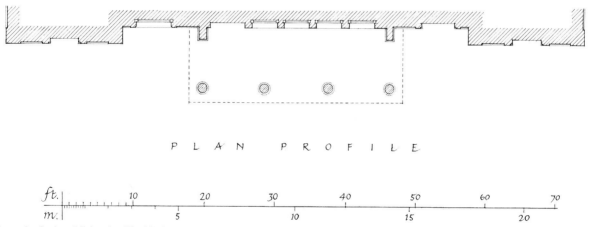

P L A N   P R O F I L E

Haymarket Station, Edinburgh; office-block

Railway Station   NT 239731
Haymarket, Edinburgh
        Lothian, City of Edinburgh   ●][1967, 1980

Haymarket Station was originally planned and built between 1840 and 1842 as the eastern terminus of the Edinburgh and Glasgow Railway Company, one of the principal constituents of the later North British Railway. The designer was John Miller, engineer. The frontal office-block of the present station, and immediately to the w a train-shed which has since been removed to the preserved railway at Bo'ness, represent all that is left of the original terminal station. In 1846 the railway line was extended eastwards to Waverley Station, and Haymarket

Haymarket Station, Edinburgh;
roof structure of original train-shed

was subsequently converted into a four-platform through-station with two sets of double tracks.

The remains of the early train-shed consisted of ten surviving bays of an elegant arcaded and canopied structure, originally twelve bays and 239 ft (72·85 m) in overall length. The bays were formed with fluted cast-iron columns and elliptical arches with decorated spandrels; the columns were hollow, serving as rainwater conductors, and on the s side of the canopy, where there was no platform, they were set on high stone pedestals. The tie-rods of the roof-structure were secured by ornate struts; the apex of each truss incorporates a pendant anthemion leaf, and on the s side the ends rest on carved scrolled brackets.

The office block has a classical 82 ft 3 in-long (25·07 m) and two-storeyed frontage to the station forecourt. It is hip-roofed and its seven bays incorporate slightly advanced end-pavilions and a central tetrastyle portico, all faced in yellowish sandstone ashlar. The openings are emphasised by broad offset margins with scrolled brackets and consoles, and a large circular clock occupies a prominent central position in the block parapet above a mutuled cornice. The main floors are set above a basement at the platform level; there is still an original external stair at the N end, but the interior has been remodelled and modernised.

St Enoch Railway Station   NS 589649
Glasgow
    Strathclyde, City of Glasgow   # 1975

St Enoch Station was the principal terminus of the Glasgow and South Western Railway Company, which operated Anglo-Scottish services jointly with the Midland Railway. The station was opened for traffic in October 1876, and the five-storeyed hotel facing St Enoch Square was completed in July 1879, evidently incorporating the earliest electric lighting-system in Glasgow.[41] The commercial success of the station led to the construction of six additional platforms between 1898 and 1902, bringing up the total number to twelve. The station was closed in 1966, the hotel in 1974, and the entire complex has since been demolished.

The special distinction of the train-shed was its pair of impressive arched overall roofs. The roof of the original (northern) shed was of five-centred elliptical form and of wrought-iron and steel construction. It had a clear span of about 204 ft (62·2 m), a height of 83 ft (25·30 m), and a length of about 525 ft (160 m) divided up by latticed arch-ribs into sixteen bays. The arch-ribs bore the date 1877 (when the station was already in operation) and the maker's name, Messrs Andrew Handyside & Co. Ltd. of Derby and London, which reflected the interest and influence of the Midland Railway in a design which would serve as a counterpart to that of their own larger and more celebrated terminal station at London St Pancras. The design engineers for St Enoch were John Fowler and James F Blair. The roof over the southern extension was of similar but smaller arched form, being 293 ft 7 in (89·48 m) long, 65 ft (19·81 m) high, and having an internal clear span of 143 ft (43·60 m). Beyond the sheds, the platforms were covered with glazed awnings.

224

A

B

St Enoch Station, Glasgow
  A.   train-sheds from SE
  B.   detail of roof-cresting
  C.   interior of N train-shed

C

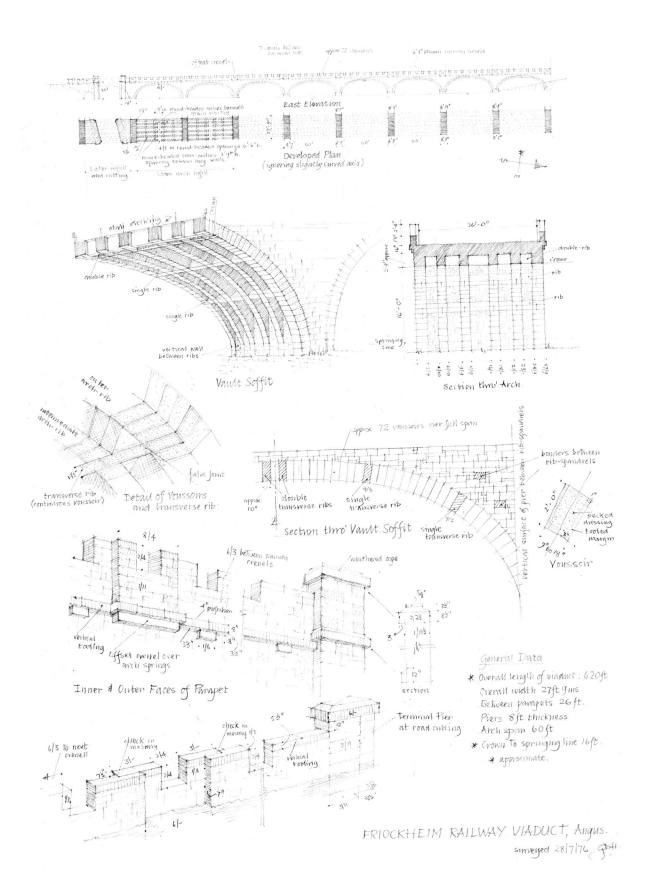

East Elevation

Developed Plan
(ignoring slightly curved axis)

Vault Soffit

Section thro' Arch

Detail of Voussoirs
and transverse rib

Section thro' Vault Soffit

Voussoir

Inner & Outer Faces of Parapet

Terminal Pier
at road cutting

General Data

* Overall length of viaduct : 620ft
  Overall width 27ft 9ins
  Between parapets 26ft.
  Piers 8ft thickness
  Arch span 60ft.
* Crown to springing line 16ft.
  * approximate.

FRIOCKHEIM RAILWAY VIADUCT, Angus.
surveyed 28/7/76.

Railway viaduct, Friockheim, Angus;
aerial view from NW

Railway Viaduct NO 588497
Friockheim, Angus
    Tayside, Angus # 1976

Built in about 1840 for the Arbroath and Forfar Railway, which was later absorbed by the Caledonian Railway, this viaduct stands on the eastern side of what was formerly a triangular junction with the Caledonian main line to Aberdeen and formed part of the earliest railway link between Arbroath and Montrose. This line was rendered obsolete when the North British Railway constructed a direct coastal route in the 1880s, and the viaduct had ceased to be used for railway traffic before 1914.

Constructed on a slightly curved N-S axis over the Lunan Water and its tributaries at the western end of Friockheim village, the viaduct has an overall length of about 620 ft (189 m) and a width of 27 ft 9 in (8·46 m). It has a battlemented parapet and a slabstone deck carried by eight out of an original series of nine ribbed elliptical arches of 60 ft (18·29 m) spans. The soffit of each arch has six ribs bonded by six transverse ribs, two of which occur at each crown. At the southern end there are two infilled blind arches and a road-cutting, all subsequently modified in association with a girder bridge. The masonry throughout is of local red sandstone with tooled or pecked ashlar dressings and snecked rubble walling which approaches ashlar standards in its quality of execution and jointing.

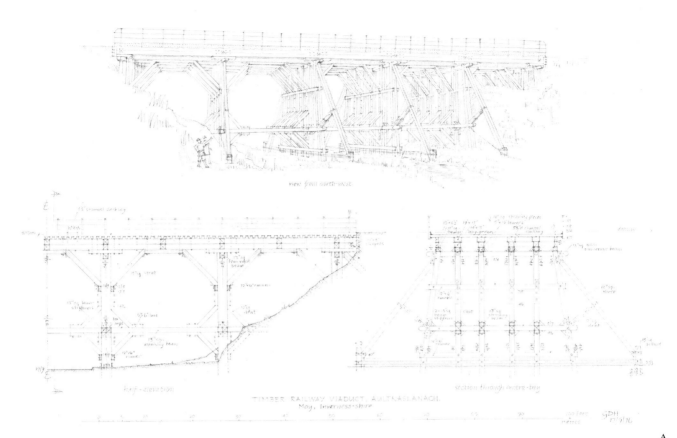

view from north-west

TIMBER RAILWAY VIADUCT, AULTNASLANACH,
Moy, Inverness-shire

half-elevation

section through centre-bay

A

B

Railway viaduct,
Aultnaslanach, Moy,
Inverness-shire
   A.   pencil drawings
   B.   detail of structural framework

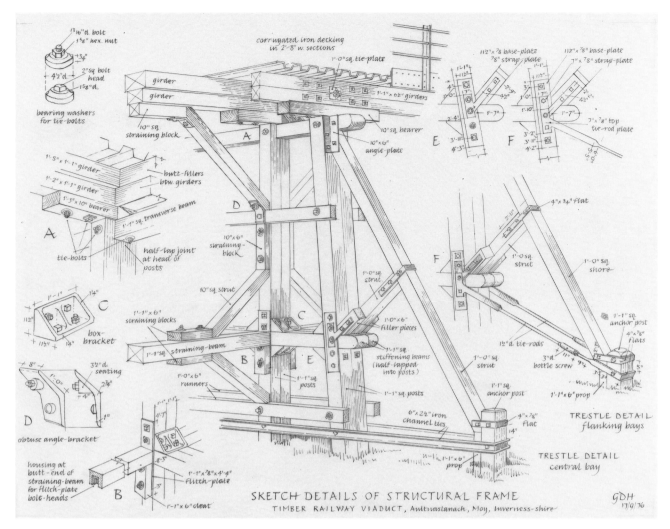

Railway viaduct,
Aultnaslanach, Moy,
Inverness-shire
  A. pencil drawings
  B. detail of structural framework

Railway Viaduct   NH 760349
Aultnaslanach, Moy, Inverness-shire
      Highland, Inverness   ● 1976

This wooden trestle bridge carries the single-track Avie-
more-Inverness railway line across the Allt Creag Bheithen
just N of the former station at Moy. This line was opened by
the Highland Railway Company in 1897, and the bridge is
now the only surviving structure of its type on a main-line
railway in Scotland, possibly in Britain.[42]

The bridge is 132 ft 7 in (40·41 m) in length by 28 ft 6 in
(8·69 m) in width with raking shores spreading the width to
60 ft (18·29 m) overall. There are five spans, varying
between 24 ft 4 in (7·42 m) and 25 ft 1 in (7·65 m) in length

centre to centre, and the decking stands 27 ft 9 in (8·46 m)
above the normal water-line of the burn.

Compared with the elaborate structures of this kind
erected by I K Brunel in England, and those on North
American railroads,[43] this bridge is of modest trestle frame
and multiple prop-and-beam construction, employing
heavy pitch-pine baulks with iron-clad joints. The sectional
corrugated-iron deck is carried on a series of six longitudinal girders, each made up of coupled baulks mounted
one on top of the other. There are six trestle bents, the two
end ones being set within the embankments. Each of the
four central frames is composed of six upright posts driven
into the ground like piles and joined together by runners,
beam-stiffeners and, at the head, a transverse beam. The
main structural components are braced laterally by raking
shores, and longitudinally by an elaborate system of raking
struts associated with the main girders and a lower
straining-beam.

A

B

Aircraft hangars, Montrose Airfield, Angus
  A.   side-door hangars (1913)
  B.   roof-truss detail

Aircraft Hangars
Montrose Airfield
    Tayside, Angus

NO 719595

][1980

The former Montrose airfield, which occupies a 38-acre (15·4 ha) site extending along the coastline immediately N of the town, was established in 1913, when it became the permanent base of Nos. 1 and 2 Flights of the Royal Flying Corps, in preference to the earlier one at Dysart because of its better landing-facilities. Between 1913 and 1919 it served primarily as a training base, though there was an attached War Flight, whose combat duties were confined to Zeppelin-fighting. Wartime aircraft known to have been in service there included the early Maurice Farman (MF7 and 11) and BE2, and the later Bristol Fighter (F2B) and Sopwith Camel.[44] Initially, in late 1913, three side-door hangars, originally designed for Dysart, were erected in a crescent-shaped layout facing eastwards at the s end of the airfield to replace temporary ones of canvas and wooden portable construction. Then in 1917 three larger hangars were built on a N-s axis at the far end of the site. After the

230 A

war the airfield was abandoned in favour of Leuchars, but in the shadow of the Second World War it was reopened, and during the period 1936–1945 several more hangars were built with standard tubular metal portal-frames. One of these, and the central 1917 hangar, were destroyed by enemy action in 1940.

The three 1913 hangars each measure 211 ft 6 in (64·47 m) by 66 ft 9 in (20·35 m) overall, over a clear roof span, and with a headroom of 16 ft (4·88 m), they are framed of timber in twenty-two closely spaced bays and clad externally with corrugated iron sheeting. The impressive range of roof trusses are of fairly conventional design, but utilise iron rods for the vertical tension members and strap reinforcement at the principal joints. Overall stiffening depends on a central row of longitudinal cross-braces supplemented by diagonal wall-ties across the angles of the building and the three central bays. The wide-span access openings, originally accommodating four timber-framed sliding-doors, are bridged by a triangulated roof at right angles to the main one. An original internal feature is the staggered row of iron rings, one strapped beneath alternate tie-beams, presumably for suspending block-and-tackle equipment.

The two surviving 1917 hangars are orthodox prefabricated structures, built on a series of timber-framed bays and

230 B

230 C

232

C

Aircraft hangars, Montrose Airfield, Angus; end-door hangar (1917)

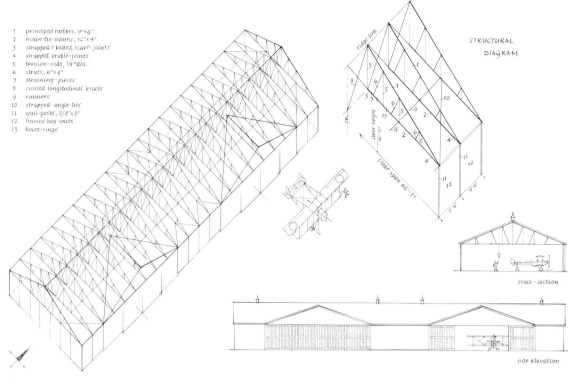

1 principal rafters, 9"×4"
2 main tie-beams, 12"×4"
3 strapped & bolted scarf-joints
4 strapped bridle-joints
5 tension-rods, 7/8"dia.
6 struts, 6"×4"
7 straining-pieces
8 crossed longitudinal braces
9 runners
10 strapped angle-ties
11 wall-posts, 2/8"×3"
12 framed bay-units
13 hoist-rings

STRUCTURAL
DIAGRAM

ridge line

clear height 10'-0"

clear span 65'-3"

cross-section

side elevation

1913 SIDE-DOOR HANGAR

1 built-up principals of 3/8"×2"
2 main-ties, 2/9"×1½"+6" spacers
3 strapped toe-joints
4 bolted scarf-joints
5 tension-rods, 7/8"dia.
6 struts, of 3/5½"×2"
7 strap-joints
8 crossed longitudinal braces
9 runners of 2/7"×2"
10 wall-struts, 2/9"×2"
11 wall-posts of 3/9"×3"
12 wall-props, 2/9"×2"+spacer
13 framed bay-units
14 trestle door-housing

STRUCTURAL
DIAGRAM

ridge line

clear height 19'-6"

clear span 80'-0"

end-elevation

side-elevation

1917 END-DOOR HANGAR

ft 10 20 30 40 50 60 70 80 90 100 110 120 130 140 150 160 170 180 190 200
m.   10   20   30   40   50   60

GDH

Aircraft hangars, Montrose Airfield, Angus

231

Aircraft hangars,
Montrose Airfield, Angus
A.   end-door hangar
B.   detail of door buffer

distinguished externally by their shallow rounded roofs, propped side-walls and massive wooden end-doors flanked by their trestle housings. The roofs were covered with bituminous felt laid on diagonal boarding; the sides, of horizontal weatherboarding, were similarly felted, but may originally have been left exposed and treated with pitch. They measured 170 ft (51·82 m) in length by 80 ft (24·38 m) in width over a clear roof span, and with headroom of 18 ft (5·49 m). The propped wall-frames and roof-trusses were constructed of built-up timber sections, lapped and bound together at the principal joints by a combination of iron bolts, straps and spacer-pieces. The trusses—strictly of polygonal profile—were braced with a system of raking struts and vertical tension rods, and the roof structure as a whole was stiffened by two rows of longitudinal wind-braces and the provision of diagonal bracing over the purlins.[45*]

The hangars were evidently of a standard type—dubbed 'black hangars' among flying personnel because of their outward appearance—once common at RFC stations situated elsewhere in the United Kingdom at, for example, Tadcaster, Beverley and Yatesbury.

Flying-boat Hangar
NO 431309

Stannergate, Dundee
Tayside, City of Dundee
1982

The former First World War seaplane base, situated at Stannergate just E of Dundee, was one of several established by the Royal Naval Air Service along the E coast of Britain for conducting reconnaissance and anti-submarine operations. Occupying a 25-acre (10·1 ha) site on the banks of the River Tay, the base was initially equipped with two hangars and a slipway, suitable for serving seaplanes such as the Short 184. The hangars were possibly transferred from an earlier base at Port Laing on the River Forth (NT 134811). By April 1918 a third hangar of more substantial dimensions had been erected, with adjacent slipway, along the E side of the site in order to house the larger Curtiss H-12 and Felixstowe F2A flying-boats. This hangar, which can be identified as the tall building in the middle background axial with the slipway, is now all that remains of the original complex.

A

B

Flying-boat hangar,
Stannergate, Dundee, Angus
  A.   seaplane base, *c.* 1918
  B.   exterior from NE

Classified as an F-type hangar—of which two later examples built in the 1920s also remain in Scotland at Evanton, Ross and Cromarty, and West Freugh, Wigtownshire,[46]—it has a structural frame of all-metal construction set out on a 17 ft (5·18 m) regular grid. The main area measures 204 ft (62·18 m) in length by 104 ft (31·70 m) over a clear roof span, with headroom ('ceiling') of 27 ft (8·23 m). There is, in addition, a single-storeyed range which extends along the w side. The trusses are of lattice-style construction, and the principal wall-members—cast with the maker's name 'THE FRODINGHAM IRON & STEEL CO LTD, ENGLAND'—are made up of U-channel sections. Externally, the end-walls are reinforced with raking members, but the main architectural feature of the building is the E wall, which was capable of being opened in sections over its entire length. Framed wheeled doors, each 51 ft (15·55 m) in width, were manually operated by a crank-and-chain drive. The minimum of fixed supports were used to carry the guide-rails and eaves-girder; these supports comprised latticed stanchions at each end and raking frames at the midpoints, where the girder spanning the double-width central opening is deeper and projects above the eaves-line. Both the roof and walls were clad with corrugated asbestos sheeting of the 'Trafford Tile' pattern, then a relatively new material.[47]

234 A

233 B

234 C,D

234 B

233

A

B

C

D

Flying-boat hangar,
Stannergate, Dundee,
Angus
  A. interior
  B. midpoint and corner
       stanchions
  C, D. details of sliding
         door mechanism

Airship sheds, Caldale, Orkney, *c.* 1916

Airship Stations

Between 1915 and 1916, as part of a strategic network defending Britain's coastline, Royal Naval airship stations were established in Scotland: on the west coast at Luce Bay, Wigtownshire (NX *c.*117597); and along the more vulnerable east coast at Caldale, Orkney (HY *c.*413104), Longside, Aberdeenshire (NK *c.*038475), and East Fortune, East Lothian (NT *c.*560795).

Caldale and Luce Bay stations were each equipped with three or four 'Sea Scout' non-rigid airships and a number of kite balloons designed to be towed behind ships for spotting enemy movements. Sheds[48*] for housing these smaller craft varied in size, the two at Caldale measuring 220 ft (67·06 m) by 109 ft (33·22 m) by 50 ft (15·24 m) high and 160 ft (48·77 m) by 70 ft (21·34 m) by 46 ft (14·02 m) high, and the one at Luce Bay 302 ft (92·05 m) by 70 ft (21·34 m) by 50 ft (15·24 m) high. The Caldale sheds were of timber skeleton construction, clad with painted corrugated iron. The principal stations of Longside and East Fortune were planned primarily to accommodate the larger 'Coastal' and 'North Sea' types of non-rigid as well as the embryo of Britain's proposed rigid fleet. Accommodation at each station comprised a rigid-airship shed, flanked by a smaller shed for Coastals on each side; these last were stepped forward to afford a sheltered area in front of the rigid shed, and the resultant formation was aligned with its long axis in the direction of the prevailing winds. Typical dimensions for a Coastal shed were 320 ft (97·54 m) by 120 ft (36·58 m) by 80 ft (24·38 m), while the rigid sheds extended in length to as much as 700 ft (213·36 m) and 110 ft (33·53 m) in clear height. The width of the Longside shed, however, was 150 ft 6 in (45·87 m), enough to house two of the earlier 23-class rigids, as compared with 180 ft (54·86 m) at East Fortune, which could hold two of the larger 33-class ships.[49*] After

July 1917 the East Fortune shed was also used as the main base for housing the new North Sea type of non-rigid.

Intimately connected with the sheds was the hazardous business of manoeuvring the ships through the end-doorways, especially in windy conditions. Designed to allow the maximum dimensional clearance, the enormous four-leaf sliding-doors ran on a wheeled double track and were operated by winch or capstan. To further assist with ground-handling, one or more giant windscreens were used in the form of walled extensions to protect the ship when walking it to and from the shed entrance—an operation which required as many as 500 men. Ranging in size from 160 ft (48·77 m) by 40 ft (12·19 m) high to 360 ft (109·73 m) by 70 ft (21·34 m), they were usually of all-metal construction, strengthened by bracing-members and faced with a latticed surface in order to break up the force of cross-winds.

The rigid-airship sheds were of all-steel construction covered with corrugated iron sheeting painted in camouflage colours and glazed with several rows of anti-actinic glass. Designed to enclose a vast, clear space by the most economical means, structurally they had to be strong enough to resist severe wind-pressures and to allow a ship to be slung from the roof-frames when it was deflated or lacking buoyancy. Basically, the framework consisted of a series of transverse frames, spaced at about 28 ft (8·53 m) centres, joined by longitudinal members. The transverse frames were usually braced with raking struts which, unlike the smaller aeroplane hangars of the time, were covered externally to form smooth sloping wall-surfaces and side-bays or annexes within. To judge from contemporary photographs, the rigid shed at East Fortune was similar, if not identical, to the 'No. 2 shed' at Pulham, Norfolk, and accordingly an impression of its structural design may be got from the reconstruction drawing. Such a shed required about 3,000 tons (3,048 tonnes) of steel, the main supports and stiffening members being of coupled channel-section, and the successive bays fabricated in a standard range of triangulated units.

A

B

Airship stations
A. East Fortune,
    East Lothian;
    aerial view from
    SE, c. 1918
B. Longside,
    Aberdeenshire;
    aerial view from
    E, c. 1917

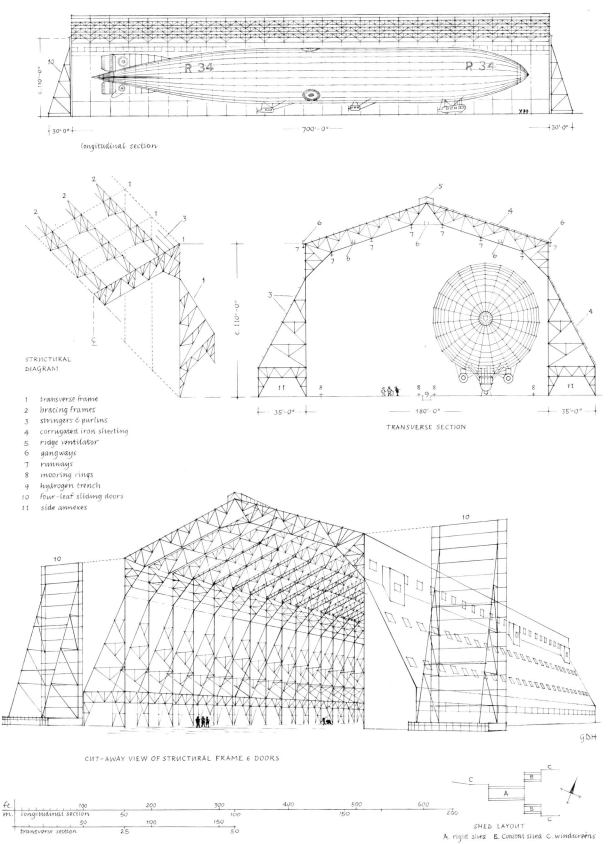

longitudinal section

STRUCTURAL
DIAGRAM

c. 110'-0"

5

6   4
6   7   7   6
7   7
3   4

11   8   8 9 8   11

35'-0"   180'-0"   35'-0"

TRANSVERSE SECTION

1   transverse frame
2   bracing frames
3   stringers & purlins
4   corrugated iron sheeting
5   ridge ventilator
6   gangways
7   runways
8   mooring rings
9   hydrogen trench
10 four-leaf sliding doors
11 side annexes

10   10

GDH

CUT-AWAY VIEW OF STRUCTURAL FRAME & DOORS

ft.   100   200   300   400   500   600
m.   longitudinal section   50   100   150   200
                    50   100   150
          transverse section   25   50

SHED LAYOUT
A. rigid shed   B. coastal shed   C. windscreens

Rigid airship shed, formerly at East Fortune, East Lothian

237

S

NOTES

n.1   E.g. *Inventory of Roxburghshire,* **2,** Appendix A, pp. 463–74; *Inventory of Stirlingshire,* **1,** Nos. 124–5; *Inventory of Peeblesshire,* **2,** Nos. 634–5; *Inventory of Lanarkshire,* Nos. 262–6. See Maxwell, G S, 'The evidence from the Roman period', in Fenton, A and Stell, G P (eds.), *Loads and Roads in Scotland and Beyond* (1984), 22–48.

n.2   E.g. *Inventory of Roxburghshire,* **1,** pp. 50–1, Nos. 116–23, 180–2, 264–6, 293, 376–83, 489–93; **2,** Nos. 616–19, 757–66, 831–4, 885–8, 890–3, 1015–21, 1069–70, and pp. 474–9 (Appendices B and C); *Inventory of Selkirkshire,* pp. 27–8, Nos. 92–117; *Inventory of Peeblesshire,* **1,** pp. 47–8; **2,** Nos. 634–53; *Inventory of Stirlingshire,* **1,** pp. 52–4; **2,** Nos. 508–9, 511–31; *Inventory of Argyll,* **2,** p. 4. See also Graham, A, *PSAS,* **83,** (1948–9), 198–206; ibid., **93** (1959–60), 217–35; *HBNC,* **35** (1959–61), 288–300; *PSAS,* **96** (1962–3), 318–47.

n.3   E.g. *Inventory of Argyll,* **4,** No. 4, pp. 142–3. See also *Post-Medieval Archaeology,* **9** (1975), 137–63.

n.4   For bridges substantially of pre-1707 date, see, e.g., *Inventory of Kirkcudbrightshire,* Nos. 74 (pp. 54–5), 375, 399, 495; *Inventory of Berwickshire,* revised edition, Nos. 68, 160, 258 (p. 132); *Inventory of Dumfriesshire,* No. 131; *Inventory of East Lothian,* Nos. 75–6, 86, 140, 151; *Inventory of Midlothian and West Lothian,* Nos. 44, 120, 140 (p. 107), 188–9, 252, 359; *Inventory of Fife, Kinross-shire and Clackmannanshire,* Nos. 102, 178, 369, 389, 405, 416–17, 470, 559, 590–1, 614; *Inventory of Orkney and Shetland,* **2,** Nos. 121–2; *Inventory of Roxburghshire,* **1,** No. 432; **2,** Nos. 567 (pp. 266, 269), 593; *Inventory of Stirlingshire,* **2,** No. 455; *Inventory of Peeblesshire,* **2,** Nos. 628, 630.

n.5   E.g. *Inventory of Stirlingshire,* **2,** No. 510; *Inventory of Argyll,* **2,** Nos. 371–2. See also Graham, A, *PSAS,* **97** (1963–4), 226–36; and for a selection of 18th- and 19th-century bridges: *Inventory of Roxburghshire,* **1,** Nos. 6, 519–20; **2,** Nos. 584, 787; *Inventory of Selkirkshire,* Nos. 68–74; *Inventory of Stirlingshire,* **2,** Nos. 452–4, 456–70; *Inventory of Peeblesshire,* **2,** Nos. 627, 629, 631–3; *Inventory of Argyll,* **1,** Nos. 353–6; **2,** Nos. 368–70; **3,** Nos. 375–6, 389–90; **5,** Nos. 430, 432.

n.6   E.g. tollhouses, *Inventory of Stirlingshire,* **2,** No. 383; *Inventory of Peeblesshire,* **2,** No. 653. For related work on the A9, see Curtis, G R, *PSAS,* **110** (1978–80), 475–96.

n.7   E.g. *Inventory of Roxburghshire,* **2,** No. 593; *Inventory of Stirlingshire,* **2,** No. 477. See also Stell, G P, *SAF,* **13** (forthcoming).

n.8   *Inventory of Argyll,* **5,** No. 432. Cf. Hume, J R, *Industrial Archaeology Review,* **2** (1977), 290–9 at 290.

n.9   The cast-iron bridge over the River Devon at Cambus (NS 853940), at one time threatened and now restored, has been ascribed to the mid-19th century by Hume, op. cit., 296.

n.10   Hume, J R, *SAF,* **8** (1977), 91–105.

n.11   For harbours and jetties, see, e.g., *Inventory of Stirlingshire,* **1,** p. 4; **2,** No. 557; *Inventory of Argyll,* **1,** p. 3, Nos. 318, 334; **2,** Nos. 298, 310 (p. 251), 348, 350, 355–6, 362 (p. 384); **3,** Nos. 361, 379, 384; **5,** Nos. 408, 415, 434, 437–8, 443, and NMRS records of Blackpots, Portmahomack, Dunoon Pier, etc. For boat-landings, anchorages and later boat-houses, see, e.g., *Inventory of Argyll,* **1,** No. 314 (p. 178); **2,** Nos. 290 (p. 216), 293 (pp. 231–2), 310 (p. 251), 317, 364; **3,** Nos. 333 (pp. 176–7), 340 (p. 202), 346 (p. 226); **4,** pp. 36, 142; **5,** Nos. 304–5, 310, 402 (pp. 265–4), 403 (p. 272), 404 (p. 275), and discussion in Stell, G P, *SAF,* **13** (forthcoming).

n.12   *Inventory of Wigtownshire,* No. 411; *Inventory of Berwickshire,* revised edition, No. 45.

n.13   *Inventory of Fife, Kinross-shire and Clackmannanshire,* No. 42.

n.14   *Inventory of Argyll,* **1,** No. 349.

n.15   *Inventory of Argyll,* **3,** Nos. 374, 391; **5,** No. 441. See also ibid., Nos. 439, 442, and *Inventory of Argyll,* **2,** No. 357.

n.16   *Inventory of Argyll,* **3,** Nos. 382 and 379 (quarry on Mull).

n.17   Lindsay, J, *The Canals of Scotland* (1968), 13–14; Hume, *Ind Archaeol Scotland,* **1,** (1976), 32–3.

n.18   Only about one-third of the Caledonian Canal's total watercourse of 60 miles (96·56 km) consists of canal cuttings.

n.19   *Inventory of Stirlingshire,* **2,** Nos. 552–3.

n.20   Ibid., No. 474.

n.21   *Inventory of Argyll,* **1,** No. 347. See also Graham, A, *PSAS,* **100** (1967–8), 170–8.

n.22   Lindsay, op. cit., 142–77; Hume, *Ind Archaeol Scotland,* **2** (1977), 202.

n.23   Lindsay, op. cit., 113–41.

n.24   *Inventory of Stirlingshire,* **2,** No. 560.

n.25   Ibid., No. 559.

n.26   Ibid., Nos. 472, 475–6. See also Nos. 471 and 473.

n.27   For the railway that ran northwards from the adjacent Canal Street Station, see Graham, A, *Book of the Old Edinburgh Club,* **33,** part 3 (1972), 159–64.

n.28   Johnston, C and Hume, J R, *Glasgow Stations* (1979), 75–91. For Glasgow Central Station (1879, extended 1906), with its grand concourse designed by Donald Mathieson as part of the later extensions, see ibid., 28–49 at 29. See above, 198A.

n.29   For British airship development, see Sinclair, J A, *Airships in Peace and War* (1934); Higham, R, *The British Rigid Airship, 1908–1931* (1961); and Hartcup, G, *The Achievement of the Airship* (1974).

n.30   Hay, G D and Stell, G P, 'Old bridge, Bridge of Earn, Perthshire', in Fenton, A and Stell, G P (eds.), *Loads and Roads in Scotland and Beyond* (1984), 92–104.

n.31   Buchanan, R A and Jones, S K, *Industrial Archaeology Review,* **4,** part 4 (1980), 214–25.

n.32   Inscribed panel on bridge; *NSA,* **11** (Kincardineshire), 184–5; Henderson, J A, *History of the Parish of Banchory-Devenick* (1890), 56–7, 277–9. The cost of the bridge was about £1,400, and Morison bequeathed a sum 'to maintain and uphold it in time coming'.

n.33   Hume, *Ind Archaeol Scotland,* **2** (1977), 70–1, 87, 112; *SAF,* **8** (1977), 95, 102.

n.34   Cf. *NSA,* **11** (Kincardineshire), 184–5.

n.35   Hume, *Ind Archaeol Scotland,* **2** (1977), 70, 258; *SAF,* **8** (1977), 95–8, 103.

n.36   Munro, R W, *Scottish Lighthouses* (1979), 42–3; Stell, G P, *TDGAS,* 3rd series, **59** (forthcoming).

n.37   Graham, A, *TDGAS,* 3rd series, **54** (1979), 39–74 at 53–6; Donnachie, I, *Industrial Archaeology of Galloway* (1971), 180–1, 238.

n.38   Lindsay, J, *The Canals of Scotland* (1968), 15–51, 212–13.

n.39   *Inventory of Stirlingshire,* **2,** No. 552.

n.40   Hume, J R, *Industrial Archaeology of Glasgow* (1974), 167.

n.41   Hume, *Ind Archaeol Scotland,* **2** (1977), 215, 139; Johnston, C and Hume, J R, *Glasgow Stations* (1979), 50–74.

n.42   Hume, *Ind Archaeol Scotland,* **2** (1977), 211.

n.43   Booth, L G, in Pugsley, A (ed.), *The Works of Isambard Kingdom Brunel* (1976), 107–35; e.g. Foster, W C, *A Treatise on Wooden Trestle Bridges* (1913).

n.44   Munson, K, *Aircraft of World War I* (edition of 1977).

n.45   Twelve trusses of an earlier hangar, possibly from Edzell airfield, have been reused to cover a store at 5 Hill Place, Montrose (NO 713574).

n.46   Information from Mr Ian Shaw, Airfield Research Group.

n.47   Hudson, K, *Building Materials* (1972), 84–5.

n.48   Dimensional and technical data of the airship sheds derived from the *Quarterly Survey of the Stations of the RAF,* part 5 (Marine), 1918. For Caldale, see an auction notice published in the *Orkney Herald,* 19 May 1920. The three main types of non-rigid airship were: the 'Sea Scout', ranging in size and capacity from 144 ft (43·89 m) in length by 28 ft (8·53 m) in maximum diameter by 65,000 cu ft (1,840·6 cu m), to 165 ft (50·29 m) by 49 ft (14·94 m) by 100,000 cu ft (2,831·7 cu m); the 'Coastal', 196 ft (59·74 m) by 52 ft (15·85 m) by 170,000 cu ft (4,813·9 cu m), to 218 ft (66·45 m) by 49 ft 3 in (15·01 m) by 210,000 cu ft (5,946·6 cu m); and the 'North Sea', 262 ft (79·86 m) by 56 ft 9 in (17·30 m) by 360,000 cu ft (10,194·1 cu m).

n.49   Dimensional data for the rigid airships based at East Fortune: R29 (23X class), 539 ft (164·29 m) by 53 ft (16·15 m) in maximum diameter by 990,600 cu ft (28,050·8 cu m); and R34 (33 class), 643 ft (195·99 m) by 78 ft 9 in (24·0 m) by 1,950,000 cu ft (55,218·2 cu m).

GLOSSARY

Air pump. In a steam-engine, a reciprocating pump designed to draw water and air from a condenser chamber.

Ashlar. In masonry, stonework dressed to a smooth or rusticated surface, carefully squared and finely jointed, usually in level courses.

Bascule bridge. A balance or counterpoise bridge which can be rotated upwards about axes at one or both ends.

Batter. An inward-sloping wall-face.

Bedstone. In milling, the lower fixed stone of a pair of millstones.

Bending moment. The total bending effect caused by external loads at any section of a beam.

Bent. In civil engineering, a self-supporting transverse frame.

Blackband ironstone. An iron ore containing coal used as fuel in hot-blast furnaces.

Boom. In bridge and roof construction, the top or bottom horizontal member of a built-up girder or truss.

Boxed section. In iron-framed buildings, a beam or stanchion of I-section strengthened by cross-ribs or diaphragms.

Breast-shot. Of a water-wheel in which the water is directed below (low breast-shot) or above (high breast-shot) the horizontal centre-line of the wheel, causing it to turn in a reverse direction.

Bridge tree. In milling-machinery, the hinged beam supporting the thrust bearing of the runner-stone spindle.

Bridging-box. In milling-machinery, the seating for the bearing of the runner-stone spindle.

Cat-slide roof. Any portion of a roof which is continued downwards below the general eaves-line.

Centrifugal governor. In a steam-engine, a pendulum device consisting of two hanging rods, the lower weighted ends of which swing outwards to control the steam-supply valve.

Collar-rafter roof. A roof comprising pairs of common rafters joined together by tie-beams (collars) fixed above wall-head level.

Condenser. In a steam-engine, the chamber in which exhaust steam from the cylinder is condensed.

Dentil band. In Classical architecture, a course of small square blocks, usually forming part of a cornice.

Double-acting cylinder. A cylinder in which the up and the down strokes of the piston act as working strokes.

Double-floor construction. A floor composed of main beams which carry a system of cross- or filler-joists.

Eccentric. In machinery, a non-concentric disc or cam for converting rotary into reciprocating motion.

Eccentric rod. An arm attached to the strap of an eccentric disc which transmits the backwards and forwards motion to a slide-valve.

English bond. In brickwork, alternate courses composed entirely of headers or stretchers.

English garden-wall bond. Brickwork in which three or five stretcher courses alternate with one header course.

Entablature. In Classical architecture, the whole of the horizontal members above the column (architrave, frieze, cornice). In engineering, the cross-beam supporting the centre of a beam-engine.

Extrados. The upper surface of an arch or vault.

Farland. A receiving-box or trough used in fish-gutting.

Finnan haddock. A haddock smoked by a specialised method first practised at Findon, near Aberdeen.

Flail. A wooden-handled and flexible-jointed device for threshing corn by hand.

Flange. In iron beam and column design, the flat strengthening member at one or both ends of the web (*q.v.*).

Flèche. A slender wooden spire mounted on the ridge of a roof.

Flemish bond. In brickwork, courses consisting of alternate stretchers and headers.

Flitched. Two wooden beams bolted together to form a single structural member.

Flume, see *Pentrough.*

Furrows, see *Lands and furrows.*

Gambrel roof. A hipped roof with gablet-ended ridge.

Gorge cornice. In Ancient Egyptian architecture, a broad cavetto cornice.

Great spur-wheel. In milling-machinery, a large horizontal gearwheel mounted on the upright shaft and engaging with the stone nuts.

Gudgeon. The pivot point at the end of an axle.

Hackle screws. In milling-machinery, screws mounted on the bridging-box (*q.v.*) to permit fine adjustment of the horizontal plane of the millstones.

Internal frame. In a building, a framework of beams and stanchions structurally integral with external load-bearing walls.

Intrados. The under-surface of an arch or vault.

Jack arch. In 'fireproof' floor construction, a shallow arch, usually of plastered brick, spanning the lower flanges of iron beams.

Jib. The principal load-bearing member of a crane.

Joggle and socket. In structural ironwork, a joint formed between two members, one tenoned and the other socketed.

King-post roof truss. A form of timber roof truss comprising principal rafters, tie-beam, raking struts and a central vertical member (the king-post).

Knapped stones. In rubble masonry, stones roughly squared off or trimmed.

Lands and furrows. In millstone dressing, a system of flat surfaces (lands) and channels (furrows) cut on the grinding face.

Launder, see *Pentrough.*

Line-shafting. A system of horizontal shafting used to transmit the main drive to individual machines.

Mutules. Regularly spaced blocks in the soffit of a Classical cornice.

Overshot. Of a water-wheel in which water is directed onto the wheel above and beyond its vertical centre-line, causing it to turn in a forward direction.

Parallel motion. A system of parallel links designed to maintain the up-and-down motion of a piston-rod in a straight line.

Penstock, see *Pentrough.*

Pentrough. A wooden trough, or chute, directing water onto a water-wheel.

Pilaster. A rectangular column of shallow projection integral with, or attached to a wall.

Pitch-back wheel. A form of water-wheel of high breast-shot type.

Pitched slope. In harbour construction, a sea-wall having a gradual slope of about 45° or less.

Pit-wheel. In milling-machinery, the primary vertical gearwheel mounted on the shaft of the water-wheel.

Plummer or pillow block. A form of clamp casing for housing the bearing of a pivot or shaft.

Queen-post roof truss. A form of timber roof truss comprising principal rafters, tie-beam, raking struts and a pair of vertical posts (queen-posts) symmetrically disposed on each side of the mid-span.

Rack ring. The toothed iron ring or rack on the top face of the horse-wheel of a horse-engine.

Raking shore. A sloping prop or strut for bracing a vertical frame or wall.

Runner stone. In milling, the upper revolving millstone.

Rynd, rind. In milling, an iron bearer, or mace, which supports and transmits the drive to the runner stone.

Saggar. A fireclay casing for protecting pottery during kiln firing.

Scarf joint. A form of lapped joint between two members which does not increase their overall cross-sectional area.

Scrib joint. A form of lapped joint between the main plate sections of a riveted still.

Slag-dam. In a blast-furnace, a dwarf wall extending across the lower forepart of the tapping-arch.

Snecked rubble. Squared rubble brought to short courses using small square stones (snecks).

Soffit. The underside of any structural or ornamental member.

Spandrel. The triangular space above the haunch of an arch.

Spigot joint. The male and female joint formed between two lengths of pipe or column.

Split bearing. A bearing which is formed in two halves and fits within a plummer block (*q.v.*).

Stilling basin. An outer basin designed to protect the entrance to an inner harbour.

Stone nuts. In milling-machinery, small spur-wheels or pinions transmitting the drive to the runner stones.

Straining beam. In structural framing, a horizontal strut or stiffening member.